VOICES OF CHEROKEE WOMEN

Voices of
Cherokee Women

Edited by Carolyn Ross Johnston

 JOHN F. BLAIR, PUBLISHER *Winston-Salem, North Carolina*

JOHN F. BLAIR,
PUBLISHER

1406 Plaza Drive
Winston-Salem, North Carolina 27103
www.blairpub.com

COVER
Earth's Sky © Jeanne Rorex Bridges

Library of Congress Cataloging-in-Publication Data

Johnston, Carolyn, 1948-
  Voices of Cherokee women / edited by Carolyn Ross Johnston.
      pages   cm. — (Real voices, real history)
  Includes bibliographical references and index.
  ISBN-13: 978-0-89587-599-0 (alk. paper)
  ISBN: 978-0-89587-600-3 (ebook)
  ISBN-10: 0-89587-599-3
 1. Cherokee women—History—Sources. 2. Cherokee women—Historiography.
 3. Cherokee women—Biography. I. Title.
  E99.C5J618 2013
  975.004'97557—dc23
                        2013022218

For Caldonia, Salina, Margaret, Alta, and all Cherokee women

Se liye'ni, a Cherokee medicine woman from 1926–27, and her son Walker Calhoun

PHOTOGRAPH SUBMITTED BY JAMES MOONEY AND FRANS OLBRECHTS; BULLETIN 99, NEGATIVE 996 D 4, NATIONAL ANTHROPOLOGICAL ARCHIVES, SMITHSONIAN INSTITUTION

CONTENTS

INTRODUCTION

Members of the Cherokee Nation gathered at Rattlesnake Springs near what is now the town of Charleston, Tennessee. They had fled from their capital at New Echota in Georgia when threatened with violence and moved their council to Red Clay, Tennessee. The Indian Removal Act passed in 1830. Eight years later, the Cherokees were driven into stockades in Tennessee, Georgia, North Carolina, and Alabama. There, they awaited the long journey. They carried live coals from their final council fire.

In 1838, William Shorey Coodey described the departure of the first of the thirteen detachments to leave on the Trail of Tears:

> At this very moment a low sound of distant thunder fell on my ear. In almost an exact western direction a dark spiral cloud was rising above the horizon and sent forth a murmur. I almost fancied a voice of divine indignation for the wrongs of my poor and unhappy countrymen, driven

by brutal power from all they loved and cherished in the land of their fathers to gratify the cravings of avarice. The sun was unclouded—no rain fell—the thunder rolled away and sounds hushed in the distance. The scene around and before me, and in the elements above, were peculiarly impressive & singular. It was at once spoken of by several persons near me, and looked upon as omens of some future event in the west. John Ross stood on a wagon and led the people in a prayer. After the thunder sounded, a bugle announced the departure of the first detachment.[1]

The Cherokees carried those live coals with them all the way over the eight-hundred-mile journey to Indian Territory. When they arrived, they lit the Eternal Flame from the coals of that last council fire.

In 1984 at Red Clay, the Cherokee Nation of Oklahoma and the Eastern Band of Cherokee Indians reunited in a joint council meeting. This was the first time the two groups had come together since the removal in 1838. Representatives of the two groups lit the Eternal Flame with torches that had been ignited a few days earlier at Cherokee, North Carolina. Cherokee runners carried the torches along 150 miles of mountainous roads.[2] Before they returned to Red Clay 146 years after their last council meeting in the East, the Cherokees had endured the Trail of Tears, the Civil War, and allotment of their lands. The live coals represented their deep commitment to Cherokee identity.

The Eternal Flame still burns.

When Cherokees met Europeans, the Europeans assumed

the Cherokees were "uncivilized" because they were not Christians and because the women had so much power. That power was tied to their role as producers and mothers. Cherokee women were farmers and Cherokee men hunters. Their society was matrilineal and matrilocal, which meant that women owned their residences and the fields they worked. Cherokee women were wives, mothers, producers, healers, and warriors. They possessed sexual freedom and could obtain divorce without difficulty. Still, the clans maintained strict incest taboos. In all their actions, women had to take the welfare of the community into account. Cherokees believed in a sexual division of labor—a division associated with complementarity and equality, not hierarchy or domination.

Cherokee women lost and gained power in a variety of ways in the eighteenth and nineteenth centuries. Intended to impress the United States government and especially Georgians that the tribe was civilized and democratic, the Cherokee Constitution of 1827 disenfranchised women politically but allowed them to retain their property rights. While such political changes were strategic moves, they also stemmed from the economic shift from hunting to intensive agriculture, and from the adoption of patriarchal values by the influential Cherokees who drafted the legislation. The Cherokees even acquired African slaves. Often, their perception was that survival as a nation hinged on selective acculturation and the appearance of civilization.

The Indian Removal Act intended to remove all southeastern Indians. Resistance was fierce. Cherokee women protested, as they were more tied to the land than were men, but they were excluded from formal political decisions. No Cherokee women were lawyers, judges, or members of juries. Cherokee women still retained covert political influence, but their formal power diminished. Approximately 10 percent of the tribe at the time of removal was highly acculturated. Cherokees often intermarried with white Americans and converted to Christianity. Yet adopting European dress or language did not necessarily imply the loss of Cherokee identity and culture. Removal and the Civil War tended to reinforce older Cherokee values and beliefs, while allotment dealt a serious blow to Cherokee women's power and to tribal sovereignty.

The following pages present the "Real Voices, Real History" of Cherokee women. Gerda Lerner, an architect of the field of women's history, asked, "What would history look like if viewed through the eyes of women?" The primary documents in this book allow a view through the eyes of Cherokee women, whose stories have been missing from the traditional narratives. Cherokee women enjoyed equality with men until the nineteenth century. Then, in the latter part of the twentieth century, they began to regain power and influence. Wilma Mankiller assumed the post of chief of the Cherokee Nation of Oklahoma in 1985, then was elected in 1987 and 1991. Joyce Dugan became chief of the Eastern Band of Cherokee Indians in 1995.

Part 1 presents the stories of the Cherokees as the shaman and storyteller Swimmer told them to James Mooney. These stories illuminate what it meant to be female and male within Cherokee culture and how Cherokees viewed the creator and their mythic world.

The book's second part offers a glimpse into the first encounters Cherokees had with Europeans through the primary accounts of early explorers and travelers.

Part 3 illustrates how Cherokee women like Catharine Brown responded to the United States government's civilization program and how they interacted with missionaries.

The Trail of Tears is the subject of Part 4. It presents the oral histories and speeches of Cherokee women as they opposed removal, were driven from their homes, and were forced to walk to Indian Territory.

No sooner had the Cherokee Nation rebuilt in Indian Territory than it confronted another crisis: the Civil War, the subject of Part 5. This section features the letters of Mary Stapler Ross and John Ross, the principal chief for decades, and Sarah and Stand Watie. The two couples, who lived through the Civil War on opposite sides, represent the fierce factionalism in the tribe that had existed since the removal crisis. Also included is Hannah Worcester Hicks, who wrote in her diary of the murder of her husband, Abijah, and her constant fear of robbers and marauders. Other Cherokee women's oral histories illuminate different experiences of that tumultuous time.

Part 6, on allotment, assimilation, and struggles for sovereignty, gives insight into the lives of Cherokee women in the post–Civil War period, when they were dispossessed of their land once again and had to face an uncertain future. It presents the voices of students of the Cherokee Female Seminary as they confronted the challenges of assimilation.

The book's final part focuses on modern Cherokee women who became educated leaders of the Cherokee Nation in the nineteenth and twentieth centuries, when they began to reclaim the power and influence their female ancestors had traditionally possessed.

The fall of 2013 marks the 175th anniversary and commemoration of the Trail of Tears. Cherokees endured great suffering in the wars with Europeans, during their forced removal from their homeland, in the Civil War, and because of the policy of allotment. Like the Phoenix, the mythical bird that rose from the ashes, the tribe rose from despair to become a thriving nation of more than three hundred thousand in the Cherokee Nation of Oklahoma and over thirteen thousand in the Eastern Band of Cherokee Indians. Tribal members have preserved their language, ceremonies, culture, and sovereignty.

For hundreds of years, the Cherokees celebrated the Green Corn Ceremony, generally in June or early July, when the first corn ripened. This ceremony affirmed the importance of women in the community and the need for men and women to live in balance. The ceremony honored Selu, the life-sustaining Corn Mother. The Green Corn Ceremony was the occasion when rebirth occurred and old grudges were laid aside. In some eras, crimes were even pardoned. As part of the purification, people fasted and went to the water to cleanse themselves. Forty-five days later, Cherokees celebrated the Ripe or Mature Green Corn Ceremony, which again featured the balance of female and male contributions to life. Cherokees still observe the Green Corn Ceremony and retain some of the original practices.

This book addresses a central question: What does Cherokee history look like when expressed by women's voices and viewed through their eyes?

Gwendolyn Brooks, the gifted African-American poet,

once told me that her work was about either celebration or lamentation. The voices of Cherokee women reflect those themes. At times, their suffering, dispossession, and losses will lead readers to despair; however, their celebrations of Cherokee language, identity, traditions, stories, ceremonies, and sovereignty inspire hope. Images flood this landscape: Nancy Ward becoming a "Beloved Woman" by picking up a rifle and fighting as a warrior in the midst of battle . . . Rebecca Neugin being carried as a child on the Trail of Tears . . . Mary Stapler Ross seeing her beautiful Rose Cottage burned to the ground during the Civil War . . . Hannah Hicks watching as marauders steal all her food . . . Elizabeth Watts seeing raiders split open the beds, feathers scattering in the wind . . . girls at the Cherokee Female Seminary studying the same curriculum as the women at Mount Holyoke . . . Joyce Dugan and Wilma Mankiller becoming the first female chiefs of the Cherokee Nation . . . men and women celebrating the Green Corn Ceremony and dancing at the Stomp dance ground.

The coals the Cherokees carried to Indian Territory and to North Carolina still glow with fire.

ENDNOTES

[1] William Shorey Coodey to John Howard Payne, John Howard Payne Papers, Edward E. Ayer Collection, Newberry Library, Chicago, quoted in Samuel Carter III, *Cherokee Sunset* (New York: Doubleday, 1976), 250.

[2] Wilma Mankiller and Michael Wallis, *Mankiller: A Chief and Her People* (New York: St. Martin's Griffin, 1993), 47–48. See also Jack Frederick Kilpatrick, "An Etymological Note on the Tribal Name of the Cherokee and Certain Place and Proper Names Derived from Cherokee," *Journal of the Graduate Research Center*, no. 30 (1962), 37–41. On April 16–18, 2009, at the Red Clay Historic Area in southern Bradley County, Tennessee, the Eastern and Western Cherokees met in a joint tribal session for the second time in

171 years. In 1951, the Eastern Band of Cherokee Indians had persuaded the Cherokee Nation of Oklahoma to allow it to ignite a fire from the Eternal Flame. It carried this flame back to North Carolina and established a second Eternal Flame. In April 1984, a torch was ignited from the North Carolina flame and relayed by runners back to Red Clay to light a third Eternal Flame. Several resolutions were read and adopted by the joint council. See Curtis Lipps, *Herald-News*, Rhea County, Tenn., Wed., Apr. 22, 2009.

—

"*Many Native Americans felt utterly violated and compromised. It seemed as if the spiritual and social tapestry they had created for centuries was unraveling. Everything lost that sacred balance. And ever since, we have been striving to return to the harmony we once had. It has been a difficult task. The odds against us have been formidable. But despite everything that has happened to us we have never given up and will never give up. There is an old Cherokee prophecy which instructs us that as long as the Cherokees continue traditional dances, the world will remain as it is, but when the dances stop, the world will come to an end. Everyone should hope that the Cherokees will continue to dance.*"

Wilma Mankiller

—

Swimmer/A'yûñ inǐ taken by James Mooney in 1888

Part 1
STORIES OF THE CHEROKEES

The following stories about how the world was made and what it means to be female or male have been told in the Cherokee Nation for hundreds of years. A late-nineteenth-century Cherokee shaman named Swimmer told these versions to James Mooney (1861–1921), who worked for the Smithsonian's Bureau of Ethnology. He began his research in 1887 and lived with the Cherokees for several years. Mooney gained the trust of Swimmer, who revealed sacred knowledge about healing and medicine. Swimmer also told him Cherokee stories of ancient origins. Mooney published three works on the Cherokees that are some of the finest ever written on their culture.

The first story, "How the World Was Made," is the creation story. It explains why a woman has only one child in a year, and also how animals, plants, and humans are related.

The second story, "The First Fire," tells how the humble Water Spider spun a thread from her own body and brought fire to the people by weaving a *tusti*—the Cherokee word for bowl, sometimes connoting a small bowl—and carrying a live coal back in it. Like Prometheus in the Greek myth, the Water Spider is the fire bringer to humans.

The third story, "Kana'tĭ and Selu," tells of the first man and woman. It emphasizes Selu's sacrifice of her life and her gift of corn. The story of her sons, the Thunder Boys, explains why Cherokees do not live in a perfect world. The boys introduce uncertainty into an ordered world by breaking rules. The story teaches that if the people show respect and gratitude and do not break taboos, the blessings of the Corn Mother might return. In contrast to a patriarchal religious system in which deities are male and women are considered subordinate to men, Cherokees believed in female and male supernatural beings. Ceremonies, rituals, warfare, and sports helped teach who they were and where they came from.

The stories about Spear-finger and Stone Coat (or Dressed in Stone) reveal a fear of women's terrifying and destructive powers. In addition to the powerful images of Selu and the sun as female, women's strength is evident in the story of Nûñ'yunu'wĭ (Stone Coat). Menstrual blood was believed to be dangerously powerful, as demonstrated by Stone Coat, who is killed by the sight of seven menstruating women. Women mysteriously bled each month without dying. Cherokee women's power derived from their ability to give and sustain life, especially through farming. However, blood was believed to be the ultimate symbol of that power. War women gained power through shedding blood and taking life in times of conflict. Selu's blood was shed as she sacrificed her life and gave the gift of corn. Clan membership was determined through the mother's bloodline. In the female version of the Stone Coat story, Spear-finger, U'tlûñ'tă, has the ability to change herself into any shape; she is also covered with a stone coat. Spear-finger represents a female monster that takes life.

The following stories teach that the relationships between men and women and their roles must be in balance for a community to flourish. They also identify femaleness with menstruation, childbirth, motherhood, blood, the sun, clan, corn, and agriculture. Masculinity is associated with warfare, hunting, animals, water, fatherhood, the moon, and ball play.

⌁ How the World Was Made

The earth is a great island floating in a sea of water, and suspended at each of the four cardinal points by a cord hanging down from the sky vault, which is of solid rock. When the world grows old and worn out, the people will die and the cords will break and let the earth sink down into the ocean, and all will be water again. The Indians are afraid of this.

When all was water, the animals were above in Gălûñ'lătĭ, beyond the arch; but it was very much crowded, and they were wanting more room. They wondered what was below the water, and at last Dâyuni'sĭ, "Beaver's Grandchild," the little Water-beetle, offered to go and see if it could learn. It darted in every direction over the surface of the water, but could find no firm place to rest. Then it dived to the bottom and came up with some soft mud, which began to grow and spread on every side until it became the island which we call the earth. It was afterward fastened to the sky with four cords, but no one remembers who did this.

At first the earth was flat and very soft and wet. The animals were anxious to get down, and sent out different birds to see if it was yet dry, but they found no place to alight and came back again to Gălûñ'lătĭ. At last it seemed to be time, and they sent out the Buzzard and told him to go and make ready for them. This was the Great Buzzard, the father of all the buzzards we see now. He flew all over the earth, low down near the ground, and it was still soft. When he reached the Cherokee country, he was very tired, and his wings began to flap and strike the ground, and wherever they struck the earth there was a valley, and where they turned up again there was a mountain. When the animals above saw this, they were afraid that the whole world would be mountains, so they called him back, but the Cherokee country remains full of mountains to this day.

When the earth was dry and the animals came down, it was still dark, so they got the sun and set it in a track to go every day across the island from east to west, just overhead. It was too hot this way, and Tsiska'gĭlĭ, the Red Crawfish, had his shell scorched a bright red, so that his meat was spoiled; and the Cherokee do not eat it. The conjurers put the sun another hand-breadth higher in the air, but it was still too hot. They raised it another time, and another, until it was seven hand-breadths high and just under the sky arch. Then it was right, and they left it so. This is why the conjurers call the highest place Gûlkwâ'gine Di'gălûñ'lătiyûñ', "the seventh height," because it is seven hand-breadths above the earth. Every day the sun goes along under this arch, and returns at night on the upper side to the starting place.

There is another world under this, and it is like ours in everything—animals, plants, and people—save that the seasons are different. The streams that come down from the mountains are the trails by which we reach this under-world, and the springs at their heads are the doorways by which we enter it, but to do this one must fast and go to water and have one of the underground people for a guide. We know that the seasons in the underworld are different from ours, because the water in the springs is always warmer in winter and cooler in the summer than the outer air.

When the animals and plants were first made—we do not know by whom—they were told to watch and keep awake for seven nights, just as young men now fast and keep awake when they pray to their medicine. They tried to do this, and nearly all were awake through the first night, but the next night several dropped off to sleep, and the third night others were asleep, and then others, until, on the seventh night, of all the animals only the owl, the panther, and one or two more were still awake. To these were given the power to see and to go about in the dark, and to make prey of the birds and animals which must sleep at night. Of the trees only the cedar, the pine, the spruce, the holly, and the laurel were awake to the end, and to them it was given to be always green and to be greatest for medicine, but to the others it was said: "Because you have not endured to the end you shall lose your hair every winter."

Men came after the animals and plants. At first there were only a brother and sister until he struck her with a fish and told her to multiply, and so it was. In seven days a child was born to her, and thereafter every seven days another, and they increased very fast until there was danger that the world could not keep them. Then it was made that a woman should have only one child in a year, and it has been so ever since.

~ The First Fire

In the beginning there was no fire, and the world was cold, until the Thunders (Ani'-Hyûñ'tĭkwălâ'skĭ), who lived up in Gălûñ'lătĭ, sent their lightning and put fire into the bottom of a hollow sycamore tree which grew on an island. The animals knew it was there, because they could see the smoke coming out at the top, but they could not get to it on account of the water, so they held a council to decide what to do. This was a long time ago.

Every animal that could fly or swim was anxious to go after the fire. The Raven offered, and because he was so large and strong they thought he could surely do the work, so he was sent first. He flew high and far across the water and alighted on the sycamore tree, but while he was wondering what to do next, the heat had scorched all his feathers black, and he was frightened and came back without the fire. The little Screech-Owl (Wa'huhu') volunteered to go, and reached the place safely, but while he was looking down into the hollow tree a blast of hot air came up and nearly burned out his eyes. He managed to fly home as best he could, but it was a long time before he could see well, and his eyes are red to this day. Then the Hooting Owl (U'guku') and the Horned Owl (Tskĭlĭ) went, but by the time they got to the hollow tree the fire was burning so fiercely that the smoke nearly blinded them, and the ashes carried up by the wind made white rings about their eyes. They had to come home again without the fire, but with all their rubbing they were never able to get rid of the white rings.

Now no more of the birds would venture, and so the little Uksu'hĭ snake, the black racer, said he would go through the water and bring back some fire. He swam across to the island and crawled through the grass to the tree, and went in by a small hole at the bottom. The heat and smoke were too much for him, too, and after dodging about blindly over the hot ashes until he was almost on fire himself he managed by good luck to get out again at the same hole, but his body had been scorched black, and he has ever since had the habit of darting and doubling on his track as if trying to escape from close quarters. He came back, and the great blacksnake, Gûle'gĭ, "The Climber," offered to go for fire. He swam over to the island and climbed up the tree on the outside, as the blacksnake always does, but when he put his head down into the hole the smoke choked him so that he fell into the burning stump, and before he could climb out again he was as black as the Uksu'hĭ.

Now they held another council, for still there was no fire, and the world was cold, but birds, snakes, and four-footed animals, all had some excuse for not going, because they were all afraid to venture near the burning sycamore, until at last Kănăne'skĭ Amai'yĕhĭ (the Water Spider) said she would go. This is not the water spider that looks like a mosquito, but the other one, with black downy hair and red stripes on her body. She can run on top of the water or dive to the bottom, so there would be no trouble to get over to the island, but the question was, How could she bring back the fire? "I'll manage that," said the Water Spider; so she spun a thread from her body and wove it into a *tusti* bowl, which she fastened on her back. Then she crossed over to the island and through the grass to where the fire was still burning. She put one little coal of fire into her bowl, and came back with it, and ever since we have had fire, and the Water Spider still keeps her *tusti* bowl.

∽ Kana'tĭ and Selu:
The Origin of Game and Corn

When I was a boy this is what the old men told me they had heard when they were boys.

Long years ago, soon after the world was made, a hunter and his wife lived at Pilot knob with their only child, a little boy. The father's name was Kana'tĭ (The Lucky Hunter), and his wife was called Selu (Corn). No matter when Kana'tĭ went into the wood, he never failed to bring back a load of game, which his wife would cut up and prepare, washing off the blood from the meat in the river near the house. The little boy used to play down by the river every day, and one morning the old people thought they heard laughing and talking in the bushes as though there were two children there. When the boy came home at night his parents asked him who had been playing with him all day. "He comes out of the water," said the boy, "and he calls himself my elder brother. He says his mother was cruel to him and threw him into the river." Then they knew that the strange boy had sprung from the blood of the game which Selu had washed off at the river's edge.

Every day when the little boy went out to play the other would join him, but as he always went back again into the water the old people never had a chance to see him. At last one evening Kana'tĭ said to his son, "Tomorrow, when the other boy comes to play, get him to wrestle with you, and when you have your arms around him hold on to him and call for us." The boy promised to do as he was told, so the next day as soon as his playmate appeared he challenged him to a wrestling match. The other agreed at once, but as soon as they had their arms around each other, Kana'tĭ's boy began to scream for his father. The old folks at once came running down, and as soon as the Wild Boy saw them he struggled to free himself and cried out, "Let me go; you threw me away!" but his brother held on until the parents reached the spot, when they seized the Wild Boy and took him home with them. They kept him in the house until they had tamed him, but he was always wild and artful in his disposition, and was the leader of his brother in every mischief. It was not long until the old people discovered that he had magic powers, and they called him I'năge-utăsûñ'hĭ (He-who-grew-up-wild).

Whenever Kana'tĭ went into the mountains he always brought back a fat buck or doe, or maybe a couple of turkeys. One day the Wild Boy said to his brother, "I wonder where our father gets all that game; let's follow him next time and find out." A few days afterward Kana'tĭ took a bow and some feathers in his hand and started off toward the west. The boys waited a little while and then went after him, keeping out of sight until they saw him go into a swamp where there were a great many of the small reeds that hunters use to make arrowshafts. Then the Wild Boy changed himself into a puff of bird's down, which the wind took up and carried until it alighted upon Kana'tĭ's shoulder just as he entered the swamp, but Kana'tĭ knew nothing about it. The old man cut reeds, fitted the feathers to them, and made some arrows, and the Wild Boy—in his other shape—thought, "I wonder what those things are for?" When Kana'tĭ had his arrows finished he came out of the swamp and went on again. The wind blew the down from his shoulder, and it fell in the woods, when the Wild Boy took his right shape again and went back and told his brother what he had seen. Keeping out of sight of their father, they followed him up the mountain until he stopped at a certain place and lifted a large rock. At once there ran out a buck, which Kana'tĭ shot, and then lifting it upon his back he started for home again. "Oho!" exclaimed the boys, "he keeps all the deer shut up in that hole, and whenever he wants meat he just lets one out and kills it with those things he made in the swamp." They hurried and reached home before their father, who had the heavy deer to carry, and he never knew that they had followed.

A few days later the boys went back to the swamp, cut some reeds, and made seven arrows, and then started up the mountain to where their father kept the game. When they got to the place, they raised the rock and a deer came running out. Just as they drew back to shoot it, another came out, and then another and another, until the boys got confused and forgot what they were about. In those days all the deer had their tails hanging down like other animals, but as a buck was running past the Wild Boy struck its tail with his arrow so that it pointed upward. The boys thought this good sport, and when the next one ran past the Wild Boy struck its tail with his arrow so that it stood straight up, and his brother struck the next one so hard with his arrow that the deer's tail was almost curled over his back. The deer carries his tail this way ever since. The deer came running past until the last one had come out of the hole and escaped into the forest. Then came droves of raccoons, rabbits, and all the other four-footed animals—all but the bear, because there was no bear then. Last came great flocks of turkeys, pigeons, and partridges that darkened the air like a cloud and made such a noise with their wings that Kana'tĭ, sitting at home, heard the sound like distant thunder on the mountains and said to himself, "My bad boys have got into trouble; I must go and see what they are doing."

So he went up the mountain, and when he came to the place where he kept the game he found the two boys standing by the rock, and all the birds and animals were gone. Kana'tĭ was furious, but without saying a word he went down into the cave and kicked the covers off four jars in one corner, when out swarmed bedbugs, fleas, lice, and gnats, and got all over the boys. They screamed with pain and fright and tried to beat off the insects, but the thousands of vermin crawled over them and bit and stung them until both dropped down nearly dead. Kana'tĭ stood looking on until he thought they had been punished enough, when he knocked off the vermin and made the boys a talk. "Now, you rascals," said he, "you have always had plenty to eat and never had to work for it. Whenever you were hungry all I had to do was to come up here and get a deer or a turkey and bring it home for your mother to cook; but now you have let out all the animals, and after this when you want a deer to eat you will have to hunt all over the woods for it, and then maybe not find one. Go home now to your mother, while I see if I can find something to eat for supper."

When the boys got home again they were very tired and hungry and asked their mother for something to eat. "There is no meat," said Selu, "but wait a little while and I'll get you something." So she took a basket and started out to the storehouse. This storehouse was built upon poles high up from the ground, to keep it out of reach of animals, and there was a ladder to climb up by, and one door, but no other opening. Every day when Selu got ready to cook the dinner she would go out to the storehouse with a basket and bring it back full of corn and beans. The boys had never been inside the storehouse, so wondered where all the corn and beans could come from, as the house was not a very large one; so as soon as Selu went out of the door the Wild Boy said to his brother, "Let's go and see what she does." They ran around and climbed up at the back of the storehouse and pulled out a piece of clay from between the logs, so that they could look in. There they saw Selu standing in the middle of the room with the basket in front of her on the floor. Leaning over the basket, she rubbed her stomach—so—and the basket was half full of corn. Then she rubbed under her armpits—so—and the basket was full to the top with beans. The boys looked at each other and said, "This will never do; our mother is a witch. If we eat any of that it will poison us. We must kill her."

When the boys came back into the house, she knew their thoughts before they spoke. "So you are going to kill me?" said Selu. "Yes," said the boys, "you are a witch." "Well," said their mother, "when you have killed me, clear a large piece of ground in front of the house and drag my body seven times around the circle. Then drag me seven times over the ground inside the circle, and stay up all night and watch, and in the morning you will have plenty of corn." The boys killed her with their clubs, and cut off her head and put it up on the roof of the house with her face turned to the west, and told her to look for her husband. Then they set to work to clear the ground in front of the house, but instead of clearing the whole piece they cleared only seven little spots. This is why corn now grows only in a few places instead of over the whole world. They dragged the body of Selu around the circle, and wherever her blood fell on the ground the corn sprang up. But instead of dragging her body seven times across the ground they dragged it over only twice, which is the reason the Indians still work their crop but twice. The two brothers sat up and watched their corn all night, and in the morning it was full grown and ripe. . . .

Soon afterward some strangers from a distance, who had heard that the brothers had a wonderful grain from which they made bread, came to ask for some, for none but Selu and her family had ever known corn before. The boys gave them seven grains of corn, which they told them to plant the next night on their way home, sitting up all night to watch the corn, which would have seven ripe ears in the morning. These they were to plant the next night and watch in the same way, and so on every night until they reached home, when they would have corn enough to supply the whole people. The strangers lived seven days' journey away. They took the seven grains and watched all through the darkness until morning, when they saw seven tall stalks, each stalk bearing a ripened ear. They gathered the ears and went on their way. The next night they planted all their corn, and guarded it as before until daybreak, when they found an abundant increase. But the way was long and the sun was hot, and the people grew tired. On the last night before reaching home they fell asleep, and in the morning the corn they had planted had not even sprouted. They brought with them to their settlement what corn they had left and planted it, and with care and attention were able to raise a crop. But ever since the corn must be watched and tended through half the year, which before would grow and ripen in a night.

~ U'tlûñ'tă, the Spear-finger

Long, long ago—*hĭlahi'yu*—there dwelt in the mountains a terrible ogress, a woman monster, whose food was human livers. She could take on any shape or appearance to suit her purpose, but in her right form she looked very much like an old woman, excepting that her whole body was covered with a skin as hard as a rock that no weapon could wound or penetrate, and that on her right hand she had a long stony forefinger of bone, like an awl or spear head, with which she stabbed everyone to whom she could get near enough. On account of this fact she was called *U'tlûñ'tă*, "Spear-finger," and on account of her stony skin she was sometimes called *Nûñ'yunu'wĭ*, "Stone-dress." There was another stone-clothed monster that killed people, but that is a different story.

Spear-finger had such powers over stone that she could

easily lift and carry immense rocks, and could cement them together by merely striking one against another. To get over the rough country more easily she undertook to build a great rock bridge through the air from Nûñyû'-tlu'gûñ'yĭ, the "Tree Rock," on Hiwassee, over to Sanigilâ'gĭ (Whiteside Mountain), on the Blue ridge, and had it well started from the top of the "Tree Rock" when the lightning struck it and scattered the fragments along the whole ridge, where the pieces can still be seen by those who go there. She used to range all over the mountains about the heads of the streams and in the dark passes of Nantahala, always hungry and looking for victims. Her favorite haunt on the Tennessee side was about the gap on the trail where Chilhowee Mountain comes down to the river.

Sometimes an old woman would approach along the trail where the children were picking strawberries or playing near the village, and would say to them coaxingly, "Come, my grandchildren, come to your granny and let granny dress your hair." When some little girl up and laid her head in the old woman's lap to be petted and combed the old witch would gently run her fingers through the child's hair until it went to sleep, when she would stab the little one through the heart or back of the neck with the long awl finger, which she had kept hidden under her robe. Then she would take out the liver and eat it.

She would enter a house by taking the appearance of one of the family who happened to have gone out for a short time, and would watch [for] her chance to stab some one with her long finger and take out his liver. She could stab him without being noticed, and often the victim did not even know it himself at the time—for it left no wound and caused no pain—but went on about his own affairs, until all at once he felt weak and began gradually to pine away, and was always sure to die, because Spear-finger had taken his liver.

When the Cherokee went out in the fall, according to their custom, to burn the leaves off from the mountains in order to get the chestnuts on the ground, they were never safe, for the old witch was always on the lookout, and as soon as she saw the smoke rise she knew there were Indians there and sneaked up to try to surprise one alone. So as well as they could they tried to keep together, and were very cautious of allowing any stranger to approach the camp. But if one went down to the spring for a drink they never knew but it might be the liver eater that came back and sat with them.

Sometimes she took her proper form, and once or twice, when far out from the settlements, a solitary hunter had seen an old woman, with a queer-looking hand, going through the woods singing low to herself:

Uwe'lana'tsĭkû'. Su' să' sai'.
Liver, I eat it. *Su' să' sai'.*

It was rather a pretty song, but it chilled his blood, for he knew it was the liver eater, and he hurried away, silently, before she might see him.

At last a great council was held to devise some means to get rid of U'tlûñ'tă before she should destroy everybody. The people came from all around, and after much talk it was decided that the best way would be to trap her in a pitfall where all the warriors could attack her at once. So they dug a deep pitfall across the trail and covered it over with earth and grass as if the ground had never been disturbed. Then they kindled a large fire of brush near the trail and hid themselves in the laurels, because they knew she would come as soon as she saw the smoke.

Sure enough they soon saw an old woman coming along the trail. She looked like an old woman whom they knew well in the village, and although several of the wiser men wanted to shoot at her, the others interfered, because they did not want to hurt one of their own people. The old woman came slowly along the trail, with one hand under her blanket, until she stepped upon the pitfall and tumbled through the brush top into the deep hole below. Then, at once, she showed her true nature, and instead of the feeble old woman there was the terrible U'tlûñ'tă with her stony skin, and her sharp awl finger reaching out in every direction for some one to stab.

The hunters rushed out from the thicket and surrounded the pit, but shoot as true and as often as they could, their arrows struck the stony mail of the witch only to be broken and fall useless at her feet, while she taunted them and tried to climb out of the pit to get at them. They kept out of her way, but were only wasting their arrows when a small bird, Utsu'gĭ, the titmouse, perched on a tree over head and began to sing "*un, un, un.*" They thought it was saying *u'nahŭ'*, heart, meaning that they should aim at the heart of the stone witch. They directed their arrows where the heart should be, but the arrows only glanced off with the flint heads broken.

Then they caught the Utsu'gĭ and cut off its tongue, so that ever since its tongue is short and everybody knows it is a liar. When the hunters let it go it flew straight up into the sky until it was out of sight and never came back again. The titmouse that we know now is only an image of the other.

They kept up the fight without result until another bird, little Tsĭ'kĭlilĭ, the chickadee, flew down from a tree and alighted up on the witch's right hand. The warriors took this as a sign that they must aim there, and they were right, for her heart was on the inside of her hand, which she kept doubled into a fist, this same awl hand with which she had stabbed so many people. Now she was frightened in earnest, and began to rush furiously at them with her long awl finger and to jump about in the pit to dodge the arrows, until at last a lucky arrow struck just where the awl joined her wrist and she fell down dead.

Ever since the Tsĭ'kĭlĭlĭ is known as a truth teller, and when a man is away on a journey, if this bird comes and perches near the house and chirps its song, his friends know he will soon be safe home.

➤ Nûñ'yunu'wĭ, Stone Coat

This is what the old men told me when I was a boy.

Once when all the people of the settlement were out in the mountains on a great hunt one man who had gone on ahead climbed to the top of a high ridge and found a large river on the other side. While he was looking across he saw an old man walking about on the opposite ridge, with a cane that seemed to be made of some bright, shining rock. The hunter watched and saw that every little while the old man would point his cane in a certain direction, then draw it back and smell the end of it. At last he pointed it in the direction of the hunting camp on the other side of the mountain, and this time when he drew back the staff he sniffed it several times as if it smelled very good, and then started along the ridge straight for the camp. He moved very slowly, with the help of the cane, until he reached the end of the ridge, when he threw the cane out into the air and it became a bridge of shining rock stretching across the river. After he had crossed over upon the bridge it became a cane again, and the old man picked it up and started over the mountain toward the camp.

The hunter was frightened, and felt sure that it meant mischief, so he hurried on down the mountain and took the shortest trail back to the camp to get there before the old man. When he got there and told his story the medicine-man said the old man was a wicked cannibal monster called

Nûñ'yunu'wĭ, "Dressed in Stone," who lived in that part of the country, and was always going about the mountains looking for some hunter to kill and eat. It was very hard to escape from him, because his stick guided him like a dog, and it was nearly as hard to kill him, because his whole body was covered with a skin of solid rock. If he came he would kill and eat them all, and there was only one way to save themselves. He could not bear to look upon a menstrual woman, and if they could find seven menstrual women to stand in the path as he came along the sight would kill him.

So they asked among all the women, and found seven who were sick in that way, and with one of them it had just begun. By the order of the medicine-man they stripped themselves and stood along the path where the old man would come. Soon they heard Nûñ'yunu'wĭ coming through the woods, feeling his way with his stone cane. He came along the trail to where the first woman was standing, and as soon as he saw her he started and cried out: "*Yu!* my grandchild; you are in a very bad state!" He hurried past her, but in a moment he met the next woman, and cried out again: "*Yu!* my child; you are in a terrible way," and hurried past her, but now he was vomiting blood. He hurried on and met the third and the fourth and the fifth woman, but with each one that he saw his step grew weaker until when he came to the last one, with whom the sickness had just begun, the blood poured from his mouth and he fell down on the trail.

Then the medicine-man drove seven sourwood stakes through his body and pinned him to the ground, and when night came they piled great logs over him and set fire to them, and all the people gathered around to see. Nûñ'yunu'wĭ was a great *ada'wehĭ* [magician] and knew many secrets, and now as the fire came close to him he began to talk, and told them the medicine for all kinds of sickness. At midnight he began to sing, and sang the hunting songs for calling up the bear and the deer and all the animals of the woods and mountains. As the blaze grew hotter his voice sank low and lower, until at last when daylight came, the logs were a heap of white ashes and the voice was still.

Then the medicine-man told them to rake off the ashes, and where the body had lain they found only a large lump of red *wâ'dĭ* paint and a magic *u'lûñsû'tĭ* stone. He kept the stone for himself, and calling the people around him he painted them, on face and breast, with the red *wâ'dĭ*, and whatever each person prayed for while the painting was being done—whether for hunting success, for working skill, or for a long life—that gift was his.[1]

Endnotes

[1] James Mooney, *Myths of the Cherokee: Nineteenth Annual Report of the Bureau of American Ethnology, 1897-98*, part 1 (Washington: GPO, 1900), 240–48, 317–20. For biographical information on Mooney, see the Papers of James Mooney and Register to the Papers of James Mooney (James R. Glenn, Apr. 1991), both in the National Anthropological Archives of the Smithsonian. Mooney's other major works include *Myths of the Cherokees* (Cambridge: Riverside Press, 1888), *The sacred formulas of the Cherokees* (Washington: Bureau of American Ethnology, 1891), and *The Swimmer Manuscript: Cherokee sacred formulas and medicinal prescriptions*, revised, completed, and edited by Frans M. Olbrechts (Washington: GPO, 1932).

Two Cherokee women sitting in front of log cabin exhibit

COURTESY OF MUSEUM OF THE CHEROKEE INDIAN, CHEROKEE, NC, 2009.002.07791, CHA PHOTO

Part 2
ENCOUNTERS

Cherokee women's sexual freedom and their considerable political, economic, and domestic power shocked most European observers from the time of first contact in 1540. Cherokees accepted sexuality as natural, and their dances were sometimes overtly sexual in nature. For example, in the friendship dance, men and women enacted the stages of courtship and became openly intimate. During the course of the dance, the male dancers began to make sexual gestures like touching their female partners' breasts and finally even the clothing over their genitals.[1] The Cherokees did not see nudity as a cause for shame and did not have laws against fornication or adultery. Their language lacked any words for heaven or hell, damnation or salvation, or grace, repentance, or forgiveness.[2]

Since Cherokee women had more freedom and power than their counterparts in Europe, Europeans viewed this reversal of patriarchal values as deviant, uncivilized, sinful, and deeply threatening. Survival depended on the balance of male and female contributions. Cherokee men and women had gender-specific tasks and complementary responsibilities in the productive and reproductive spheres: men hunted and women cultivated the earth and gathered food. The division of labor based on one's sex did not imply hierarchy, but equality. Social identity and rules of conduct were tied to clan; the tribe was matrilineal. The recognized clans today are Deer, Wolf, Bird, Long Hair, Wild Potato, Blue, and Paint.[3]

Although the land was held communally, Cherokee women owned their dwellings and domestic hearths, and husbands lived in the women's houses.[4] Women were influential in political affairs. The females of each clan selected an elder woman to serve on the women's council, a highly influential body. The Beloved Woman, who also represented her clan, presided over the council.[5] Frequently, Beloved Women who had been courageous in battle decided the fate of prisoners.

Travelers, traders, and missionaries recorded their observations about Cherokee women's appearance, sexual practices, marriage customs, menstrual taboos, and labor. Generally, their accounts portrayed the women's sexual freedom as licentious and dangerous and their crucial economic role as evidence of their oppression by Cherokee men. When Europeans first encountered the Cherokees, they wrote about the radical differences in their cultures.

The Cherokees' encounter with the gold-seeking Hernando de Soto and his men marked their first contact with Europeans and Africans. De Soto's Spanish army arrived on May 30, 1540, at Guasili (or Guaxule), a village in western North Carolina. His expedition also went through Georgia and Tennessee villages that were later identified as

Cherokee. De Soto believed the villages were under a Coosa chiefdom, while a Chalaque nation was described around the region where North Carolina, South Carolina, and Georgia meet near the Keowee River.[6] The Spaniards encountered the queen of Cofitachiqui (a Muskogean woman of great wealth), whom they captured and made a prisoner. She managed to escape with some of the slaves in de Soto's entourage. Years later, in 1567, another Spanish expedition, led by Juan Pardo, encountered the Cherokees. As a result of the two *entradas*, the Cherokees and other tribes contracted diseases that decimated their populations.[7]

In the following eighteenth- and nineteenth-century documents, James Adair, Henry Timberlake, John Haywood, William Bartram, Louis Philippe, and Daniel Butrick reveal their impressions of the Cherokee people and Cherokee women. Their accounts tend to be brief, as they had limited access to the women's world. Like other travelers and traders, Louis Philippe saw Cherokee women as libertine and as oppressed by the men. Adair, Timberlake, Haywood, and Butrick sought to prove that the Cherokees were descended from the ancient Hebrews. In contrast to the others, Bartram perceived Cherokee women as happy and equal to their husbands. The following selections reveal glimpses of the daily lives of Cherokee women and a great deal about the European values of the observers.

ENDNOTES

[1] Frank G. Speck and Leonard Broom in collaboration with Will West Long, *Cherokee Dance and Drama* (1951; reprint, Norman: University of Oklahoma Press, 1983), 65–68.

[2] William G. McLoughlin, *Champion of the Cherokees: Evan and John B. Jones* (Princeton, N.J.: Princeton University Press, 1990), 35; Raymond D.

Fogelson, "On the 'Petticoat Government' of the Eighteenth-Century Cherokee," in *Personality and Cultural Construction of Society*, edited by David K. Jordan and Marc J. Swartz (Tuscaloosa: University of Alabama Press, 1990), 170.

[3] John Howard Payne Papers, Edward E. Ayer Collection, Newberry Library, Chicago, vol. 4: 92, 4: 65, 4: 270, part 2.

[4] John Ridge, Washington City, Feb. 27, 1826, John Howard Payne Papers, Edward E. Ayer Collection, Newberry Library, Chicago, vol. 8: 109.

[5] John P. Brown, *Old Frontiers: The Story of the Cherokee Indians from Earliest Times to the Date of Their Removal to the West, 1838* (Kingsport, Tenn.: Southern Publishers, 1938), 18.

[6] Lawrence A. Clayton, Vernon James Knight Jr., and Edward C. Moore, editors, *The De Soto Chronicles: The Expedition of Hernando De Soto to North America in 1539–1543*, vol. 2 (Tuscaloosa and London: University of Alabama Press, 1993), 308–9.

[7] Mooney, *Myths of the Cherokee*, 23–29.

~ James Adair Excerpt ~

James Adair was a trader born in Ireland who lived with southeastern tribes for forty years. His book *The History of the American Indians; Particularly Those Nations adjoining the Mississippi, East and West Florida, Georgia, South and North Carolina, and Virginia* (1775) shed light on Cherokee culture. Like John Haywood and Daniel Butrick, Adair believed Cherokees descended from the Jews.

In 1736, he was a trader among the Cherokees. Evidently, he moved to northern Mississippi to live with the Chickasaw Nation in 1744.

In the following excerpt, Adair describes the ways in which Cherokee women's menstrual retreats resembled those of the ancient Hebrews and Mosaic laws regarding uncleanness.

~

The Indians have customs consonant to the Mosaic Laws *of uncleanness*. They oblige their women in their *lunar retreats*, to build small huts, at as considerable a distance from their dwelling-houses, as they imagine may be out of the enemies reach; where, during the space of that period, they are obliged to stay at the risk of their lives. Should they be known to violate that ancient law, they must answer for every misfortune that befalls any of the people, as a certain effect of the divine fire; though the lurking enemy sometimes kills them in their religious retirement. Notwithstanding they reckon it conveys a most horrid and dangerous pollution to those who touch, or go near them, or walk anywhere within the circle of their retreats; and are in fear of thereby spoiling the supposed purity and power of their holy ark, which they always carry to war; yet the enemy believe they can so cleanse themselves with the consecrated herbs, roots, etc. which the chieftain carries in the beloved war-ark, as to secure them in this point from bodily danger, because it was done against their enemies.

The non-observance of this separation, a breach of the marriage-law, and murder, they esteem the most capital crimes. When the time of the women's separation is ended, they always purify themselves in deep running water, return home, dress, and anoint themselves. They ascribe these monthly periods, to the female structure, not to the anger of *Ishtohoollo Aba*.[1]

ENDNOTES

[1] James Adair, *History of the American Indians* (London: Edward & Charles Dilly, 1775), 123–24. *Ishtohoollo Aba* has been translated as meaning "holy, exalted, sacred Fire Father" (or "Great Spirit"), who lived in the Heavens.

～ Henry Timberlake Memoir ～

Lieutenant Henry Timberlake encountered the Cherokees as a British emissary. He wrote his account of his observations of the Overhill Cherokees in the 1760s. His memoir is a highly valuable ethnological study. Timberlake arrived after Fort Loudon in Tennessee was abandoned in 1760. He was especially impressed by the Cherokee designation of Nancy Ward as a Beloved Woman and War Woman. Timberlake wrote,

> These chiefs, or headmen, likewise compose the assemblies of the nation, into which the war-women are admitted. The reader will not be a little surprised to find the story of *Amazons* not so great a fable as we imagined, many of the Indian women being as famous in war, as powerful in council. . . . This is the only title females can enjoy; but it abundantly recompenses them, by the power they acquire by it, which is so great that they can, by the wave of a swan's wing, deliver a wretch condemned by the council, and already tied to the stake.

In the following passage, Timberlake describes the Cherokees' appearance, dress, and disposition.

> The Cherokees are of a middle stature, of an olive color, though generally painted, and their skins stained with gunpowder, pricked into it in very pretty figures. The hair of their head is shaved, though many of the old people have it plucked out by the roots, except a patch on the hinder part of the head, about twice the bigness of a crown-piece, which is ornamented with beads, feathers, wampum, stained deer hair, and such like baubles. The ears are slit and stretched

to an enormous size, putting the person who undergoes the operation to incredible pain, being unable to lie on either side for near forty days. To remedy this, they generally slit but one at a time; so soon as the patient can bear it, they are wound round with wire to expand them, and are adorned with silver pendants and rings, which they likewise wear at the nose. This custom does not belong originally to the Cherokees, but taken by them from the Shawnees, or other northern nations.

They that can afford it wear a collar of wampum, which are beads cut out of clamshells, a silver breast-plate, and bracelets on their arms and wrists of the same metal, a bit of cloth over their private parts, a shirt of the English make, a sort of cloth-boots, and moccasins, which are shoes of a make peculiar to the Americans, ornamented with porcupine-quills; a large mantle or match-coat thrown over all completes their dress at home; but when they go to war they leave their trinkets behind, and the mere necessaries serve them. The women wear the hair of their head, which is so long that it generally reaches to the middle of their legs, and sometimes to the ground, club'd, and ornamented with ribbons of various colours; but, except their eyebrows, pluck it from all the other parts of the body, especially the looser part of the sex. The rest of their dress is now become very much like the European; and, indeed, that of the men is greatly altered. The old people still remember and praise the ancient days, before they were acquainted with the whites, when they had but little dress, except a bit of skin about their middles, moccasins, a mantle of buffalo skin for the winter, and a lighter one of feathers for the summer. The women, particularly the half-breed, are remarkably well featured; and both men and women are straight and well-built, with small hands and feet.

The warlike arms used by the Cherokees are guns, bows and arrows, darts, scalping-knives, and tomahawks, which are hatchets; the hammer-part of which being made hollow, and a small hole running from thence along the shank, terminated by a small brass-tube for the mouth, makes a complete pipe. There are various ways of making these, according to the country or fancy of the purchaser, being all made by the Europeans; some have a long spear at top, and some different conveniences on each side. This is one of their most useful pieces of field-furniture, serving all the offices of hatchet, pipe, and sword; neither are the Indians less expert at throwing it than using it near, but will kill at a considerable distance.

They are of a very gentle and amicable disposition to those they think their friends, but as implacable in their enmity, their revenge being only completed in the entire destruction of their enemies. They were pretty hospitable to all white strangers, till the Europeans encouraged them to scalp; but the great reward offered has led them often since to commit as great barbarities on us, as they formerly only treated their most inveterate enemies with. They are very hardy, bearing heat, cold, hunger and thirst, in a surprising manner; and yet no people are given to more excess in eating and drinking, when it is conveniently in their power: the follies, nay mischief, they commit when inebriated, are entirely laid to the liquor; and no one will revenge any injury (murder excepted) received from one who is no more himself: they are not less addicted to gaming than drinking, and will even lose the shirt off their back, rather than give over play, when luck runs against them.

They are extremely proud, despising the lower class of Europeans; and in some athletic diversions I once was present at, they refused to match or hold conference with any but officers.[1]

ENDNOTES

[1] Henry Timberlake, *The Memoir of Lieut. Henry Timberlake* (London: printed for the author, 1765), 49–53.

～ John Haywood Excerpt ～

Born in North Carolina in 1762, John Haywood was a judge and historian who moved to Tennessee. His book *The Natural and Aboriginal History of Tennessee* is a valuable source of the history of the Cherokees. In addition to commenting on the Cherokees' appearance, temperament, and menstrual taboos, Haywood described the tribe's marriage customs.

In his book, he sought to prove that the native people of Tennessee descended from the ancient Hebrews. To back up his thesis, Haywood included biblical references. He also helped perpetuate the view of Cherokee women as oppressed drudges, even going so far as to make an unsubstantiated claim that Cherokees destroyed their female offspring.

～

The Cherokee women are elegantly formed, have sprightly eyes, accompanied with modesty and chastity, which render them very far from uninteresting objects. They love their husbands; are attached to domestic duties and devotion to their children. With them the marriage contract is purchase. The suitor either devotes his services for a time to the parents of the maid whom he courts, hunts for them, assists in making canoes, or offers them presents. The woman has not the power of refusing. The price which he pays generally consists of wearing apparel, with which the bride is dressed out. On the appearance of the bridegroom, she is stripped of it by her relations, who claim it, and in that state she is presented to him as his wife. He receives her with cold indifference whilst she, with modesty and humility, retires to the hut which he has prepared for her reception. The culture of the farm, the preparing and dressing of food, and the bearing of burthens [burdens] in their travels, are all imposed upon her. The husband stalks about, with his gun and pipe, regardless of the fatigue and pain which she endures. After she has served him as a slave, contributed to his pleasures as a mistress, borne him children, and taken care of his hut, he often takes another wife, and parts with her as unfeelingly as if she had never existed. Such is the barbarous treatment which women experience, that they not infrequently destroy their female offspring, that they may escape the hardships which have fallen on the mother. They use for the cure of disorders, what is called the Indian sweat, by pouring water on heated stones in a confined place, from whence the fumes arising soon produce a copious perspiration. The same practice precisely has prevailed in Scythia [central Eurasia], from the earliest times.[1]

ENDNOTES

[1] John Haywood, *The Natural and Aboriginal History of Tennessee: Up to the First Settlements Therein by the White People in the Year 1768* (Nashville, Tenn.: George Wilson, 1823), 279–80.

~ William Bartram Excerpts ~

William Bartram's views on Cherokee women differed radically from those of Henry Timberlake and John Haywood. Bartram traveled extensively throughout the Southeast in the eighteenth century. A keen observer and naturalist, he commented on Cherokee women's appearance and grace. He is unique among the commentators because he did not see Cherokee women as oppressed but rather quite happy. He went so far as to claim that "there is no people anywhere who love their women more than these Indians do."

The first passage below is from Bartram's famous *Travels*. The second was published after his lifetime.

~

The women of the Cherokees, are tall, slender, erect and of a delicate frame; their features formed with perfect symmetry, their countenance cheerful and friendly, and they move with a becoming grace and dignity.

. . . The Cherokees in their dispositions and manners are grave and steady; dignified and circumspect in their deportment; rather slow and reserved in conversations; yet frank, cheerful, and humane; tenacious of the liberties and natural rights of man; secret, deliberate and determined in their councils; honest, just and liberal, and ready always to sacrifice every pleasure and gratification, even their blood, and life itself, to defend their territory and maintain their rights.

What is the condition of the women among the tribes of Indians which you visited? We are told by many writers that the condition or state of the Indian women is the picture of misery and oppression; is this actually the case? Do the Indian women ever, so far as you know, preside at the councils of the Sachems, especially when war and other matters of consequence are considered in their councils? Have you ever heard or known of any instance of women who have presided over any nation or nations of Indians?

Answer. I have every reasonable argument from my own observation, as well as the accounts of the whites residing among the Indians, to be convinced that the condition of the women is as happy, compared with that of the men, as the condition of women in any part of the world. Their business or employment is chiefly in the house, as it is with other women, except at the season when their crops are growing, when they generally turn out with their husbands or parents, but they are by no means compelled to such labor. There are not one-third as many females as males seen at work in their plantations: for, at this season of the year, by a law of the people, they do not hunt, the game not being in season till after their crops or harvest is gathered in, so the males have little else with which to employ themselves; and the Indians are by no means that lazy, slothful, sleepy people, they are commonly reported to be. Besides, you may depend upon my assertion that there is no people anywhere who love their women more than these Indians do, or men of better understanding in distinguishing the merits of the opposite sex, or more faithful in rendering suitable compensation. They are courteous and polite to the women, and gentle, tender and fondling, even to an appearance of effeminacy, to their offspring. An Indian never attempts, nay, he cannot use towards a woman amongst them any indelicacy or indecency, either in action or language.

I never saw or heard of an instance of an Indian beating his wife or other female, or reproving them in anger or in harsh language. And the women make a suitable and grateful return; for they are discreet, modest, loving, faithful, and affectionate to their husbands.[1]

ENDNOTES

[1] William Bartram, *Travels Through North & South Carolina, Georgia, East & West Florida, the Cherokee Country, the Extensive Territories of the Muscogulges, or Creek Confederacy, and the Country of the Cha[o]ctaws* (Philadelphia: James and Johnson, 1791), 483–85. See also http://babel. hathitrust.org/cgi/pt?id=mdp.39015021105773;view=1up;seq=59. The question-and-answer section—from Bartram's "Observations on the Creek and Cherokee Indians"—was written in 1789, probably in response to inquiries from naturalist Benjamin Smith Barton, but appeared after Bartram's lifetime. His manuscript, edited by E. G. Squier, was first published in *Transactions of the American Ethnological Society* 3, part 1 (1853), 1–81. The excerpt is on pages 15–17.

~ Louis Philippe Excerpt ~

Louis Philippe was king of France from 1830 to 1848. He traveled to the United States in 1796–97. Louis Philippe's moralistic commentary on the Cherokees in 1797 emphasized the sexual freedom of the women. Cherokees accepted sexual activity before marriage, and although they expected fidelity afterward, they had an interesting attitude toward adultery. In 1807, Major John Norton remarked that, in contrast to the Creeks, "the Cherokees have no such punishment for adultery; the husband is even disgraced in the opinion of his friends, if he seeks to take satisfaction in any other way, than that of getting another wife."

Although he recognized Cherokee women's sexual autonomy, Louis Philippe portrayed Indian women more generally as drudges. This image of Indian women as degraded and overworked persisted into the nineteenth century. Euro-Americans did not realize that Indian women's strenuous work brought them power and control over the products of their labor.

The other distinct image of the Indian woman was that of the princess—a woman such as Pocahontas, a beautiful daughter of a chief. Thus, when Europeans encountered Cherokees, who possessed a radically different gender system from theirs, their misconceptions about gender were used to justify campaigns to civilize American Indians and eventually remove them from the Southeast.[1]

In the following excerpt, Louis Philippe portrays Cherokee women as drudges but emphasizes their sexual freedom as well.

. . . The Cherokees, on the other hand, are exceedingly casual. If a Cherokee's woman sleeps with another man, all he does is send her away without a word to the man, considering it beneath his dignity to quarrel over a woman. And all Cherokee women are public women in the full meaning of the phrase: dollars never fail to melt their hearts.

It is notable that this freedom of concubinage, this polygamy, invariably renders the women contemptible in the men's eyes and deprives them of all influence. That is an awkward forecast for Frenchwomen; new divorce laws have made their marriage an Indian concubinage. It is quite true that women can free themselves from the dependence due to their weakness only by the nobler feelings they arouse in men, and not by the pleasures they offer. If these pleasures are not to degrade the emotions, they must serve exclusively to heighten the affections of a man who loves and believes himself loved. But if they are lavished on legions, the magic of the emotion vanishes, and women fall into degradation and thence into dependence. But back to my story: the Indians have all the work done by women. They are assigned not only household tasks; even the corn, peas, beans, and potatoes are planted, tended, and preserved by the women. The man smokes peacefully while the woman grinds corn in a mortar (this mortar is not more than a h[o]llowed tree trunk, and the pestle is a long piece of wood, one end about as wide as the hollow).[2]

ENDNOTES

[1] Fogelson, "On the 'Petticoat Government,' " 169. See also Rayna Green, *Women in American Indian Society* (New York: Chelsea House, 1992), 47, 51; Charles Hudson, *Southeastern Indians* (Knoxville: University of Tennessee Press, 1976), 260, 319–20.

[2] Louis Philippe, *Diary of My Travels in America: Louis-Philippe, King of France, 1830–1848* (New York: Delacorte Press, 1977), 72–73.

⮜ Payne-Butrick Papers ⮞

The United States government and missionaries regarded Christian conversion as a crucial step toward becoming civilized. Cherokees who did join churches were sometimes expelled for adultery or drunkenness. Some refused to abandon their traditional beliefs and practices. For example, Cherokees who already had two wives did not want to forsake one of them, and many converts still wanted to consult conjurers and participate in ball play and ceremonies.

Daniel Sabin Butrick, a missionary sent in 1818 by the American Board of Commissioners for Foreign Missions, recorded that Cherokee women observed all the traditional rules of the Hebrews regarding female "uncleanness," as stated in the twelfth and fifteenth chapters of Leviticus, with the exception that, among the Cherokees, the restrictions did not last any longer after the birth of a daughter than that of a son. Following childbirth, Cherokee women observed restrictions for twelve to twenty-four days. During their menstrual periods, they remained alone for seven days, touching only their own food, clothes, and furniture. They bathed before reentering their communities. Warriors remained separate from women for three days before and after going on a raid.

John Howard Payne, who wrote the famous song "Home, Sweet Home," became the guest of Chief John Ross in 1836, just two years before the Cherokees' removal from their homeland. He engaged in research about their history and culture. Like Butrick, James Adair, John Haywood, and many others, Payne believed the Cherokees to be descended from the ancient Hebrews. He recorded his observations, collected many documents while living among the Cherokees, and collaborated with Daniel Butrick to preserve them.

The following excerpts from the Payne-Butrick Papers describe traditional practices that the majority of Cherokees observed. They differ dramatically from later selections in this book that espouse white, Victorian views of womanhood adopted by a small, elite, highly acculturated group of Cherokees.

Nutsawi and Epenetus, both Cherokees, were informants, as were T. Smith and A. Sanders.

⇍

⤳ Marriage

At first one man had one wife. Polygamy was forbidden before the flood, and has never been lawful. (Nutsawi)

Second marriages were not approved; and widows and widowers generally remained single. Others were afraid to marry them.

Anciently girls were not allowed to marry till after their first separation [menstrual period], nor without the consent of parents, brothers and sisters, and uncles. (Nutsawi)

Cherokees could not marry any blood connections, and no one of the same clan with either of their father or mother. The consent of the relatives on both sides was required, and when two came together they promised to forsake all other men and women, and live together as long as they lived. (Nutsawi)

When a young man wished to marry a young woman, he gave her parents something for her, of whatever he could spare; and if the young woman had a brother, this brother and the intended bridegroom exchanged clothes, horses & then were as if own brothers. (T. Smith)

The Cherokee were not allowed to marry in the same clan with themselves nor any near descendants of their mother's relatives though they might marry any of the descendants of their father's connections.

Anciently the Cherokees, it is said, seldom married a second time. Second marriages not being approved of (unless as among the Creeks).

A priest was not allowed to marry a widow, nor a woman who [had] been put away by her husband, nor any other woman of bad character.

And as their God, the moon, had but one wife, the sun (or on the other hand, among those who consider the sun, the male, as the sun had but one wife, the moon) therefore they supposed it improper for them to have more than one wife each. When a young man desired a young woman for his wife, he consulted her parents, whose consent was deemed absolutely essential. All parties being agreed, the time was appointed for the marriage; and the priest, who was to officiate, was notified of their wishes. Accordingly on the day appointed for the marriage, early in the morning, the priest got two roots of a certain kind, and laid them on his hand, a little distance from each other. He then, with his face toward the east, or rising sun, prayed to that God, or goddess, to let him know whether those two persons were designed for each other; and whether, if married, they would live long and happily together. If the persons were not for each other, and would not, if married, live well together, the roots would not move. If, in case of marriage, they would live well together a short time, and then one die, the roots would move together, but one would quickly wilt away. In either case the priest forbid the marriage,

& nothing more was said about it. But if the roots moved quickly together, & continued so till put down, the marriage was to be consummated.

All parties then assembled and the priest commended the couple to God (the sun)[,] praying that they might be enabled to live long and happily together. He then told them that if either should prove unfaithful to the other, that one especially must go to the bad place. They supposed that nothing would break the marriage covenant but adultery. Nothing else could justify a separation. . . .

Cherokee girls were not allowed to marry till after their first separation (the commencement of their monthly courses) nor without the consent of parents, brothers, sisters and uncles. (Nutsawi)

~ *Childbirth*

Cherokee women generally have but little difficulty in bringing forth their children. A mother, or grandmother, in common cases, affords all the assistance needed. The presence of men is disgusting to them on such occasions. The priest, however, or conjurer, in some instances prayed for a speedy & safe delivery. If the child, at birth, happened to fall on its breast, the omen was bad, and it was wrapped up immediately, and thrown into the creek. When the cloth about it was disengaged, or unwrapped and began to float, the child was taken up, & carried back, while the cloth, supposed to have taken the ill fortune, was suffered to float away. But if the child at birth fell on its back, the event was ominous of good. Sometimes soon after birth, the child [was] waved over the fire, or [was] held before it, while a prayer was made to the element, to take care of it.

Either on the fourth or seventh day, (sometimes on one

& sometimes on the other) the priest, (or, in late days) the conjurer, took the child to a creek or river. He there commended it to its creator (the sun) and prayed that it might have a long and happy life in this world. He then dipped the child in the water (seven times) and returned it to its parents.

Children were named at 4 or 7 days old. But sometimes at birth & washed immediately. (Epenetus)

⌁ *Menstrual Taboos*

With regard to female uncleannesses, the views & customs of the Cherokee and Creeks can scarcely be expressed more accurately than by referring to a strict obedience of the directions given in the 12th and 15th chapters of Leviticus; only as these Indians have not the Jewish Tabernacle, or Temple worship in all its forms, "except" the common uncleanness of seven days, only after childbirth, is observed.

During the time of their uncleanness they must touch no person, but stay by themselves (among the Creeks, as anciently among the Cherokee also) and must touch nothing but their own food, their own bed, & wearing apparel. And at the end of the seven days, they are by washing and other means purified, & permitted to return to the family circle. Unless the cause of uncleanness in some instances may be prolonged, in which case the uncleanness continues also.

The same uncleanness was communicated by the touch of a bone or a grave as of a dead body & the same rules with regard to purifying. Warriors observed the same kind or more rigid method of purification.

For a man to sleep with a woman during the time of her uncleanness, was considered among the most filthy crimes. He was obliged to take an emetic formed of a root, called *u-yo-ti* (bearing a high stalk and red blossom) and then dip himself seven times in a river, & continue alone, in his uncleanness till night. Unless he did this he was declared unfit to hunt or go to war. (Nutsawi)

Females in their uncleanness must not eat anything but hominy or thin drink. (A. Sanders)

If, after childbirth, a woman was sick so as to require doctoring, then at her purification a sacrifice was offered of a certain kind of bird.

If a woman pregnant or unclean happens to look on a person snake bit, the person will die. (Nutsawi)[1]

ENDNOTES

[1] John Howard Payne Papers, Edward E. Ayer Collection, Newberry Library, Chicago, Payne-Butrick Papers, vol. 4: 373–74; 376–84; 403–12 (manuscript pages). See also *The Payne-Butrick Papers*, edited by William Anderson, Jane L. Brown, and Anne F. Rogers, Vols. 4–6 (Lincoln and London: University of Nebraska Press, 2010). The editors included invaluable annotations. For more on missionaries' battle to control Cherokee women's sexuality, see Carolyn Johnston, "Burning Beds, Spinning Wheels, and Calico Dresses: Controlling Cherokee Women's Sexuality," *Journal of Cherokee Studies* 19 (1998), 3–17. For more on Cherokee conversions and backsliding, see McLoughlin, *Champion of the Cherokees;* Adair, *History of the American Indians*, 133–65; Fogelson, "On the 'Petticoat Government,' " 165.

Part 3

THE CIVILIZATION PROGRAM

After the American Revolution, when the Cherokee Nation lost large tracts of its land, the United States government and missionaries sought to transform Cherokee gender roles and attitudes toward sexuality and the body. This involved transforming Cherokee men into farmers and Cherokee women into submissive housewives. Traditional Cherokees resisted, but eventually wealthier members of that society, many of them of mixed ancestry, began to accept a radical alteration of gender roles. American presidents from Thomas Jefferson to Andrew Jackson agreed that the Indians must either be removed from the East or become civilized. The spinning wheel and plow became the symbols of the civilization program. Many Cherokee women welcomed the spinning wheels so they could clothe their families. This was especially true after the deerskin trade expanded, when they faced a scarcity of deerskins for family use.

Thomas Jefferson assumed the Indians were capable of civilization but believed that they would become extinct unless they turned to agriculture and adopted Western European gender roles, the practice of owning private property, and Christianity. Since Jefferson doubted they would adopt these values, he planned to move the Indians who lived east of the Mississippi River to the northern part of the Louisiana Purchase. Like Jefferson, Presidents Monroe, Adams, and Madison all supported civilization programs. Monroe signed an appropriation bill in 1819 that provided ten thousand dollars annually for the civilization of the Indians. These early presidents envisioned Cherokee lands as eventually becoming part of the United States.[1]

Since Cherokee women contributed significantly to the sustenance of their families, Europeans saw them as exploited drudges. Jefferson addressed the role of women in his *Notes on the State of Virginia*:

> The women are subjected to unjust drudgery. This I believe is the case with every barbarous people. With such, force is law. The stronger sex imposes on the weaker. It is civilization alone that replaces women in the enjoyment of their natural equality. That first teaches us to subdue the selfish passions, and to respect those rights in others which we value in ourselves. Were we in equal barbarism, our females would be equal drudges. The man with them is less strong than with us, but their women stronger than ours; and both for the same obvious reason; because our man and their woman is habituated to labor, and formed by it. With both races the sex which is indulged with ease is the least athletic.[2]

Jefferson misunderstood that women's economic and political power stemmed from the work he saw as drudgery. Before long, missionaries and the United States government would attempt to change all that. Both justified their "civilization program" as a means for liberating Cherokee women from drudgery. But the practical effect was to undermine women's sources of power and destabilize gender and class relations.

As part of its plan, the federal government helped fund the Brainerd Mission, in East Tennessee near Chattanooga, in 1817. The missionaries of the American Board of Commissioners for Foreign Missions (ABCFM) set up the mission as an exemplary one to convert and civilize the Cherokees. The school educated three hundred Cherokee men and women over two decades. The ABCFM missionaries—among them Daniel Butrick, Ard Hoyt, Sophia Sawyer, Cyrus Kingsbury, and Samuel Worcester—were Congregationalists from Boston.

A central goal of this initiative was controlling women's sexual behavior. The missionaries disapproved of participation in ceremonies, polygamy, fornication, nudity, gambling, drinking, conjuring, dancing, infanticide, witchcraft, ball play, and card playing. The Cherokees received more missionaries and missionary funds in the early nineteenth century than did any other tribe. The missionaries sought to "elevate" Cherokee women through submission to patriarchal values.[3] Those at the Brainerd Mission extolled the virtues of their most famous convert, Catharine Brown.

Cherokee women lost and gained power in a variety of ways in the nineteenth century. The disruption of gender roles was integrally tied to the dispossession of the Cherokees' land. The following documents reveal voices—those of Catharine

Brown, missionaries, Wahnenauhi, and selected authors of articles in the *Cherokee Phoenix*, the Cherokee newspaper—espousing the ideals of true womanhood.

ENDNOTES

[1] Theda Perdue, "Women, Men, and American Indian Policy: The Cherokee Response to Civilization," in *Negotiators of Change*, edited by Nancy Shoemaker (New York: Routledge, 1995), 90–114; Laurel Thatcher Ulrich, *The Age of Homespun: Object and Stories in the Creation of an American Myth* (New York: Alfred A. Knopf, 2001); Michael Paul Rogin, *Fathers and Children: Andrew Jackson and the Subjugation of the American Indian* (New York: Alfred A. Knopf, 1975), 179–80.

[2] Roy Harvey Pearce, *The Savages of America: A Study of the Indian and the Idea of Civilization* (Baltimore: Johns Hopkins University Press, 1953), 92–93.

[3] Jeremiah Evarts, Memorandum, April–May 1822, American Board of Commissioners for Foreign Missions Papers (hereafter ABCFM Papers), by permission of the Houghton Library, Harvard University, Cambridge, Mass., quoted in William G. McLoughlin, *Cherokees and Missionaries, 1789–1839* (Norman: University of Oklahoma Press, 1995), 139. See also Harriet J. Kupferer, *Ancient Drums, Other Moccasins: Native North American Cultural Adaptation* (Englewood Cliffs, N.J.: Prentice Hall, 1988); William G. McLoughlin, "Who Civilized the Cherokees?" *Journal of Cherokee Studies* 13 (1988), 65.

～ Memoir of Catharine Brown ～

Catharine Brown arrived at the Brainerd Mission on July 9, 1817. The missionaries of the ABCFM believed that her life epitomized the virtues of piety, purity, submissiveness, and domesticity and symbolized the taming of female sexuality. Rufus Anderson, the editor of her memoir, published in 1825, praised Brown as a paragon of virtue.[1]

While Brown remained chaste, she inspired lust in at least one missionary. Daniel Sabin Butrick felt such sexual passion for Brown that he agonized over it in his diary, guiltily confided to its pages, "My wicked passions rage, the storm beats on my foundering bank, and gaping waves and towering surges threaten my immediate ruin."[2]

Brown began to show symptoms of tuberculosis in 1822. She died on the morning of July 18, 1823. Her death was romanticized in her memoir. Brown quickly became a martyr in the eyes of Christians, and a symbol of true womanhood. In the years following her death, she assumed almost mythic proportions. The missionaries' admiration of her was so great that they regarded her as a model of what every young woman should be.[3]

Yet Brown's life was likely more complicated. Although she was a Christian convert, she continued to fast and to rely on the help of traditional healers; she also participated in women's prayer groups in the mountains or forests. Thus, she may have retained more of her Cherokee beliefs than the missionaries' accounts acknowledged.[4]

The following excerpts from her memoir tell the story of a Cherokee woman of the nineteenth century who bridged two worlds. Rufus Anderson wrote the first and third sections; Anderson quotes missionaries Cyrus Kingsbury and Jeremiah Evarts and Dr. Campbell, Brown's physician. The second part contains material from Catharine Brown's diary.

‑

[Rufus Anderson excerpts]

The reader will be prepared to credit what will be said, in the progress of this memoir, respecting Catharine's intellectual condition, when she first came under the care of the missionaries.

It is pleasing to observe here, that her moral character was ever irreproachable. This is the more remarkable, considering the looseness of manners then prevalent among the females of her nation, and the temptations to which she was exposed, when, during the war with the Creek Indians, the army of the United States was stationed near her father's residence. Were it proper to narrate some well authenticated facts, with reference to this part of her history, the mind of the reader would be filled with admiration of her heroic virtue, and especially of the protecting care of providence. Once she even forsook her home and fled into the wild forest, to preserve her character unsullied.[5]

. . . Catharine was of the middle stature, erect, of comely features, and blooming complexion; and, even at this time, she was easy in her manners, and modest and prepossessing in her demeanor.

"It was, however, manifest," says Mr. Kingsbury, "that, with all her gentleness and apparent modesty, she had a high opinion of herself, and was fond of displaying the clothing and ornaments, in which she was arrayed. At our first interview, I was impressed with the idea that her feelings would not easily yield to the discipline of our schools, especially to that part of it which requires manual labor of the scholars. This objection I freely stated to her and requested that, if she felt any difficulty on the subject, she would seek admission to some other school. She replied that she had no objection to our regulations. I advised her to take the subject into consideration, and to obtain what information she could, relative to the treatment of the scholars, and if she then felt a desire to become a member of the school, we would receive her.

"She joined the school, and the event has shown that it was of the Lord, to the end that his name might be glorified. I have often reflected, with adoring gratitude and thankfulness, on the good providence, which conducted that interesting young female to Brainerd, and which guided her inquiring and anxious mind to the Savior of sinners."

Sometime before this, it is not known precisely how long, while residing at the house of a Cherokee friend, she had learned to speak the English language, and had acquired, also, knowledge of the letters of the alphabet. She could even read in words of one syllable. These acquisitions, which were of no particular service at the time they were made, are to be noticed with gratitude to God, as the probable means of leading her to Brainerd. They excited desires, which she could gratify nowhere else.

Her teachers declare, that, from her first admission to the school, she was attentive to her learning, industrious in her habits, and remarkably correct in her deportment. From reading in words of one syllable, she was able, in sixty days, to read intelligibly in the Bible, and, in ninety days, could read as well as most persons of common education. After writing over four sheets of paper, she could use the pen with accuracy and neatness, even without a copy.

From the testimony of different persons it appears, that, when she entered the school, her knowledge on religious subjects was exceedingly vague and defective. Her ideas of

God extended little further than the contemplation of him as a great Being, existing somewhere in the sky; and her conceptions of a future state were quite undefined. Of the Savior of the world, she had no knowledge. She supposed, that the Cherokees were a different race from the whites, and therefore had no concern in the white people's religion; and it was some time before she could be convinced, that Jesus Christ came into the world to die for the Cherokees. She has been known, also, to remark, subsequently to her conversion, that she was much afraid, when she first heard of religion; for she thought Christians could have no pleasure in this world, and that, if she became religious, she too should be rendered unhappy. How much her opinions and sentiments on this subject were, in a short time, changed, will abundantly appear as we proceed.

That the reader may be duly sensible of the singleness of heart and Christian devotedness of the men, under whose instruction this interesting female had placed herself, he is informed, that, not long after her introduction to them, they adopted the following resolution, which develops an economical principle, carried through all the missions to the Indians, under the direction of the American Board of Commissioners for Foreign Missions.—"That, as God in his providence has called us to labor in the great and good work of building up his kingdom among the Aborigines of this country, a work peculiarly arduous, and which will be attended with much expense; and above all, considering that we have solemnly devoted ourselves, and all that we have, to the prosecution of this work; we declare it to be our cordial, deliberate, and fixed resolution, that, so far as it respects our future labors, or any compensation for them, we will have no private interests distinct from the great interests of this institution. And, that if it meets the views of the Prudential Committee, we will receive no other compensation for our services, than a comfortable supply of food and clothing for ourselves and families, and such necessary expenses as our peculiar circumstances may require; observing at all times that frugality and economy, which our duty to the Christian public and the great Head of the Church demands."

Catharine had been in the school but a very few months, before divine truth began to exert an influence upon her mind. This was manifested in an increased desire to become acquainted with the Christian religion, and in a greater sobriety of manners. A tenderness of spirit, moreover, was, at the same time observed in several others.

~

[After Jeremiah Evarts, the treasurer of the ABCFM, visited Brainerd, he wrote Dr. Worcester, the corresponding secretary of the board, about the children of the mission, including Catharine Brown. Rufus Anderson quoted Evarts as follows.]

"Her parents are half-breeds, who have never learnt to speak English; yet if you were to see her at a boarding-school in New England, as she ordinarily appears here, you would not distinguish her from well-educated females of the same age, either by her complexion, features, dress, pronunciation, or manners. If your attention were directed to her particularly, you would notice a more than ordinary modesty and reserve. If you were to see her in a religious meeting of pious females, you would not distinguish her, unless by her more than common simplicity and humility. When she joined the school in July last, (having come more than one hundred miles for that sole purpose,) she could read in syllables of three letters, and was seventeen years old. From her superior manners and comely person she had probably attracted more attention, than any other female in the nation. She was vain, and excessively fond of dress, wearing a profusion of ornaments in her ears. She can now read well in the Bible, is fond of reading other books, and has been particularly pleased with the Memoirs of Mrs. Newell. Last fall she became serious, is believed to have experienced religion in the course of the autumn, and was baptized in January. Since that time, she has been constantly in the family; and all the female members of it have the most intimate knowledge of her conduct, and receive a frank disclosure of her feelings. It is their unanimous opinion, that she gives uncommon evidence of piety. At meetings for social prayer and religious improvement, held by them on every Thursday afternoon and Sabbath evening, Catharine prays in her turn, much to the gratification of her sisters in Christ. Her prayers are distinguished by great simplicity as to thought and language, and seem to be the filial aspirations of the devout child. Before Mrs. Chamberlain took charge of the girls, Catharine had, of her own accord, commenced evening prayer with them, just as they were retiring to rest. Sometime after this practice had been begun, it was discovered by one of the missionaries, who, happening to pass by the cabin where the girls lodge, overheard her pouring forth her desires in very affecting and appropriate language. On being inquired of respecting it, she simply observed, that she had prayed with the girls, because she thought it was her duty. Yet this young woman, whose conduct might now reprove many professing Christians, who have been instructed in religion from their infancy, only ten months ago had never heard of Jesus Christ, nor had a single thought whether the soul survived the body, or not. Since she became religious, her trinkets have gradually disappeared, till only a single drop remains in each ear. On hearing that pious females have, in many instances, devoted their ornaments to the missionary cause, she has determined to devote hers also. In coming to this determination, she acted without influence from the advice of others."[6]

⁓

[Rufus Anderson added, "Time fled rapidly away, in pious employments and in Christian intercourse, and brought the long expected, much dreaded separation."]

[Cyrus Kingsbury began taking notes about the mission in 1817, and Ard Hoyt assumed that role in 1818. Daniel Butrick and William Chamberlain also wrote in the Brainerd Journal. *Those missionaries kept daily notes on the life of the Brainerd Mission and sent regular letters to ABCFM headquarters in Boston. The Journal thus developed from notes, letters, and reports.*

[Rufus Anderson quoted the following passage from the Brainerd Journal.*]*

"In the spring of 1821, while making the necessary preparations for a settlement at Creek-Path, Mr. Potter and myself, for two months, made Mr. Brown's house our home. Here we had an opportunity of noticing Catharine's daily deportment, as a member of the domestic circle.

"For sweetness of temper, meekness, gentleness, and forbearance, I never saw one, who surpassed her. To her parents she was uncommonly dutiful and affectionate. Nothing, which could contribute to their happiness, was considered a burden; and her plans were readily yielded to theirs, however great the sacrifice to her feelings. The spiritual interests of the family lay near her heart, and she sometimes spent whole evenings in conversation with them on religious subjects.

"Before our arrival, she had established a weekly prayer-meeting with the female members of the family, which was also improved as an opportunity for reading the word of God, and conversing upon its important truths. Such was her extreme modesty, that she did not make this, known to me, until more than a week after my arrival; and the usual period had passed without a meeting. She at length overcame her diffidence, and informed me what their practice had been, in a manner expressive of the most unfeigned humility. These meetings were continued while we remained in the family, and I believe they were highly useful. A monthly prayer-meeting among the sisters of the church was soon after established, in which Catharine took a lively interest; nor did she ever refuse, when requested, to take an active part in the devotional exercises.

"Soon after we removed to our station, Catharine became a member of our family, and of the school. All her energies were now bent towards the improvement of her mind, with a view to future usefulness among her people. Both in school, and in the family, her deportment was such as greatly to endear her to our hearts, and she was most tenderly loved by all the children.

"She was not entirely free from the inadvertences of youth; but always received reproof with great meekness, and it never failed to produce the most salutary effect.

"She was deeply sensible of the many favors she had received from Christian friends, and often, in the strongest terms, expressed her gratitude.

"She was zealous in the cause of Christ, and labored much to instruct her ignorant people in the things, that concern their everlasting peace. The advancement of the Redeemer's kingdom was to her a subject of deep interest, and she read accounts of the triumphs of the cross in heathen countries with peculiar delight. Not many months after we settled here, a plan was devised to form a female charitable society. This plan was proposed to Catharine. She was much pleased with it, and spared no pains to explain it to the understandings of her Cherokee friends. And so successful were her exertions that, at the meeting for the formation of the society, at which a considerable number were present, not one refused to become a member. For the prosperity of this society she manifested the most tender concern till her death; and she had determined, if her life should be spared to reach the Arkansas country, to use her exertions to form a similar society there."

—

[The following are excerpts from Catharine Brown's diary.]

Creek-Path[,] May 1, 1821. Commenced boarding with Mr. and Mrs. Potter. My parents live two miles from this place. I think I shall visit them almost every week, and they will come to see me often.

[May] 2. I love to live here much. It is retired, and a good place for study. Everything looks pleasant around the school-house. The trees are covered with green leaves, and the birds sing very sweetly. How pleasant it is to be in the woods, and hear the birds praising the Lord. They remind me of the divine command, "Remember thy Creator." O may I never be so stupid and senseless [as to forget my Creator,] but may I remember to love and serve him, the few days I live in this world; for the time will soon come, when I must appear before him. Help me, Lord, to live to thy glory, even unto the end of my life. I think I feel more anxious to learn, and, to understand the Bible perfectly, than I ever did before. Although I am so ignorant, the Savior is able to prepare me for usefulness among my people.

[**May**] **5**. Saturday evening. Again I am brought to the close of another week. How have I spent my time the past week? Have I done anything for God and any good to my fellow creatures? I fear I have done nothing to glorify his holy name. Oh, how prone I am to sin, and to grieve the Spirit of a holy God, who is so kind in giving me time to prepare for heaven. May I improve these precious moments to the glory of my God.

[**May**] **6**. Sabbath evening. How thankful I ought to be to God, that he has permitted me once more to commemorate the love of a Savior, who has shed his precious blood for the remission of sin. It was indeed a solemn season to me, and I hope refreshing to each of our souls. While sitting at the table, I thought of many sins, which I had committed against God, through my life, and how much I deserved to be cast out from his presence forever. But the Son of God, who was pleased to come down from the bosom of his Father, to die on the cross for sinners like me, will, I hope, save me from death, and at last raise me to mansions of eternal rest, where I shall sit down with my blessed Jesus.

[**May**] **8**. This evening I have nothing to complain of, but my unfaithfulness both to God and my own soul. Have not improved my precious moments as I ought. Have learned but little in school, though my privileges are greater than those of many others. While they are ignorant of God, and have no opportunity to hear or learn about him, I am permitted to live with the children of God, where I am instructed to read the Bible and to understand the character of Jesus. O may I be enabled to follow the example of my teachers, to live near the Savior, and to do much good. I wish very much to be a missionary among my people. If I had an education— but perhaps I ought not to think of it. I am not worthy to be a missionary.

[**May**] **14**. Mr. Hoyt called on us this week, on his return from Mayhew [in what is now Oklahoma]. He gives us much interesting intelligence respecting the Choctaw Missions. Mr. Hoyt expected to have brought Dr. Worcester with him, but he was too sick to travel, and was obliged to stay behind. He hopes to be able to come on soon. I long to see him. He has done a great deal towards spreading the Gospel, not only in this nation but in other heathen nations of the earth. May the Lord restore his health that he may see some fruits among the heathen, for whom he has been so long laboring.

[May] 29. This day I spent my time very pleasantly at home with my dear friends. Find that brother John is the same humble believer in Jesus, walking in the Christian path. I am truly happy to meet my dear parents and sisters in health, and rejoicing in the hope of eternal glory. O may God ever delight to bless them, and to pour his spirit richly into their hearts. I am much pleased to see them making preparations for the Sabbath. They have been engaged to-day in preparing such food, etc. as they thought would be wanting tomorrow. I think brother John and sister Susannah have done much good here with respect to the Sabbath.

[May] 30. This day attended another solemn meeting in the house of God. Mr. Potter preached by an interpreter. I think more people than usual attended. All seemed attentive to hear the word of God. Mr. P. spoke of the importance of keeping the Sabbath holy. I hope it will not be in vain to all those who were present.

June 4. This day being the first Monday in the month, the people met to pray and receive religious instructions. It was truly an interesting time. The congregation, though small, was serious. One man and his wife, who have been for some time in an anxious state of mind, remained after the meeting, and Mr. and Mrs. P earnestly entreated them to seek the Lord while he was near unto them. They appeared very solemn, and said they wished to know more about God, that they might serve him the rest of their days.

We hope and pray, that they may be truly converted, and become our dear brother and sister in the Lord.

July 1. This day I have enjoyed much. Was permitted once more to sit down at the table of the Lord, and commemorate his dying love. O how good is the Savior in permitting me to partake of his grace. May I improve my great privileges in the manner I shall wish I had done, when I come to leave the world.—P.M. Went to Mr. G.'s, where Mr. Potter preaches once in two weeks. Most of the people present were whites, from the other side of the river. It was pleasant to hear a sermon preached without an interpreter.

Sept. 2. Think I have had a good time today in praying to my heavenly Father. I see nothing to trouble me, but my own wicked heart. It appears to me that the more I wish to serve God, the more I sin. I seem never to have done anything good in the sight of God. But the time is short, when I shall be delivered from this body of sin, and enter the kingdom of heaven.

[September] 3. The first Monday in the month. No doubt many Christians have been this day praying for my poor nation, as well as for other heathen nations of the earth. O why do I live so little concerned for my own soul and for the souls of others? Why is it that I pray no more to God? Is it because he is not merciful? Oh no, He is good, kind, merciful, always ready to answer the prayers of his children. O for more love to my Savior than I now have.

~

[In the following passage, Rufus Anderson sums up Catharine's final illness and her strong religious faith.]

As she approached nearer to eternity, her faith evidently grew stronger and she became more and more able cheerfully to resign, not only herself, but her parents, her friends, her people, her all, to the disposal of her Lord.

May 15th she was reduced very low by a hemorrhage from the lungs and for a few days was viewed as upon the borders of the grave.

Before this alarming symptom, it had been proposed to send again for Dr. Campbell, but her parents were persuaded first to try the skill of some Indian practitioners. Their prescriptions were followed, until the hemorrhage occurred. Then her alarmed parents sent immediately for Mr. Potter, hoping he could do something to relieve their darling child. Providentially, the Rev. Reynolds Bascom . . . had just arrived from the Choctaw Nation, on his way to the northern States; and having been afflicted in a similar manner himself, he was able to administer effectual remedies.

~

[Here, Anderson quotes Dr. Campbell,
Catharine's physician, in her final hour.]

"As death advanced, and the powers of nature gave way, she frequently offered her hand to the friends around her bed. Her mother and sister weeping over her, she looked steadily at the former, for a short time, filial love beaming from her eyes; and then, she closed them in the sleep of death.

"She expired without a groan, or a struggle. Even those around the bed scarcely knew that the last breath had left her, until I informed them she was gone.

"Thus fell asleep this lovely saint, in the arms of her Savior, a little past 6 o'clock, on the morning of July 13th, 1823."

~

*[In the passage below, Anderson describes
Catharine's brief life and her legacy.]*

Her afflicted relatives conveyed her remains to Creek-
Path, where they were, on the 20th, deposited near the
residence of her parents, and by the side of her brother
John, who had died about a year and a half before, in the
triumphs of the same faith.

Her age was about twenty-three; and six years had
elapsed from her first entering the school at Brainerd. She
was then a heathen. But she became enlightened and sanc-
tified through the instrumentality of the Gospel of Jesus,
preached to her by the missionaries of the cross; and her
end was glorious.

A neat monument of wood, erected by her bereaved
relatives, covers the grave where she was laid. And though,
a few years hence, this monument may no longer exist to
mark the spot where she slumbers, yet shall her dust be precious in the eyes of the Lord and her virtues shall be told for
a memorial of her. . . .

Such was Catharine Brown, the converted Cherokee.
Such, too, were the changes wrought in her, through the
blessing of Almighty God on the labours of missionaries.
They, and only they, as the instruments of divine grace, had
the formation of her Christian character; and that character, excellent and lovely as it was, resulted from the nature
of their instructions. Her expansion of mind[,] her enlarge-
ment of views, her elevated affectations[,] her untiring benevolence, are all to be traced under God to her intercourse
with them. The glory belongs to God; but the instrumental
agency, the effective labor, the subordinate success, were
theirs.

In her history, we see how much can be made of the
Indian character. Catharine was an Indian. She might
have said, as her brother did to thousands, while passing

through these States, "Aboriginal blood flows through my veins." True, it was not unmixed; but the same may be affirmed of many others of her people. Her parentage, her early circumstances and education, with a few unimportant exceptions, were like those of the Cherokees generally. She dwelt in the same wilderness, was conversant with the same society, was actuated by the same fears, and hopes and expectations, and naturally possessed the same traits of character. Yet what did she become! How agreeable as an associate, how affectionate as a friend, how exemplary as a member of the domestic and social circle and of the Christian church, how blameless and lovely in all the walks of life! Her Christian character was esteemed by all who knew her while she lived, and will bear the strictest scrutiny now she is dead. To such an excellence may the Indian character attain; for, to such an excellence did it actually attain in her.

And why may it not arrive at the same excellence in other Indians? Are there no other minds among them as susceptible of discipline and culture? No other spirits, that, in the plastic hands of the Divine Agent, can receive as beautiful a conformation? Are there not dispositions as gentle, hearts as full of feeling, minds as lively and strong? And cannot such minds be so fashioned and adorned, that heavenly grace shall beam as charmingly from them, as it did from hers?

The supposition, that she possessed mental and moral capabilities, which are rare among her people, while it adds nothing to our respect for her, does injustice to her nation. In personal attraction, and in universal propriety of manner, she was, undoubtedly, much distinguished. But, in amiableness of disposition, in quickness of apprehension, in intellectual vigor, it is believed there are hundreds of Cherokee youth, who are scarcely less favored.[7]

ENDNOTES

[1] Rufus Anderson, editor, *Memoir of Catharine Brown: A Christian Indian of the Cherokee Nation* (Boston: Samuel T. Armstrong, Crocker and Brewster, 1825), 13–15.

[2] Daniel Sabin Butrick, Journal, Jan. 27, 1820, ABCFM Papers, by permission of the Houghton Library, Harvard University, Cambridge, Mass., 18.3.3, vol. 4–5.

[3] Anderson, ed., *Memoir of Catharine Brown*, 98, 111, 132, 177.

[4] See Theda Perdue, "Catharine Brown: Cherokee Convert to Christianity," in *Sifters: Native American Women's Lives*, edited by Theda Perdue (New York: Oxford University Press, 2001), 77–91. Still, the missionaries held on to their image of the saintly Catharine Brown and their belief that Christianity would liberate Cherokee women from the heavy labor of cultivating the earth and elevate them as moral guardians of the hearth. See Bernard Sheehan, *Seeds of Extinction: Jeffersonian Philanthropy and the American Indian* (Chapel Hill: University of North Carolina Press, 1973), 165–67; Robert Sparks Walker, *Torchlights to the Cherokees: The Brainerd Mission* (1931; reprint, Johnson City, Tenn.: Overmountain Press, 1994), 97, 118, 138, 176.

[5] A note here in the text reads, " 'I was pleased to find,' says a friend, 'that General Jackson, (who commanded in the war with the Creeks,) had a high opinion of Catharine. In the course of our conversation he remarked, *She was a woman of Roman virtue, and above suspicion.*' " Anderson, ed., *Memoir of Catharine Brown*, 15.

[6] Evarts later published his report in *Panoplist* 14, 344. Mrs. Newell's memoirs were known among missionaries. Harriet Newell and her husband, Samuel, were ABCFM missionaries to India. Her memoirs also contained a sermon by Leonard Woods on the occasion of her death. See the following: Harriet Newell, *Memoir of Mrs. Harriet Newell, Wife of the Rev. Samuel Newell, Missionary to India* (Andover, Mass.: American Tract Society, 1812); Harriet Newell and Leonard Woods, *A Sermon Preached at Haverhill, Mass., in Remembrance of Mrs. Harriet Newell, Wife of the Rev Samuel Newell, Missionary to India Who Died at the Isle of France, Nov. 30, 1812, aged 19 Years; to which are added Memoirs of her Life* (Boston: Samuel T. Armstrong, 1814).

[7] Anderson, ed., *Memoir of Catharine Brown*, 20–25, 34–36, 84–93, 131–32, 148–49, 171–73.

~ Wahnenauhi Excerpt ~

The Cherokee woman Wahnenauhi ("Over-There-They-Just-Arrived-With-It") had the English name Lucy Lowrey Keys. Born in 1831 in Willstown, Alabama, she bridged two cultures. Her father, Dr. Milo Hoyt, was a missionary. Lydia Benge, her mother, was a Cherokee and a relative of Sequoyah, who invented the Cherokee syllabary. Lydia Benge attended the Brainerd Mission. After her conversion to Christianity and baptism, she had a dream in which the words of a hymn came to her. The next morning, she wrote down the hymn, which became the first credited to a Cherokee. *The Cherokee Hymn Book* printed it under the name "The Lord and I Are Friends."

Wahnenauhi was a graduate of the first class of the Cherokee National Female Seminary. She married Monroe Calvin Keys, a graduate of the Cherokee National Male Seminary. In 1889, she sent a manuscript that she had written to the Bureau of Ethnology. Her manuscript provides rare insights into Cherokee history and culture. It is the fascinating work of a highly acculturated mixed-blood young Cherokee woman who took great pride in traditions and wanted to honor both cultures to which she belonged. She describes ancient Cherokee stories like that of the first fire and Kana'tï and Selu as resembling Bible stories. She describes conjurors, dress, food, medical practices, festivals, and dances. She offers insights into such luminaries as Sequoyah and her maternal grandfather, Major George Lowrey, a Cherokee leader whom George Washington employed to carry a secret message to the French in Canada. George Lowrey also served as assistant chief and chief of the Cherokee Nation.

Wahnenauhi died in 1912. In the following selection, she recalls how the tribal leaders warmly received missionaries.

About the year 1803, Mr. and Mrs. Gambold, Moravian Missionaries, came to the Cherokees, who received them joyfully.

Arrangements were immediately made by the Chiefs and Headmen to select a suitable locality for a Mission Station. A school was soon put into operation, and . . . influential men immediately availed themselves of the privilege of sending their children to a Christian School. In 1804, Presbyterian Missionaries were sent to the Cherokee Nation, and in a short time several Mission Stations were located in different parts of the Nation, Schools were established and Churches organized. But many of the people still adhered to the old ways, would have nothing to do with the Missionaries, and ignored all their efforts made for educating and civilizing the Indians.

At their dances and ball-plays, whiskey was brought in and freely used; very often the gatherings were broken up by drunken quarrels, and sometimes by brutal murder.

However, the most influential persons, who were followed by the greater part of the Nation, anxious to secure educational advantages for their children, made great exertions to assist the Missionaries in building houses, and providing things necessary for their comfort while working among them.

In 1817 the Station at Brainerd was begun and the school put into successful operation. And in a few years several other Mission Stations were established, and the schools well attended and prosperous. The Baptist[s] and

Methodist[s] also had Mission Stations among the Cherokees. As a Nation, they were now prepared to receive the
Gospel, brought to them by the Missionaries.

Many were converted. . . . The Missionaries were greatly loved by the Cherokees, who had by this time received
such an impetus towards Christianity and Civilization that
it was impossible for them to return to barbarism.[1]

ENDNOTES

[1] *The Wahnenauhi Manuscript: Historical Sketches of the Cherokees, Together with Some of Their Customs, Traditions, and Superstitions*, edited and
with an introduction by Jack Frederick Kilpatrick, Anthropological Papers,
Bureau of Ethnology, no. 77, Bulletin 196 (Washington: GPO, 1966), 201–2.

~ *Cherokee Phoenix* Articles ~

The *Cherokee Phoenix* was the first Indian newspaper to be published. The inaugural edition came out in 1828 with Elias Boudinot (Gallegina Uwati or Buck Watie) as editor. Boudinot (1802–1839) was educated in Cornwall, Connecticut. He married Harriet Ruggles Gold, a white woman, and returned to Georgia. They had six children. Boudinot converted to Christianity and initially worked tirelessly to oppose removal. Along with Major Ridge and John Ridge, he later signed the infamous Treaty of New Echota, which ceded Cherokee land in the Southeast. Since the tribe considered that action treasonous, the three were murdered in Indian Territory in 1839.

The newspaper Boudinot edited is still published today. For seven years the official voice of the Cherokee Nation, it was published in New Echota. Because of the remarkable creation of Sequoyah's syllabary, the Cherokees were first among the indigenous people of the continent to have a written language. Within a brief time, the whole Cherokee Nation was literate.

The following articles from the *Cherokee Phoenix* provide a fascinating window into the ways in which the civilization program was promulgated in its pages. The articles promote an image of women as genteel and highly acculturated to white values—an image that contrasts sharply with the traditional Cherokee values of gender equality.

∼Woman

Never shrink from a woman of strong sense. If she becomes attached to you, it will be from seeing and valuing similar qualities in yourself. You may trust her, for she knows the value of your confidence; you may consult her, for she is able to advise; and does so at once with the firmness of reason, and the consideration of affection. Her love will be lasting, for it will not have been lightly won; it will be strong and ardent, for weak minds are not capable of the loftier grades of the passion. If you prefer attaching to yourself a woman of feeble understanding, it must be either from fearing to encounter a superior person, or from the poor vanity of preferring that admiration which springs from ignorance, to that which arises from appreciation.

A woman who has the beauty of feminine delicacy & grace, who has the strong sense of a man, yet softened and refined by the influence of womanly feeling—whose passions are strong, but chastened and directed by delicacy and principle—whose mind is brilliant, alike from its natural emanations and its stores of acquirement—whose manners have been formed by the imperceptible influence of good society, in its broad sense, yet are totally free from the consciousness and affectation of any *clique*, though it be the highest—who, though she shines in and enjoys the world, finds her heart's happiness at home—is not this the noblest and the sweetest of the creatures formed by God?[1]

∼Female Influence

Everywhere throughout the circle of her intercourse, her influence is felt like the dew of heaven; gentle, silent, and unseen yet pervading & efficient. But, in the domestic circle its power is concentrated; and is like the life-giving beams of the sun, awakening, illustrating, and almost creating the moral aspect of the scene. To speak first of the filial relation—none can conceive how much a daughter may promote the comfort and the moral benefit of her parents, but those who have seen the female character exhibited under the influence of an enlightened understanding, and an improved heart; which, by their mutual action, have produced the most extended views of duty, with the strongest desire to fulfill it. As a sister, a female may exert a most important influence. With no strong counteracting circumstances, she may give what features she pleases to the moral and intellectual character of those with whom she is connected in this relation. All the sweet endearments of mutual affection and confidence will give weight to her influence. An intelligent, high-aiming female, of a well disciplined mind and pious heart, has been known to give a much higher cast of character, attainment, and condition, to a large circle of brothers and sisters, than they would otherwise have received. But it is as a *mother* that woman has all the powers with which the munificence of her Divine Benefactor has endowed her, matured to their highest perfection, and exercised in their greatest strength.[2]

[The following piece was reprinted in the Cherokee Phoenix *from the publication* Ariel. *It was credited to the writer Viator, a pseudonym sometimes taken to mean "traveler."]*

⌁Female Delicacy

Female delicacy is a subject upon which my thoughts delight to ruminate, and upon which I shall now attempt to form a speculation. Altho' I am conscious of being unequal to the task, which requires so delicate a hand, such refinement of sentiment and such purity of thought, as well as such elegance of language, yet my fair readers will forgive the attempt, when I assure them that I wish for no higher satisfaction than to notice their advancement in mental and moral, as well as external perfection; and to share in that happiness which such perfection will ensure to themselves and to the rest of the world.

It ill becomes him who is born of a woman to speak degradingly of the sex. It less becomes him who is not only born of a woman, but is indebted, in a considerable degree, to female attention and assiduity, to female conversation and example, and to female tenderness and delicacy; that his mind was early opened to intelligence, and his appetites and passions have been inured to control; that his sentiments have been refined, his manners polished, his steps withheld from danger and directed to safety and wisdom; his bosom relieved of its cares, and his life illumined with pleasures. And least of all does it become him to disparage the sex, who, to his personal obligations, can add his philanthropy; who professes to be a friend of mankind; who knows the influence which woman has upon a man, and the hand she has, or might have, in promoting the virtue and happiness of families, of larger communities, and of the world.

Our omnipotent Creator, whose wisdom and benignity shine conspicuous in all his works, has formed the female sex, if I may be indulged the expression, with a *delicate hand*. The slender texture of their bodies, the softness of their features, the tunefulness of their voices, the general placidness of their tempers, and tenderness of their hearts, together with a similar niceness in their intellectual powers, denote a characteristic, delicacy, with which their educations and employment, their sentiments and views, their conversation and behavior, and ours with and towards them, should exactly correspond. So that my idea of female delicacy is complex and comprehensive. It includes whatever is delicate in the structure of their frames, in the faculties of their minds, in the disposition of their hearts, in their sentiments, in their tastes, in their words, in their actions. But while it excludes not that delicacy in their bodies or minds which is merely natural, it regards principally that which is acquired; which is the effect of culture and education; which results from an early and assiduous care to preserve and establish the native innocence and purity of the heart, to correct and govern the passions, to refine and elevate the sentiments, and to render the conversation and manners more and more engaging. In short, the delicacy which I mean, and which I wish to recommend is an inward sense of propriety which regulates and beautifies the whole conduct; and a settled, unsullied, and inflexible virtue and sweetness of temper, beaming forth in everything that is done. This will heighten the delicacy of the features and air—for it is loveliness itself.

Every moral writer and thinker knows, and every moral liver feels, that there is something so deformed and ugly in vice, as to excite aversion in every rightly tempered breast. It argues, therefore, an indelicacy of mind to cherish perverse humors and give way to faulty propensities. The more delicate the taste of the soul is, the greater is its abhorrence of everything that borders on vice, or savors of impiety. The heart which is attuned to the refined exercises of virtue, of devotion, and religion, and which cannot consent to any deficiency in its gratitude and obedience to God, or in justice and benevolence to man, discovers a delicacy superior to the most exquisite taste in economy, cookery, and embroidery, and in music, painting, and poetry. The mind that does not wish to possess and exercise all the virtues and graces which are prescribed for the adorning of human nature, and for the attainment of perfection and felicity, is as deficient in taste and delicacy as it is in goodness.

Such are my ideas of female delicacy: And though they may be tho't by some to be too refined or diffuse, yet it must be owned that a behavior in the sex corresponding with such ideas, a course of conduct formed upon such maxims, will exalt their characters, add a luster to all other charms and secure their hearts from seduction, their lives from blemish, and their bosoms from remorse. And it is easier to conceive than to describe the happy alterations which such sentiments and manners would produce in the other sex, both as to exalted morals and rational enjoyment. Vice and misery would be greatly diminished, virtue and happiness proportionably advanced. It is the wish of my heart that wives, mothers, and daughters would pursue with candor and docility the hints here offered, and by reducing them to practice, try the experiment, how amiable and happy they will render them.[3]

⌐ The Female Heart

The female heart may be compared to a garden, which when well cultivated, presents a continued succession of fruits and flowers to regale the soul, and delight the eye; But when neglected, producing a crop of the most noxious weeds; large and flourishing because their growth is in proportion to the warmth and richness of the soil from which they spring. Then let the ground be faithfully cultivated; let the mind of the young and lovely female be stored with useful knowledge, and the influence of women, though undiminished in power, will be like the "diamond of the desert," sparkling and pure, whether surrounded by the sands of desolation, forgotten and unknown, or pouring its refreshing streams through every avenue of the social and moral fabric.[4]

Endnotes

[1] http://neptune3.galib.uga.edu/ssp/News/chrkphnx/18280813d.pdf, *Cherokee Phoenix*, vol. 01/08131828, no. 24, 4. For biographical information on Elias Boudinot, see Thurman Wilkins, *Cherokee Tragedy: The Story of the Ridge Family and the Decimation of a People* (London: Macmillan, 1970), 235–37, 242–44.

[2] http://neptune3.galib.uga.edu/ssp/News/chrkphnx/18280820d.pdf, *Cherokee Phoenix*, vol. 0108201828, no. 025, 4.

[3] *Cherokee Phoenix*, vol. 01/11191828, no. 38, 4.

[4] *Cherokee Phoenix*, vol. 02/11251829, no. 33, 4.

Part 4

THE TRAIL OF TEARS

Stockades imprisoned Cherokees in the summer of 1838 in Tennessee, North Carolina, Georgia, and Alabama. Soon, tribal members would begin the long westward journey of eight hundred miles to Indian Territory.

The policy of removing the Indians from the Southeast had supporters as early as 1803, after the Louisiana Purchase. In the years 1808 through 1810, and in 1817 and 1818, about two thousand Cherokees moved to Indian Territory. They became known as the Old Settlers. Pressure for removal grew strong in the 1820s, leading to the passage of the Indian Removal Act of 1830, signed into law by Andrew Jackson. Under Chief John Ross's leadership, Cherokees resisted in the courts and had allies especially in New England, among them Catherine Beecher, Henry David Thoreau, and Ralph Waldo Emerson.

A small group of twenty-two Cherokees signed the Treaty of New Echota in 1835. The Senate passed it by one vote in 1836, and the government ordered forcible removal of the

Cherokees within two years. Although the members of the Treaty Party did not have authority to sign for the tribe, and although nearly sixteen thousand Cherokees formally protested the treaty, the tribe was forced to cede all its lands in the Southeast for land in Indian Territory. It was promised five million dollars to be disbursed on a per capita basis and an additional half a million for education. The treaty also promised compensation to individuals for their buildings and fixtures and pledged to pay the cost of relocation. The United States promised to honor the title of the Cherokee Nation's new land, respect its political autonomy, and protect the tribe from trespassers. As late as 1907, the Cherokees were still trying to recover much of the promised money.

Federal troops arrived in 1838 and forced three detachments of a thousand Cherokees each westward that summer. So many deaths occurred that John Ross persuaded the government to allow the Cherokees to remove themselves. Ross put his brother Lewis in charge of the provisioning. Thirteen detachments left for Indian Territory in the winter of 1838–39.

The Trail of Tears claimed the lives of at least four thousand Cherokees, a fourth of the tribe. Women faced more hardships than men on the journey because many of them were pregnant. They bore children while in the stockades and on the road. At least sixty-nine newborns arrived in the West, but many infants died on the way. Women's experiences also differed from men's because they were vulnerable to rape. Along with the elderly and the very young, women were especially susceptible to disease and death.[1]

The following selections record the protests of Cherokee women against removal and the personal testimonies of those who went on the Trail of Tears or whose parents made the long journey.

ENDNOTES

[1] "Emigration Detachments," *Journal of Cherokee Studies* 3 (1978), 186–81. Theda Perdue, "Women and the Trail of Tears," *Journal of Women's History*, vol.1, no. 1 (Spring 1989), 14–30. Around one thousand Cherokees in North Carolina escaped into the mountains. Their descendants are members of the Eastern Band of Cherokee Indians. Descendants of the Cherokees who went on the Trail of Tears eventually established the Cherokee Nation of Oklahoma.

~ Petitions by Cherokee Women ~
1817, 1818

Cherokee women tried repeatedly to defend and preserve their land. In an attempt to encourage a peaceful resolution of existing land disputes, Nancy Ward, the Beloved Woman (or War Woman) of Chota, addressed the treaty conference at Hopewell, South Carolina, in 1785. That conference was the last occasion when women played an official role. Subsequently, the Cherokees lost large areas of land south of the Cumberland River in Tennessee and Kentucky and west of the Blue Ridge Mountains in North Carolina. Cherokee women unofficially continued to oppose further cession of lands.

In 1787, a Cherokee woman delivered a speech urging her people to embrace peace with the American nation. She appealed to the respect the Cherokees held for the power of women as mothers. She also wrote to Benjamin Franklin and sent him some of the same tobacco she had used to fill the peace pipe for the warriors. She entreated her people to heed women's counsel: "I am in hopes that if you Rightly consider that woman is the mother of All—and the Woman does not pull Children out of Trees or Stumps nor out of old Logs, but out of their Bodies, so that they ought to mind what a woman says."[1]

Common ownership of land promoted harmony within the culture and made the sale of land dependent on the consensus of the nation. Cherokee women collectively opposed the allotment of land to individuals in 1817 and 1818. They urged the council to continue to hold the land in common.

When the United States attempted to acquire more of the tribe's land in 1817, a group of thirteen women, in a petition delivered to the council, equated removal with destroying Cherokee mothers. In an appeal in 1818, they lamented the influence of whites who had intermarried with Cherokees. Still, they argued against removal because the Cherokees had become civilized. Finally, the women expressed their concern about the influence of whites within Cherokee society. They claimed that although whites had been agents of civilization, they seemed more interested in gaining economic and political power over the society than in Americanizing Indians.

Cherokee women sent the following messages to the National Council in 1817 and 1818.

⌒ *Cherokee Women*
Petition
May 2, 1817

The Cherokee ladys [ladies] now being present at the meeting of the chiefs and warriors in council have thought it their duty as mothers to address their beloved chiefs and warriors now assembled.

Our beloved children and head men of the Cherokee Nation, we address you warriors in council. We have raised all of you on the land which we now have, which God gave us to inhabit and raise provisions. We know that our country has once been extensive, but by repeated sales has become circumscribed to a small track, and [we] never have thought it our duty to interfere in the disposition of it till now. If a father or mother was to sell all their lands which they had to depend on, which their children had to raise their living on, which would be indeed bad and to be removed to another country. We do not wish to go to an unknown country which we have understood some of our children wish to go over the Mississippi, but this act of our children would be like destroying your mothers.

Your mothers, your sisters ask and beg of you not to part with any more of our land. We say ours. You are our descendants; take pity on our request. But keep it for our growing children, for it was the good will of our creator to place us here, and you know our father, the great president [James Monroe], will not allow his white children to take our country away. Only keep your hands off of paper talks for it's our own country. For [if] it was not, they would not ask you to put your hands to paper, for it would be impossible to remove us all. For as soon as one child is raised, we have others in our arms, for such is our situation and will consider our circumstance.

Therefore, children, don't part with any more of our lands but continue on it and enlarge your farms. Cultivate and raise corn and cotton and your mothers and sisters will make clothing for you which our father the president has recommended to us all. We don't charge anybody for selling any lands, but we have heard such intentions of our children. But your talks become true at last; it was our desire to forewarn you all not to part with our lands.

Nancy Ward [spoke] to her children: ["]Warriors to take pity and listen to the talks of your sisters. Although I am very old yet [I] cannot but pity the situation in which you will hear of their minds. I have [a] great many grand-children which [I] wish them to do well on our land.["][2]

~ Cherokee Women
Petition
June 30, 1818

Beloved Children,

We have called a meeting among ourselves to consult on the different points now before the council, relating to our national affairs. We have heard with painful feelings that the bounds of the land we now possess are to be drawn into very narrow limits. The land was given to us by the Great Spirit above as our common right, to raise our children upon, and to make support for our rising generations. We therefore humbly petition our beloved children, the head men & warriors, to hold out to the last in support of our common rights, as the Cherokee Nation have been the first settlers of this land; we therefore claim the right of the soil.

We well remember that our country was formerly very extensive, but by repeated sales it has become circumscribed to the very narrow limits we have at present. Our Father, the President, advised us to become farmers, to manufacture our own clothes, & to have our children instructed. To this advice we have attended in everything as far as we were able. Now the thought of being compelled to remove [to] the other side of the Mississippi is dreadful to us, because it appears to us that we, by this removal, shall be brought to a savage state again, for we have, by the endeavor of our Father the President, become too much enlightened to throw aside the privileges of a civilized life.

We therefore unanimously join in our meeting to hold our country in common as hitherto. Some of our children have become Christians. We have missionary schools among us. We have heard the gospel in our nation. We have become civilized and enlightened, and are in hopes that in a few years our nation will be prepared for instruction in other branches of sciences & arts, which are both useful and necessary in civilized society.

There are some white men among us who have been raised in this country from their youth, are connected with us by marriage, and have considerable families who are very active in encouraging the emigration of our nation. These ought to be our truest friends but prove our worst enemies. They seem to be only concerned [with] how to increase their riches, but do not care what becomes of our Nation, nor even of their own wives and children.[3]

ENDNOTES

[1] Perdue, "Cherokee Women and the Trail of Tears," 14–30.

[2] Presidential Papers microfilm, 1961, series 1, reel 22, Andrew Jackson Papers, Manuscript Division, Library of Congress, Washington.

[3] See Ard Hoyt, Moody Hall, Daniel Butrick, and William Chamberlin to Samuel Worcester, July 25, 1818, ABCFM Papers, by permission of the Houghton Library, Harvard University, Cambridge, Mass., 18.3.1, vol. 2: 113. See also *Brainerd Journal*, Feb. 13, 1817, for note about the women's intentions to protest removal.

~ Catherine Beecher Letter ~

In 1825, Cherokee women argued against removal. They presented a string of shells (of the wampum) to General William Clark, urging him to resist the policy and to "pursue in our undertaking and not give it up."[1] However, women lost political power under the Constitution of the Cherokee Nation in 1827, when voting rights were limited to "all free male citizens (excepting Negroes and descendants of white and Indian men by negro women who may have been set free) who shall have attained the age of eighteen years." In fact, official female participation in the Cherokee political system had ended after 1794. Stone Carrier took two women in his delegation to Washington in 1808, but only in an unofficial capacity. Women continued to exercise rights of petition but could no longer command obedience; they could only plead for support.[2]

A letter appearing in the January 6, 1830, issue of the *Cherokee Phoenix* restated the arguments made in the women's petitions of 1817 and 1818. Catherine Beecher, a white woman, wrote the letter in an appeal to other white females to exert their influence to save the Indian people from disaster. The sister of Harriet Beecher Stowe and a strong advocate for women's education, Beecher urged immediate action to protect the Indians' land. But in doing so, she also made clear whites' ignorance of Cherokee women's traditional power and authority.

Circular
Addressed to Benevolent Ladies of the U. States
December 25, 1829

The present crisis in the affairs of the Indian nations in the United States demands the immediate and interested attention of all who make any claims to benevolence or humanity. The calamities now hanging over them threaten not only these relics of an interesting race, but, if there is a being who avenges the wrongs of the oppressed, are causes of alarm to our whole country.

The following are the facts of the case:—This continent was once possessed only by the Indians, and earliest accounts represent them as a race numerous, warlike, and powerful. When our forefathers sought refuge from oppression on these shores, this people supplied their necessities, and ministered to their comfort; and though some of them, when they saw the white man continually encroaching upon their land, fought bravely for their existence and their country, yet often, too, the Indian has shed his blood to protect and sustain our infant nation. As we have risen in greatness and glory, the Indian nations have faded away. Their proud and powerful tribes have gone; their noble sachems [chiefs] and mighty warriors are heard of no more; and it is said the Indian often comes to the borders of his limited retreat to gaze on the beautiful country no longer his own, and to cry with bitterness at the remembrance of past greatness and power.

Ever since the existence of this nation, our general government, pursuing the course alike of policy and benevolence, have acknowledged these people as free and independent nations, and has protected them in the quiet possession of their lands. In repeated treaties with the Indians, the United States, by the hands of the most distinguished statesmen, after purchasing the greater part of their best lands, have *promised* them "*to continue the guarantee of the remainder of their country forever.*" And so strictly has government guarded the Indian's right to his lands that even to go on to their boundaries to survey the land, subjects [trespassers] to heavy fines and imprisonment.

Our government also, with parental care, has persuaded the Indians to forsake their savage life, and to adopt the habits and pursuits of civilized nations, while the charities of Christians and the labours of missionaries have sent to them the blessings of the gospel to purify and enlighten. The laws and regular forms of a civilized government are instituted; their simple and beautiful language, by the remarkable ingenuity of one of their race, has become a written language with its own peculiar alphabet, and, by the printing press, is sending forth among these people the principles of knowledge, and liberty, and religion. Their fields are beginning to smile with the labors of the husbandman; their villages are busy with the toils of the mechanic and the artisan; schools are rising in their hamlets, and the temple of the living God is seen among their forests.

Nor are we to think of these people only as naked and wandering savages. The various grades of intellect and refinement exist among them as among us; and those who visit their chieftains and families of the higher class, speak with wonder and admiration of their dignified propriety, nobleness of appearance, and refined characteristics as often exhibited in both sexes. Among them are men fitted by native talents to shine among the statesmen of any land, and who have received no inferior degree of cultivation. Among them, also, are those who, by honest industry, have assembled around them most of the comforts and many of the elegancies of life.

But the lands of this people are *claimed* to be embraced within the limits of some of our southern states, and as they are fertile and valuable, they are demanded by the whites as their own possessions, and efforts are making to dispossess the Indians of their native soil. And such is the singular state of concurring circumstances, that it has become almost a certainty that these people are to have their lands torn from them, and to be driven into western wilds and to final annihilation, unless the feelings of a humane and Christian nation shall be aroused to prevent the unhallowed sacrifice.

Unless our general government interferes to protect these nations, as by solemn and oft-repeated treaties they are bound to do, nothing can save them. The states which surround them are taking such measures as will speedily drive them from their country, and cause their final extinction....

Have not then the females of this country some duties devolving upon them in relation to this helpless race?—They are protected from the blinding influence of party spirit and the asperities of political violence. They have nothing to do with any struggle for power, nor any right to dictate the decisions of those that rule over them.—But they may *feel* for the distressed; they may stretch out the supplicating hand for them, and by their prayers strive to avert the calamities that are impending over them. It may be that female petitioners can lawfully be heard, even by the highest rulers of our land. Why may we not approach and supplicate that we and our dearest friends may be saved from the awful curses denounced on all who oppress the poor and needy, by Him whose anger is to be dreaded more than the wrath of man; who can "blast us with the breath of his nostrils," and scatter our hopes like chaff before the storm. It may be this will be *forbidden*; yet still we remember the Jewish princess who, being sent to supplicate for a nation's life, was thus reproved for hesitating even when *death* stared her in the way: "If thou altogether hold thy peace at this time, then shall deliverance arise from another place; but thou and thy father's house shall be destroyed.

And who knoweth whether thou art come to the kingdom for such a cause as this?"

To woman it is given to administer the sweet charities of life and to sway the empire of affection; and to her it may also be said, "Who knoweth whether thou art come to the kingdom for such a cause as this?" . . .

You who gather the youthful group around your fireside, and rejoice in their future hopes and joys, will you forget that the poor Indian loves his children too, and would as bitterly mourn over all their blasted hopes? And, while surrounded by such treasured blessings, ponder with dread and awe these fearful words of Him, who thus forbids the violence, and records the malediction of those, who either as individuals, or as nations, shall oppress the needy and helpless. . . .

This communication was written and sent abroad solely by the female hand. Let every woman who peruses it exert that influence in society which falls within her lawful province, and endeavor by every suitable expedient to interest the feelings of her friends, relatives, and acquaintances, on behalf of this people, that are ready to perish. A *few weeks* must decide this interesting and important question, and after that time sympathy and regret will all be in vain.[3]

ENDNOTES

[1] Green, *Women in American Indian Society*, 46.

[2] William McLoughlin, *Cherokee Renascence in the New Republic* (Princeton, N.J.: Princeton University Press, 1986), 398.

[3] *Cherokee Phoenix*, Jan. 6, 1830, no. 39, 2. See also *Christian Advocate and Journal*, Dec. 25, 1829.

~ Evan Jones Journal ~

Cherokees learned that neither accommodation nor resistance would save them from removal. The pleas of Cherokee women and their white supporters could not stop the process. Cherokees had lost 90 percent of their pre-colonial territory by 1819. Approximately one million whites in Georgia, Alabama, the Carolinas, and Tennessee surrounded seventeen thousand Cherokees. When Andrew Jackson assumed the presidency on March 4, 1829, removal became imminent. The discovery of gold on Cherokee land in Georgia later that year virtually sealed the tribe's fate.[1]

Nine contingents left in October 1838 and four that November. The first detachments, led by John Benge on October 1 and Jess Bushyhead on October 5, boarded Blythe's Ferry and crossed the Tennessee River where the Hiwassee intersected it. As the Cherokees looked back, they saw their homeland fade into the distance. Their journey of eight hundred miles would take three and a half months.[2]

In the following excerpt, Evan Jones, a Baptist missionary among the Cherokees, records the suffering of tribal members and comments on the effects on women. Jones served the Cherokee Nation for fifty years, opposed removal, walked with the Cherokees on the Trail of Tears, and continued to minister to them in Indian Territory. Here, he describes how they were brutally forced from their homes into camps by soldiers.

~

The Cherokees are nearly all prisoners. They have been dragged from their houses and camped at the forts and military posts all over the Nation. In Georgia, especially, the most unfeeling and insulting treatment has been experienced by them, in a general way. Multitudes were not allowed time to take anything with them but the clothes they had on. Well-furnished houses were left prey to plunderers who like hungry wolves, follow the progress of the captors and in many cases accompany them. These wretches rifle the houses and strip the helpless, unoffending owners of all they have on earth. Females who have been habituated to comforts and comparative affluence are driven on foot before the bayonets of brutal men. Their feelings are mortified by the blasphemous vociferations of these heartless creatures. It is a painful sight. The property of many has been taken and sold before their eyes for almost nothing; the sellers and buyers being in many cases combined to cheat the poor Indian. . . . Cherokees are deprived of their liberty and stripped of their entire property at one blow. Many who a few days ago were in comfortable circumstances are now the victims of abject poverty. . . . I say nothing yet of several cold-blooded murders and other personal cruelties, for I would most conscientiously avoid making the slightest erroneous impression on any persons, being not in possession of precise and authentic information concerning all the facts in these cases of barbarity.[3]

ENDNOTES

[1] David Williams, *The Georgia Gold Rush: Twenty-Niners, Cherokees, and Gold Fever* (Columbia: University of South Carolina Press, 1993), 14, 19.

[2] For more on the Trail of Tears, see Carolyn Ross Johnston, *Cherokee Women in Crisis: Trail of Tears, Civil War, and Allotment, 1838–1907* (Tuscaloosa and London: University of Alabama Press, 2003), 56–78.

[3] Evan Jones, Journal, June 16, 1838, Missionary Correspondence, 1800–1900, microfilm reel 98, American Baptist Historical Society, Atlanta, Ga. See Cherokee Nation Papers, reel 44, RG 2, Treaty Fund Claims, 1831–83, Western History Collections, University of Oklahoma, Norman, Okla., for details of typical claims.

Petitions of
～ Ross's Landing Prisoners ～

When the Cherokees were driven from their homes into camps for removal to Indian Territory, some were taken to Ross's Landing, located on the Tennessee River. The site is now in Chattanooga.

The following petition found its way into the Records of the Cherokee Indian Agency in Tennessee. This rare document reveals the desperation of the prisoners and pleads particularly for the women and children of the tribe.

～

The humble petitions of the Cherokee prisoners
at and near Ross's Landing, June 11, 1838

We your prisoners wish to speak to you—We wish to speak humbly for we cannot help ourselves. We have been made prisoners by your men but we did not fight against you. We have never done you any harm. For we ask you to hear us. We have been told we are to be sent off by boat immediately. Sir[,] will you listen to your prisoners. We are Indians. Our wives and children are Indians and some people do not pity Indians. But if we are Indians we have hearts that feel. We do not want to see our wives and children die. We do not want to die ourselves and leave them widows and orphans. We are in trouble and our hearts are very heavy. The darkness of night is before us. We have no hope unless you will help us. We do not ask you to let us go free from being your prisoners unless it should please yourself. But we ask that you will not send us down the river at this time of the year. If you do we shall die, and our wives will die and our children will die. We want you to keep us in this country till the sickly time is over so that when we get to the West that we may be able to work to make boards to cover our families. If you send us there now the sickly time be commenced, we shall have no thought to work. We should be in the open air in all the deadly time of sickness, or we shall die and our poor wives and children will die too. And if you send the whole nation, the whole nation will die. We ask your pity. Pity our women and children if they are Indians. Do not send us off at this sickly time. Some of our people are Christians. They will pray for you. If you pity us, we hope your Lord will be pleased and that He will pity you and your wife and your children and do you good. We cannot make a good talk, our hearts are too full of sorrow. This is all we say.[1]

ENDNOTES

[1] Records of the Bureau of Indian Affairs, Records of the Cherokee Indian Agency in Tennessee, 1801–35, RG 75, microcopy 208, History Branch and Archives, Cleveland Public Library, Cleveland, Tenn.

~ Rebecca Neugin Interview ~

Throughout this book are documents from the Indian Pioneer Papers. This project, sponsored by the federal government in the 1930s, recorded the oral histories of hundreds of elderly Indians in many tribes in Oklahoma. The Oklahoma Historical Society and the Department of History at the University of Oklahoma secured a WPA Writers' Project grant for the interview program. Over one hundred writers conducted over eleven thousand interviews of early settlers, many of them Indians. When compiled, the Indian Pioneer Papers consisted of 112 volumes. Like the WPA slave narratives, this archive on Indians is an invaluable source for hearing the voices of ordinary people long silent in the historical record.

Rebecca Neugin recorded her personal recollections of the Trail of Tears in an interview with Grant Foreman in 1932. Almost a hundred years old at the time, she had been only three or four on the journey. She died near Hulbert, Oklahoma, during the same year she was interviewed. One of the vivid incidents she recalled was of her pet duck she would not leave behind. She held it so hard that she squeezed the life out of it. For ninety years afterward, she grieved its death. The Cherokees had to leave it on the roadside.

Neugin was born Wa-ki. She had nine siblings. Her first husband was John Smith, a full-blooded Cherokee, with whom she had two children. Her second husband was Bark (or Bock) Neugin. She had several children by him.

When the soldiers came to our house my father wanted to fight, but my mother told him that the soldiers would kill him if he did and we surrendered without a fight. They drove us out of our house to join other prisoners in a stockade. After they took us away my mother begged them to let her go back and get some bedding. So they let her go back and she brought what bedding and a few cooking utensils she could carry and had to leave behind all of our other household possessions. My father had a wagon pulled by two spans of oxen to haul us in. Eight of my brothers and sisters and two or three widow women and children rode with us. My brother Dick, who was a good deal older than I was, walked along with a long whip which he popped over the backs of the oxen and drove them all the way. My father and mother walked all the way also. The people got so tired of eating salt pork on the journey that my father would walk through the woods as we traveled, hunting for turkeys and deer which he brought into camp to feed us. Camp was usually made at some place where water was to be had and when we stopped and prepared to cook our food other emigrants who had been driven from their homes without opportunity to secure cooking utensils came to our camp to use our pots and kettles. There was much sickness among the emigrants and a great many little children died of whooping cough.[1]

ENDNOTES

[1] Rebecca Neugin, Interview, 1932, Indian Pioneer Papers, Western History Collections, University of Oklahoma, Norman, Okla. See references to Neugin in Grant Foreman, *Indian Removal: The Emigration of the Five Civilized Tribes of Indians* (Norman: University of Oklahoma Press, 1932), 242, 302 n. 18.

～ Kate Rackleff Interview ～

Nannie Lee Burns recorded the following interview with Mrs. Kate Neugin Rackleff in Fairland, Oklahoma, on August 31, 1937.

～

My mother, Rebecca Neugin nee Ketcher, was the daughter of John Ketcher. I do not know the name of his wife. Both were fullbloods. My mother was born in Georgia about 1829. [Different sources place Rebecca Neugin's birth as anywhere from 1827 to 1835; it is usually accepted as 1834.]

My mother, said to be the last survivor of those who came over the Trail of Tears, was about ten years old [Rebecca Neugin herself said she was around three] when they left Georgia.

They came in rude wagons drawn by oxen, each family furnishing its own transportation or at least my grandfather did, and he loaded his wagon with provisions for his family for the trip. This left little room as he had a wife and six children, of whom my mother was next to the youngest. They were compelled to have a little bedding. They left Georgia in the summer and did not reach this state till the next summer.

These people were brought through Tennessee and southern Missouri, under soldiers commanded by General Winfield Scott. General Scott left these people under command of his assistant about the middle of the trip [so] that he might attend the National Whig Convention, which was at that time contesting the nominations of Henry Clay and William Henry Harrison, for President of the United States.

Mother started with a little pig that she named "Toby." When they started he was no larger than a large rat and each day at noon and at night mother would let him run around and watched him and she kept him till he was a large hog and he disappeared one day at the noon hour and she was never able to find him.

In those days there were no roads and few trails and very few bridges. Progress of travelers was slow and often times they would have to wait many days for the streams to run down before they could cross. Each family did its own cooking on the road. People then had no matches and they started a fire by rubbing two flint rocks together and catching the spark on a piece of dry spunk held directly underneath the rocks. Sometimes, they would have to rake away the snow and clear a place to build the fire. Travelers carried dry wood in the wagons to build their fires. The wagons were so heavily loaded and had travelled so many days that when they came to a hill the persons in the wagons would have to get out and walk up the hill. They did not ride much of the time but walked a good deal, not only to rest themselves but to save their teams.

Often, teams would give out and could go no farther and then those who were with that wagon would be divided up among the other wagons and hurried along. One day mother saw a team of oxen fall dead, hitched to their wagon. The party she was with were in a severe snowstorm on the way which caused much suffering. Many died from exposure on the trip and mother said that she thought that a third of those who started died on the way, although all of her family lived to reach the new country. Those who came over the Trail of Tears would not stop for sickness and would stop only long enough to dig a rude grave when anyone died and then the bereaved family was forced to move right along.

Mother said that their food lasted them till they

reached the Indian Territory but towards the last of the trip that they had little to eat and had to plan to make it last. It was indeed a pitiful band that finally reached the new home promised them for they had been a year on the road, food had become scarce, their clothes which were home-made were wearing out, many had died on the trail, some had lost their teams and wagons and had been placed with other families and there were small children in the band who had lost their parents.[1]

ENDNOTES

[1] Kate Neugin Rackleff, Interview 7382, vol. 74, Fairland, Okla., Aug. 31, 1937, 75–77, Indian Pioneer Papers, Western History Collections, University of Oklahoma, Norman, Okla.

～ Wahnenauhi Excerpt ～

Wahnenauhi's description of the removal crisis is poignant. She was eight years old when she had to go on the Trail of Tears.

～

This was a critical time for the Cherokee Nation, its very existence threatened, and all was to be determined by the Chiefs now in Council. How this great responsibility pressed on them! perish or remove! It might be,—remove *and* perish! a long journey through the Wilderness,—could the little ones endure? and how about the sick? the old people and infirm, could they possibly endure the long tedious journey; Should they leave?

This had been the home of their Ancestors from time out of mind. Every thing they held dear on earth was here, *must* they leave?

The graves of their kindred forsaken by them would be desecrated by the hands of the White Man! The very air seemed filled with an undercurrent of inexpressible sadness and regret.

They could almost hear the reproaches and wailings of the dear dead they were leaving.

How must these Chiefs decide for their people? No wonder it seemed that Despair in its thickest blackness had settled down and enfolded in gloom this assemblage of brave and true hearted Patriots.

But no time could they spend in regrets and for[e]boding, although their own hearts were torn with grief. Throwing aside their private troubles, they set themselves to the task of preparing the people for the inevitable journey. A Delegation was appointed and authorized to make arrangements with Major General Scott for Supplies required for the Removal.

For convenience in protecting, providing for and distributing to, so large a Body of people, they were divided into Companies, or Detachments, as they were called, each provided with a Captain, whose duties were to attend to the necessities of all in his particular Detachment.

Some of the Cherokees, remained in their homes, and determined not to leave.

For these[,] soldiers were sent, by Georgia, and they were gathered up and driven, at the point of the bayonet, into camp with the others[. T]hey were not allowed to take any of their household stuff, but were compelled to leave as they were, with only the clothes which they had on. One old, very old man, asked the soldiers to allow him time to pray once more, with his family in the dear old home, before he left it forever. The answer was, with brutal oath, "No! no time for prayers. Go!" at the same time giving him a rude push towards the door.

In many instances, the families of settlers were at hand, and as the Indians were evicted, the whites entered, taking full possession of everything left.

It is useless to attempt to describe the long, wearisome passage of these exiled Indians.

The journey had but just begun when sickness attacked them.

Many of the old people, already enfeebled by age, were unable to endure the fatigue and hardships of the way, and sank unresistingly.

Every camping place was strewn with the graves of the dead.

Not one family was exempted from the tax of the Death-Angel.[1]

ENDNOTES

1 *The Wahnenauhi Manuscript*, 206–7.

~ Daniel Sabin Butrick Journal ~

Daniel Sabin Butrick, an American Board of Commissioners for Foreign Missions minister, went with the Cherokees on the Trail of Tears and served the tribe for twenty-five years. He also collaborated with John Howard Payne to collect sources from the Cherokees that became the *Indian Antiquities* volume, an invaluable source on Cherokee culture and history.

The following excerpts from his journal on the trail provide a view of the depth of suffering, especially among women and children.

~

Sabbath July 1 [1838]

Soon in the morning a large company of United States troops came up and stopped in the lane. Then a number of volunteers from the camps made their appearance about the saw mill. Every thought and every view was painful. Nothing of the Holy Sabbath. Br. Vail concluded not to leave home as so many were about and therefore I rode alone to the camps.

On the way I met crowds of people, some with dishes as if going after berries, and many I feared were going to the creek.

On arriving at the camps, I spoke from 2 Tim 4:8. Before closing my meeting I told our dear friends that I had before come to the conclusion not to visit the camps on the Sabbath, lest I should see them playing cards, though I had been persuaded to come today. I told them however, that if they continued to profane the Lord's Day by playing cards, they might depend upon it, that the wrath of God would pursue them to death.

Their almost universal Saturday night frolics, carried through the Holy Sabbath, had already drawn down Divine wrath upon them. True, they might say their enemies were cruel, but suppose they were, how did they get this power over them unless the Lord was angry with them, why should He thus give them up[?]

On returning home I met the soldiers and Cherokees, who had been to Brainerd [a Christian mission to the tribe at what is now Chattanooga, Tennessee]; and on arriving found that the women had been in the creek, swimming while the soldiers stood by them on the bank and other young men were in the creek, naked but just below. We held a prayer meeting.

Soon after on going to the creek for water, found a company of young men and boys in the creek, close by the road. I talked at length and persuaded them to put on their clothes. But almost immediately another company was there. I talked again, and told the men we could not endure such conduct any longer. Some also were fishing. We were pained to the heart at the profanations of the Holy Sabbath.

But the few Cherokees of whom I speak above are evidently exceptions, the women who infested the place by going into the creek while the soldiers were standing by, might be some who had been seduced by the soldiers.

Br. Vail, the other day, on going to the landing, saw six soldiers about two Cherokee women. The women stood by a tree, and the soldiers with a bottle of liquor were endeavoring to entice them to drink though the women, as yet, were resisting them. Br. Vail made this known to the commanding officer, yet we perceive no notice was taken of it, because it was reported afterwards that those soldiers had the two women out with them all night.

A young married woman, a member of the Methodist society, was at the camps with her friends, though her husband was not there, I believe, at the time. The soldiers, it is said, caught her, dragged her about, and at length either through fear or other causes [she] was induced to drink, and yield to their seduction, so that she is now an outcast, even in the view of her own relatives. How many of the poor captive women are thus debauched, that eye which never sleeps alone can tell.

The United States have now ascended about to the top of the climax. For about ten years, it would seem that the power, the wisdom and the funds of the whole union have been employed for the temporal and eternal ruin of this little handful of Indians.

In the first place, they were rendered lawless, and it was made a penitentiary crime for any of their rulers to execute their laws. Thus all the laws which the council had wisely enacted respecting liquor and gambling were at once annulled and every one led to follow his own inclination.

The country was soon filled with liquor to overflowing; and stores of liquor & cards were set up to induce gambling, while white gamblers were strolling through the country, seeking whom they could destroy. Many of the white men who established little stores to induce drinking and gambling go in with some Cherokees, who thus become engaged with them in carrying the plans of government into effort, thus gambling spread like wild fire through the country with none to check it.

The young people were not only almost compelled to disregard their own chiefs, but also taught to despise their parents and teachers, except such as would countenance all their wicked ways.

Thus the young men have been taught to treat the Bible, the Holy Sabbath, the ministers of the gospel, and all the duties and ordinances of religion, not as unenlightened heathen, but with all that contempt and acrimony peculiar to the Voltaires of the present age.

The young women who have been educated at mission schools, and by great expense and labour, taught to read and understand the Holy Bible, are the first victims of these emissaries of darkness. Because they understand English, the dark rhetoric of hell has an immediate and distinct effect on their minds, and they are pressed into the service of darkness, and become the ringleaders of wickedness. On this account most of the labour and expenses of the mission have been wrested into the service of Satan.

I have often been led to regret that any Cherokee had the least knowledge of the English language. They have not only been engaged in drinking and gambling, but also in profaning the Holy Sabbath, and the sainted Name of God. And with regard to the Holy Sabbath many professors of religion in the surrounding states are among the first to exert an unholy influence by travelling on business, visiting and talking entirely on worldly subjects.

But notwithstanding all the warning and sacrifices and example of men in high standing, the distraction of the poor Cherokees was not effected but by the direct power of the United States. An army containing as many soldiers probably, as there are adult Indians in the nations, was thrust into the country. These soldiers were armed with guns, bayonets, swords, pistols and all the horrid artillery of death. The few guns the Indians had were taken from them, and in the heat of the summer they were crowded into camps, or driven in most distressing manner to the West.

The fever and dysentery are now desolating the camps, yet thus far the mortality is not greater than might be expected.

Monday July 2

A child died at the camps last night and the friends wished it to be buried here; but while we were making preparations, word came that it was buried near the place where it died. Soon after a measure was brought for a coffin to bury an aged black man, who had just died. Thus we are becoming almost familiar with death.

Our dear Christian friends are often put to blush, in their present sufferings. A minister of the gospel, who professed to have been the cause of sending or leading the A. Board to send missionaries to this country, was the agent who induced a few individuals to dispose of the whole country, in opposition to the will of the council, and of almost the whole nation.

Wednesday July 23 [actually July 25]

Rode to the camps near the agency. Here are about eight thousand Cherokees in camps waiting the first of September, then to be sent off to the West. The National council house requested the privilege of moving the Nation themselves, instead of having them driven by soldiers. This request was sent to General [Winfield] Scott on Monday and an answer was expected on Tuesday but did not come and is expected today.

On arriving at the council place, I requested Mr. Taylor to mention the subject of our going to the West to Mr. [John] Ross and the other chiefs generally, as we should not wish to go without their approbation. . . .

On returning, found the council had adjourned till tomorrow and that the answer of General Scott would be presented tomorrow morning. I saw Mr. Ross and spoke with him about going with the Cherokees to the West. He said there would be no objections to our going.

O Thou Dear Redeemer, wilt thou direct and assist us in every place, and at all times, and make us a blessing to this dear people.

Thursday, July 26

Rode to Brainerd. A little child had been buried since I left home.

Just before arriving at the creek I met several wagons and learned afterwards that they had been employed in conveying the last detachment of Cherokee prisoners to Waterloo on Tennessee River, where they were put on board steam boats.

One of those wagoners stopped at br. Vails, as he passed. He said there was very great sickness and mortality among the Cherokees on the road, in so much that he could not but pity them though they were Indians. They were not allowed to stop or rest on account of sickness. They were driven on as long as they could walk, and then thrown into the wagons. And when the wagoners perceived some to be in the agonies of death, and informed the wagon master, his order was; Drive on! Drive on! And when it was known that one was dead, the lifeless body was left to the care of some stranger who might be employed to put it away, though in some instances the friends were allowed to perform the services.

Let us fancy the feeling of a dear sister, an aged father or mother, or a beloved wife or child, driven by strangers (of adamantine hearts)[,] scorching with fever, under a burning sun, parching with thirst, rendered more tormenting by the heated dust filling the air, see this dear wife of our bosom, languishing and almost ready to drop to the ground every step, and yet handing to her friends, choosing rather to die in their arms, than to be torn from them and thrown into a heated wagon, to be separated forever from all she held dear. See her last despairing look at her dead husband, as she sinks at his feet and falls in the road.

Now she is taken and thrown into a great wagon, covered with thick cloth, and all the air confined and heat[ed] by a burning sun. Here she has no cordial, no kind friend to wipe the cold sweat from her face.

As she awakes from a swoon and calls for water to quench her thirst, no kind voice replies, no hand can minister to her relief. The wagoner is in all the noise of the crowd and cannot hear her faint lispings and when he does hear, cannot understand. Thus she must lie perhaps from morning till night parching with thirst, or in the most excruciating pains of body, thrown, as it were upon the rack, by every heavy jolt of the wagon rolling over a rough road.

And thus from day to day till death kindly releases her departing spirit.

And now where is the dear partner of her bosom, the children of her love, or the fond mother of her childhood? They are mingled in the crowd and perhaps scarcely permitted to take even a parting view of the dear object of all their delight. The first they know, perhaps, someone accidentally remarks that such a person died and was left at such a place to be buried.

Let us imagine such scenes daily and for a long time together; and then inquire why the dear Cherokees are doomed to such miseries; have they murdered their white friends? Have they robbed or plundered? Or have they done any wrong to the United States for which that powerful nation is thus putting them to torture? They have done no wrong to merit any part of this evil, their enemies themselves being judges, but by refusing to acknowledge the justice of that treaty made by a few individuals, in direct opposition to the whole national council and the voice of the people.

Friday [July 27]

Visited the camps but found most of the people absent whom we wished to see. The poor old woman with us is very sick with the dysentery. Last night a small child was brought from the camps and buried in the graveyard.

Saturday [July 28]

We hear that General Scott has resigned the business of moving the Indians to the council, allowing for the removal [of] 300,000.

Went to see the poor, old, sick woman. While standing by her, a number of wagons passed swiftly by. An involuntary sigh from her heaving bosom led me to consider how dreadful that sound was to her ears. Such carriages brought her from her peaceful house, from her aged husband, from her children and grandchildren, and also racked her aged and withering frame and hurried her away, far away from all the scenes of her childhood, to cruel camps where she was guarded as a prisoner of war, denied that kind of food congenial to her feeble stomach, almost unable to rise, and yet torn from all those on whose kind arms she had been accustomed to lean for support.

When the soldiers went to the town where this family lived, such as were able [fled] to the woods. But the old man and woman could not run. The soldiers therefore took this dear old distressed woman and as her husband was too heavy to be handled without some inconvenience, he was left alone. The poor old woman was therefore at the camps a number of weeks before she could have any satisfactory evidence that she should ever again see her earthly friends. The old man, her husband, being unable to walk, came to the point of starvation, when some white children found him in the house and fed him. At length those who fled to the woods were taken and together with the old man brought to the camps.

Thursday, Dec. 13

Within ten miles of Ohio River, or Golconda.

Last week on Thursday [December 6] we passed Isaac Bushyhead, Colo. Powell, and another man, left sick about three weeks before by Rev. Jesse Bushyhead's detachment. Isaac's father and sister Susan were with him.

As we camped about two miles beyond I returned and spent the evening with them and was pleased to find them disposed to converse on religious subjects. As I was about leaving, Mr. Bushyhead requested me to pray with him, as I was myself desirous to do. Sixty persons had died out of their detachment previous to their arrival at that place.

During the night a Cherokee woman died in the camps. Though she had given birth to a child but a few days before, yet last evening she was up & no danger was apprehended, but in the morning she was found dead with the infant in her arms. As the man living near was not willing to have her buried there, and as no place could be obtained for a coffin, the corpse was carried all day in the wagon and at night a coffin was made and the next morning she was buried near the graves of some other Cherokees who had died in a detachment that had preceded us.

Also on Saturday night of last week an infant, a few

months old, died with the bowel complaint. The corpse was interred after meeting on the Sabbath.

Friday [December 14]

Last night a child about twelve months old died. This is the 15th dead since we crossed the Tennessee River. We travelled about 6 miles and camped 2 miles from the Ohio River.[1]

ENDNOTES

[1]Daniel S. Butrick, "The Journal of Rev. Daniel S. Butrick, May 19, 1838–April 1, 1839," ABCFM Papers, by permission of the Houghton Library, Harvard University, Cambridge, Mass., 18.3.3, vol. 4.

⊸ Lilian Lee Anderson Interview ⊸

Margaret McGuire conducted the following interview with Lilian Lee Anderson in Eufaula, Oklahoma, on August 20, 1937.

⟿

In 1838 my grandfather, Washington Lee, came to the Territory and stopped at Westville. He was driven from his home in Georgia over the Trail of Tears with all the other Cherokee Indians and while on the trail somewhere he lost his father and mother and sister, and never saw them anymore. He did not know whether they died or got lost.

The Cherokees had to walk; all the old people who were too weak to walk could ride in the government wagons that hauled the food and the blankets which they were allowed to have. The food was most always cornbread or roasted green corn. Sometimes the men who had charge of the Indians would kill a buffalo and would let the Indians cut some of it and roast it.

The food on the Trail of Tears was very bad and very scarce and the Indians would go for two or three days without water, which they would get just when they came to a creek or river as there were no wells to get water from. There were no roads to travel over as the country was just a wilderness. The men and women would go ahead of the wagons and cut the timber out of the way with axes.

This trail started in Georgia and went across Kentucky, Tennessee, and through Missouri into the Territory and ended at Westville [in what is now Oklahoma], where old Fort Wayne was. Old Fort Wayne was built to shelter the Indians until some houses could be built.

Aunt Chin Deenawash was my grandmother's sister

and she came from Georgia on the Trail of Tears. Her husband died shortly after they got out of Georgia and left her to battle her way through with three small children, one who could not walk. Aunt Chin tied the little one on her back with an old shawl, took one child in her arms and led the other one by the hand. The two larger children died before they had gone so very far and the little one died and Aunt Chin took a broken case knife and dug a grave and buried the little body by the side of the Trail of Tears.

The Indians did not have food of the right kind to eat and Aunt Chin came on alone and lived for years after this.

She married another man in the Territory and raised two sons and the first hanging they had in the Territory was that of her two sons. Joe Mayes was the chief of the Cherokees then and they had a double hanging at Tahlequah. My grandfather had no people left and he made his home with Aunt Chin Deenawash; she was half Cherokee and half white.[1]

ENDNOTES

[1]Lilian Lee Anderson, Interview 7326, vol. 2., Eufaula, Okla., Aug. 20, 1937, 337–39, Indian Pioneer Papers, Western History Collections, University of Oklahoma, Norman, Okla.

~ Bettie Perdue Woodall Interview ~

James R. Carselowey interviewed Bettie Perdue Woodall in Welch, Oklahoma, on September 20, 1937. She talked about the "old Indian days" and the Trail of Tears.

～

My name is Elizabeth Perdue Woodall, but I have always been called "Bettie." I was born near Westville, Indian Territory, December 6, 1851. My father's name was James Perdue, a half-breed Cherokee Indian. My mother, Dollie Thornton Perdue, was a white woman. Both were born in Georgia. They were married in 1838, and came immediately with the eastern emigrants over the Trail of Tears to their new home west of the Mississippi, settling in Going-snake District, in the new Cherokee Nation. . . .

Some histories say that on the Trail of Tears all the women and children were allowed to ride; but my mother told me that not a single woman rode unless she was sick and not able to walk. My mother walked every step of the way over here.

The government furnished green coffee in the grain for the Indians along the route. Many of them had never seen coffee and did not know how to make it. Some of them put the coffee in a pot with meat and were trying to cook it like beans when my mother came along and some Indian woman said, "Ask her, She white woman." My mother said she just had to laugh the way they were trying to cook that coffee. She took some of the green coffee, roasted it in a pan over their fire, put the parched grains in a cloth and pounded it up, and made them a pot of coffee. They all liked it and said she was a smart white woman.

She also showed them how to cook their rice. It seems they all thought everything had to be cooked with meat,

but in this way the young white woman became very popu-
lar and much loved by her newly made friends.

My mother told me about many of the hardships and
privations she and the rest of the women suffered while on
their way from Georgia. Some of them were almost unbe-
lievable, yet I know they are true, for my mother would
have had no motive in telling it if it had not been so.

On one occasion she told of an officer in charge of one
of the wagons who killed a little baby because it cried all the
time. It was only four days old and the mother was forced
to walk and carry it, and because it cried all of the time
and the young mother could not quiet it, the officer took it
away from her and dashed its little head against a tree and
killed it.

After my mother's quarrel with the officer in charge of
our wagon, my father made arrangements with some of the
other officers in front to move to another wagon. He was
afraid the officer might kill her to keep her from telling on
him.

My parents settled near the present site of Westville
and my father taught school and farmed. They were married quite a while before I was born and I was their only
child. There was a peculiarity about my father and mother.
He was an Indian, but was blue eyed and had brown hair;
while my mother, who was white, had piercing black eyes
and black hair.[1]

ENDNOTES

[1]Bettie Perdue Woodall, Interview 7551, vol. 100, Welch, Okla., Sept. 20,
1937, 66–68, Indian Pioneer Papers, Western History Collections, University of Oklahoma, Norman, Okla.

~ Ida Mae Hughes Interview ~

Robert L. Thomas interviewed Ida Mae Hughes in Muskogee, Oklahoma, on November 15, 1937. She talked about her churchgoing and an ancestor's experience of the Trail of Tears.

⟋

I was born at Tahlequah, Oklahoma, Cherokee Nation, March 14, 1879. I am three-fourths Cherokee.

I was educated in the country schools east of Stilwell, Oklahoma. I grew up in Cherokee Nation and married Lee Hughes, a one-eighth Cherokee. He died in 1919 with the influenza. . . .

When I was a girl I attended Elm Hill Baptist Church with my mother, who was a full blood Cherokee.

She was educated and was a leader in the Baptist Missionary work for thirty years. She did the interpreting for the ministers who were sent there from the east.

They had the Bible in Cherokee language and would read a verse then pass it down the line and every person would read. I was very small but it impressed me very much. I am still trying to follow out the teachings of my mother and the Bible.

I enjoyed going to church and most all my people are Baptist. The old church was called the Elm Hill Church and it is about nine miles east of Stilwell, in Adair County. The building has been torn down but the old family graveyard is still in my memory and it has grown to be a large graveyard. It was started by our family in 1845.

My grandfather's name was Alford Miller. He was born in Georgia in 1812 and came to Oklahoma with the Cherokees over the Trail of Tears. I have heard him talk of his journey here. He said they walked part of the way, came on a steamboat part of the way and had to suffer great hardships. They were driven like slaves by the masters of the expedition. The weather was cold and the Cherokees suffered; many of them died on the way.[1]

ENDNOTES

[1]Ida Mae Hughes, Interview 12184, vol. 45, Muskogee, Okla., Nov. 15, 1937, 218–19, Indian Pioneer Papers, Western History Collections, University of Oklahoma, Norman, Okla.

~ Eliza Whitmire Interview ~

James Carselowey interviewed Eliza Whitmire, a former slave, in Estella, Oklahoma, on February 14, 1936. She was past age one hundred at the time. Whitmire talked about slavery in Georgia, her experiences during the removal, and the establishment of the Cherokee capital at Tahlequah, Oklahoma.

~

My name is Eliza Whitmire. I live on a farm near Estella where I settled shortly after the Civil War and where I have lived ever since. I was born in slavery in the state of Georgia, my parents having belonged to a Cherokee Indian of the name of George Sanders who owned a large plantation in the old Cherokee Nation in Georgia. He also owned a large number of slaves but I was too young to remember how many he owned.

I do not know the exact date of my birth, although my mother told me I was about five years old when President Andrew Jackson ordered General [Winfield] Scott to proceed to the Cherokee country in Georgia with two thousand troops and remove the Cherokees by force to the Indian Territory. This bunch of Indians were called the Eastern Emigrants. The Old Settler Cherokees had moved themselves in 1835 when the order was first given to the Cherokees to move out.

The weeks that followed General Scott's order to remove the Cherokees were filled with horror and suffering for the unfortunate Cherokees and their slaves. The women and children were driven from their homes, sometimes with blows, and close on the heels of the retreating Indians came greedy whites to pillage the Indians' homes, drive off their cattle, horses and hogs, and they even rifled the graves for any jewelry or other ornaments that might have been buried with the dead.

The Cherokees, after being driven from their homes, were divided into detachments of nearly equal size and late in October, 1838, the first detachment started, the others following one by one. The aged, sick and the young children rode in the wagons which carried the provisions and bedding, while others went on foot. The trip was made in the dead of winter and many died from exposure from sleet and snow and all who lived to make this trip, or had parents who made it, will long remember it as a bitter memory.

When we arrived here from Georgia my parents settled with their master, George Sanders, near Tahlequah, or near the place where Tahlequah now is located, for at that time the capital had not been established. I well remember the time when a commission of three men was selected from the Illinois Camp Ground to look out [scout] the location for a capital and when the date was set to meet at a big spring, where the present town of Tahlequah now stands, there were only two of the commissioners present. They waited and waited for the third man to come, but finally gave him up and selected the site on account of the number of springs surrounding the town. I remember too, the great Inter-Tribal Council which was held in Tahlequah during the year of 1843 under the leadership of Chief John Ross. My mother assisted with the cooking at that gathering, while my duty was to carry water to those at the meeting from the near-by springs. About ten years after we arrived in the Indian Territory, I witnessed the erection of four little log cabins to house the officers of the Cherokee Government. I have seen a dashing young slave boy acting as coachman for Chief John Ross, drive him in from his home near Park Hill and let him out at the Capitol Square, where he would spend the day at the little log cabins, then the seat of government of the Cherokee tribe. The old square was first surrounded by a rail fence at that time and many horses could be seen tied there while their owners spent the day in the new capital. I remember a few years after we arrived here, that Major General Ethan Allen Hitchcock came here from Washington to hold a conference with Chief John Ross and the Cherokee people with reference to a new treaty, seeking to pay the Cherokees for their loss and wrongs during their removal from Georgia. This meeting was held under a big shed erected in the center of the square and was attended by a large number of people. Chief John Ross addressed the audience in English and Chief Justice Bushyhead interpreted it in Cherokee. The government agreed to indemnify the Indians for their losses but I am told that they now have claims filed in the court of claims for some of this very money.[1]

Endnotes

[1] Eliza Whitmire, Interview 12963, vol. 97, Estella, Okla., Feb. 14, 1936, 398–401, Indian Pioneer Papers, Western History Collections, University of Oklahoma, Norman, Okla.

⌁ Elizabeth Watts Interview ⌁

L. D. Wilson interviewed Elizabeth Watts—whose address was Route 2, Box 168, Muskogee, Oklahoma—on April 27, 1937. Mrs. Watts talked about the removal stories she heard from her grandparents. Wilson related her account mostly in the third person.

⌁

The Cherokees owned a large acreage in Georgia. After Jefferson was elected president by the United States, he had agents to come to the different tribes to induce them to come West. Their inducement was much more land than they had there. They had lived there in Georgia for years and years. They had good land that was left, for already the white people had encroached and taken much of their land. Naturally, most of them did not want to leave and go out into the wilderness and start life anew. To do so, was like spending a nickel these days for a grab bag, or like saying, "Buying a cat in a sack." They did not willingly want to do this. Time passed. The War of 1812 came and removal was delayed. A new president, Madison, was elected and he traded land in Arkansas, north of Ft. Smith, for their land and agreed to move them and give them supplies, guns, clothing, ammunition and utensils. A few of them agreed and came. The most of them still refused. This greatly separated the Cherokees. Those that came to Arkansas had trouble there. The government then moved them to what we call the Strip Country [part of the northern section of what is now Oklahoma].

Those left in Georgia began building larger homes, put in larger crops, planted orchards and advanced by leaps and bounds. It was during this period the Cherokees adopted the Sequoyah alphabet in Georgia. Sequoyah also came west to the ones in the Strip Country and taught it there.

The white people used all means to get the Indians out of Georgia. Claimed they were barbarians, and they, the Cherokees, made new laws just like the ones we had here in the Nation. John Ross was elected Chief of all the Tribes of Cherokees. Ross did all he could to get to stay there, but the Georgia white man passed laws and more laws, and law or no law, they destroyed the Indian's fences, and crops, and killed their cattle, burned their homes and made life a torment to them.

The Cherokees began to think of joining the West Cherokees. They simply could endure no longer. Like everything, it took a leader, and Major Ridge, his son, John Ridge, and two nephews, Elias Boudinot and Stand Watie, became leaders. Of course, John Ross was the Chief and they all got to squabbling. Ross did not want to move his people, but by some hook or crook, Boudinot and Ridge signed a treaty [New Echota] to move, and claimed it was the will of the majority, but it was not and the government waited a little while and sent Gen. Scott and two or three thousand soldiers. The soldiers gathered them up, all up, and put them in camps. They hunted them and ran them down until they got all of them. Even before they were loaded in wagons, many of them got sick and died. They were all grief stricken. They lost all on earth they had. White men even robbed their dead's graves to get their jewelry and other little trinkets.

They saw to stay was impossible and the Cherokees told Gen. Scott they would go without further trouble and the long journey started. They did not all come at once. First one batch and then another. The sick, old and babies rode on the grub and household wagons. The rest rode a horse, if they had one. Most of them walked. Many of them died along the way. They buried them where they died, in unmarked graves. It was a bitter dose and lingered in the mind of Mrs. Watts' Grandparents and parents until death took them. The road they traveled, History calls the "Trail of Tears." This trail was more than tears. It was death, sorrow, hunger, exposure and humiliation to a civilized people as were the Cherokees. Today, our greatest Politicians, Lawyers, Doctors and many of worthy mention are Cherokees. Holding high places, in spite of all the humiliation brought on their forefathers.

Yes, they reached their Western Friends and started all over again.

Lands promised, money promised, never materialized[,] only with a paltry sum, too small to recall, for what they parted with and the treatment received.[1]

ENDNOTES

[1] Elizabeth Watts, Interview 0000, vol. 95, Muskogee, Okla., Apr. 27, 1937, 527–31, Indian Pioneer Papers, Western History Collections, University of Oklahoma, Norman, Okla.

~ Mary Cobb Agnew Interview ~

L. W. Wilson interviewed Mary Cobb Agnew at her home at 917 North M Street in Muskogee, Oklahoma, on May 25, 1937.

~

My name was Mary Cobb and I was married to Walter S. Agnew before the Civil War.

I was born in Georgia on May 19, 1840. My mother was a Cherokee woman and my father was a white man. I was only four years old when my parents came to the Indian Territory and I am now ninety-three years old.

My mother and father died when I was but seven years old and I was raised by an aunt, my mother's sister. I never attended school and my education is practical except what I was taught by my husband.

My parents did not come to the Territory on the "Trail of Tears" but my grand-parents on my mother's side did. I have heard them say that the United States Government drove them out of Georgia. The Cherokees had protested to the bitter end. Finally the Cherokees knew that they had to go some place because the white men would kill their cattle and hogs and would even burn their houses in Georgia. The Cherokees came a group at a time until all got to the Territory. They brought only a few things with them[,] travelling by wagon train. Old men and women, sick men and women would ride but most of them walked and the men in charge drove them like cattle and many died en route and many other Cherokees died in Tennessee waiting to cross the Mississippi River. Dysentery broke out in their camp by the river and many died, and many died on the journey but my grandparents got through all right.

I have heard my grandparents say that after they got out of the camp, and even before they left Georgia, many Cherokees were taken sick and later died.

The Cherokees came through Tennessee, Kentucky, part of Missouri and then down to Indian Territory on the "Trail of Tears."

Some Cherokees were already in the country around Evansville, Arkansas, before my grandparents came. They called them Western Cherokees. It was in 1838 when my grandparents came and I heard them say it was in the winter time and all suffered with cold and hunger.

My mother and father remained in Georgia about six years after mother's folks came on the "Trail of Tears" and Mother worried continually about her parents. Then when I was four years old, I with my parents and other kin, came west to join my grandparents. I don't know why the Government let mother stay longer than the rest of the Cherokees in Georgia unless it was because she married a white man. We came by wagons to Memphis, Tennessee. At Memphis we took a steamboat and finally landed at Fort Gibson, Indian Territory, in June, 1844. I don't know how long it took us to come from Memphis nor do I remember the names of the towns we came through but I have heard my folks say that we had to change boats two or three times because the rivers became shallow and we had to change to smaller boats.

After our arrival at Fort Gibson, Indian Territory, we met our kinspeople in the Flint District and settled in the Territory a short way from Evansville, Arkansas. It was in the Flint District and around Fort Gibson that I grew to be a young lady.[1]

ENDNOTES
[1] Mary Cobb Agnew, Interview 5978, vol. 1, Muskogee, Okla., May 25, 1937, 289–91, Indian Pioneer Papers, Western History Collections, University of Oklahoma, Norman, Okla.

Part 5

THE CIVIL WAR

William P. Ross, John Ross's nephew, was elected twice as principal chief of the Western Cherokees. The first editor of the newspaper *Cherokee Advocate*, he described the devastating effects of the Civil War in 1864:

> Everything has been much changed by the destroying hand of War. . . . [B]ut few men remain at their homes. . . . [N]early all the farms are growing up in bushes and briars, houses abandoned or burnt. . . . [A] great and melancholy change . . . has come over our once prosperous and beautiful country. . . . [L]ivestock of all kinds has become very scarce. . . . We have not a horse, cow or hog left that I know of. . . . [S]ome few have a yoke of oxen or a mule. . . . [There has been a] great increase in the number of wild animals. The wolves howl dismally over the land and the panther's scream is often heard.[1]

As a result of wartime disruptions, Cherokee women had to assume new responsibilities and greater burdens. They suffered from refugee status and violence in the form of rape, raids, and robberies. The Civil War intensified class, political, and racial divisions within the nation. At the same time, it emphasized the role of men as warriors and elevated the role of women as providers and cultivators of the earth.[2]

The Cherokees were drawn into the war because of their geographical location and because many of them owned slaves. Loyalty to either side was problematic for them. The Southern states had dispossessed them of their homeland in the East, and the federal government had enforced their removal, withdrawn its troops from the territory, and suspended annuity payments. Bitterness between the Ridge and Ross factions grew out of the removal period when the Ridge family endorsed the Treaty of New Echota, which ceded Cherokee land in the Southeast. The Ross faction steadfastly opposed removal. The turmoil continued into the Civil War, with loyalties divided between the North and the South.

John Ross, the principal chief of the Cherokee Nation for thirty-eight years, sought to maintain neutrality when the Civil War broke out. Albert Pike, who supported the Confederate side, wrote prophetically to Colonel John Drew on July 14, 1862, warning the Cherokees of the probable results of Union loyalty: "Surely the Cherokees are sagacious enough to know that soft as the paw of the panther may be, its treacherous nature will not long allow it to keep its claws concealed. The northern states will never forgive you. They may profess that until the war is over; but if they hold possession of your country they will punish you by parceling out your lands; and licking their lips they will think they have done God good service."[3]

The Union did not offer any support or protection when Confederate troops surrounded the Cherokee Nation. Ross was forced to abandon neutrality. On October 7, 1861, the council passed resolutions supporting a treaty with the Confederacy. Stand Watie and John Drew recruited troops for the South. When Union forces moved into Tahlequah in the spring of 1862, they arrested Ross and accompanied him to Washington in order to confer with Abraham Lincoln. In early 1863, Ross's faction declared its allegiance to the Union, freed its slaves, and repudiated the alliance with the Confederacy. The Cherokee Nation was divided in two until the end of the war because Watie and his followers refused to accept this position.[4]

Cherokee and black women interacted with each other in complex ways before and throughout the Civil War. Prior to their emancipation, female slaves owned by the Cherokees did the work previously allotted to Cherokee women. They were instrumental in enabling a small class of acculturated women to pursue gentility and leisure. Thus, the relationship between black women and Cherokee women played a critical role in shaping gender distinctions. Elite Cherokees came to associate patriarchal gender roles with being civilized.[5]

Most Cherokee women expressed no support for the ideals of either the Union or the Confederacy. They hated the war, wanted it to end, and often urged their husbands and sons to return home. They spent the duration of the war at home with their families or as refugees, barely managing to survive. During the war, Cherokee women had to raise crops; spin, weave, and sew if they were to have any clothes; haul wood and supplies; care for the sick; and bury the dead. The women showed courage and strength as they faced the terror of destruction of their homes and property, robberies, and violence. Some of them relied on their religious faith to sustain them.

After the horrors of the war, the Western Cherokee Nation once again began to rebuild its institutions of government and education. Because many Cherokees had supported the South, the United States government punished the entire nation during Reconstruction. It demanded railroad access through Indian Territory, insisted that the Indian nations give citizenship and land to their freed slaves, and thwarted their sale of neutral lands and the Cherokee Outlet (a piece of land in Indian Territory owned by the Cherokees and leased for cattle grazing). The government stalled payments owed to the tribe and refused to remove white intruders. By the late nineteenth century, the Cherokee Nation became destabilized and faced possible loss of sovereignty.[6]

More than one-third of adult Cherokee women were widows at the close of the Civil War, and a quarter of Cherokee children (twelve hundred total) were orphans. For these survivors, the cessation of hostilities left deep scars. The loss of so many husbands and fathers was a devastating blow psychologically, economically, and politically. Widows had to live in the midst of a shattered nation that had lost four thousand people. Many husbands who returned from the war were disabled or seriously wounded.[7] The "panther's scream" was often heard.

The following selections present the voices of Cherokee women on both sides of the Civil War. The letters, diary, and oral histories reveal their courage and strength during that tumultuous time.

ENDNOTES

[1] Mary Elizabeth Good, editor, "The Diary of Hannah Hicks," *American Scene* 13, no. 3 (1972), editor's epilogue, 22.

[2] William McLoughlin, *After the Trail of Tears: The Cherokees' Struggle for Sovereignty, 1839–1880* (Chapel Hill: University of North Carolina Press, 1993), 74.

[3] Albert Pike to Colonel John Drew, July 14, 1862, Grant Foreman Collection, Box 6, 83–229, Oklahoma Historical Society, Oklahoma City, Okla.

[4] Edward Everett Dale and Gaston Litton, editors, *Cherokee Cavaliers: Forty Years of Cherokee History As Told in the Correspondence of the Ridge-Watie-Boudinot Family* (Norman: University of Oklahoma Press, 1995), xx, xxi; Alvin M. Josephy Jr., *The Civil War in the American West* (New York: Alfred A. Knopf, 1991), 319, 322.

[5] Theda Perdue, "Southern Indians and the Cult of True Womanhood," in *The Web of Southern Social Relations: Women, Family and Education*, edited by Walter I. Fraser, R. Frank Saunders Jr., and Jon I. Wakelyn (Athens: University of Georgia Press, 1985), 35–51.

[6] See Carolyn Ross Johnston, "The 'Panther's Scream Is Often Heard': Cherokee Women in Indian Territory during the Civil War," *Chronicles of Oklahoma* 78, no. 1, edited by Mary Ann Blochowiak (2000): 84–107; Mary Jane Warde, "Now the Wolf Has Come: The Civilian War in the Indian Territory," *Chronicles of Oklahoma* 71, no. 1 (1993): 69–87.

[7] Morris L. Wardell, *A Political History of the Cherokee Nation, 1838–1907* (1938; reprint, Norman: University of Oklahoma Press, 1977), 175; McLoughlin, *After the Trail of Tears*, 220.

~ Ella Coody Robinson Interview ~

Mrs. Ella Coody (or Coodey) Robinson was interviewed by Ella Robinson (likely her daughter) in Muskogee, Oklahoma, on May 6, 1938. She talked extensively about the Civil War and her life as a Cherokee woman during Reconstruction and beyond.

~

I was born April 28, 1847, at the home of my parents, "Frozen Rock," four miles east of the present site of Muskogee, on the Arkansas River. My father was William Shorey Coody, and my mother was Elizabeth Fields Coody, both Cherokees. Her father was Richard Fields, a prominent man in the Cherokee Nation. My father was a native of Tennessee, born across the line between Alabama and Tennessee. Mother was born near Gunter's Landing in Alabama.

Such were the prosperous, peaceful conditions of the Cherokees when the war clouds began to gather in 1860 and broke with all their fury in 1861. The Cherokees, with the other tribes attempted to remain neutral and not take any part in the conflict, as they had no part in the trouble in Congress. A convention was called and the Five Tribes decided to keep out of the conflict and abide the result of the war whichever side was victorious. But when the Southern states began to secede, things began to take on a war-like aspect in the Territory and confusion began. Pressure was brought to bear from Texas and Arkansas, asking that they join forces with them. Raiding parties from Kansas preceded the regular army, driving off stock and pilfering. Those were known as "Kansas Jay Hawkers." For self protection alone, the Indians had to take steps to defend themselves.

When it became apparent that the Cherokees had to take action, a regiment was recruited under General Stand Watie. My stepfather (Mr. Vann) was made captain. My brother, Will, seventeen years old, enlisted. Real fighting began in 1862. Our men went to the army and we children were left at home with mother.

Some years prior to that Mr. Vann had gotten a man from Kentucky to come out and he had been Mr. Vann's overseer and cared for the race horses. He was not drafted into the army, so Mr. Allen stayed with us.

The Northern Army set up headquarters in the little village of Webbers Falls [in what is now Oklahoma], and things were at high tension. Mr. John Drew raised a company of full-bloods and was appointed their captain. General Watie's troops were sent to the aid of Missouri troops and were in the disastrous battle of Pea Ridge [in northwestern Arkansas]. When things began to be so uncertain and dangerous my parents wanted to place me in the Catholic Convent at Fort Smith [Arkansas] for safety they thought, as well as school advantages, as the Cherokee schools had been forced to close. Two cousins, Emma Vore, Emma Drew and myself all were taken to Ft. Smith, but owing to over-crowded conditions, only one girl was taken—Emma Drew, daughter of John Drew. Afterward I went to Van Buren [Arkansas] and attended school at the academy. I saw the Confederate troops march through the town on their way to the northern part of the country; they went through in perfect order and looked fine. It took four hours for them to pass through. They participated in the battle of Pea Ridge and came back a terrible looking crowd, bringing their wounded with them. Schools were dismissed and every church, school and store was thrown open to care for the wounded and dying. I went once to see the wounded but didn't go again as I felt sure they took a man out to bury him that wasn't quite dead.

I stayed one year in Van Buren when that school, too, was forced to close. I came home and found things in terrible confusion. The battle of Honey Springs was the biggest battle fought near us. Just at dawn the cannons began to roar and kept up until dark. We could hear them, and each one struck terror to our hearts, for our men folks were in the midst of it. I remember how frightened Mrs. Perry Brewer was when she came to our house after nothing had been heard from the men. She was Mr. Vann's sister, and when she became panic stricken, she always came to my mother, who at all times tried to keep her balance. On that particular morning she had ridden from her home some ten miles up the river to our house, and wanted mother to go with her to try to hear from the men. Mother put her off by saying, "If we don't hear today, we'll go tomorrow," when Aunt Dee said, "Lizzie, the buzzards will have them eaten up by that time."

Mother's father, Mr. Richard Fields, was taken prisoner at Prairie Grove, Arkansas, with another Cherokee named Reece. They were taken to Union prison in Illinois, where they were held for some months, with no prospects of being exchanged for Northern soldiers held in the South. Grandfather was sick and one day when the commanding officer came through the prison, grandfather said, "Do you know General Sacket [Union general Delos B. Sackett]?" The officer said, "What do you want to know that for?" Grandfather replied, "Nothing, only he is my son-in-law and I wondered where he was now." In a day or so both he and Reese were discharged. They made their way through the line and got into the Southern Army where they rested and were given assistance in getting home. When they walked up to the house barefooted and in rags, no one knew them.

Another source of annoyance with which we had to contend was the "Pin Indians," a band of full-bloods who were not slave owners, nor did they belong to either army, although they were Union sympathizers. Their main object was stealing—taking milk cows and pilfering homes. A band of women also would go to a house in day time, go through the house and take what they wanted. One day a group of them came to our home. Mother talked to the one who seemed to be the leader and told her that she was Richard Fields' daughter and he had been such a good friend to the full-bloods. They went away but one little woman took the new water bucket from the back porch as she went. White men came down from the North ostensibly to preach to the Negroes, but instead of preaching, they were inciting them to all kinds of meanness and deviltry. The Negroes tried to be faithful to their owners and at the same time were bewildered by what was being told them by these men. The women stayed at home and tried to keep things together and care for their families but it was a terrible ordeal for they never knew what a day would bring forth. . . . Everything was being done by the agitators from the Northern army to get the Negroes to desert their owners and take refuge in the Union headquarters in the village; many did but most of ours stayed on. One white man in particular sneaked about among the Negroes, telling them they would be taken care of at the Union headquarters. He had been warned to leave the neighborhood but stayed on. One morning he was found dead on Mr. I. G. Vore's place. Mr. Vore had been away since the beginning of the war. He was stationed at Fort Washita in charge of the Creek Commissary, so they couldn't accuse him of having done it. They laid it on Mr. Vann and his brother, David, who were many miles away. They used that as an excuse and proceeded to burn our house. In April of 1863, Kansas troops commanded by Colonel [William A.] Phillips had moved into the Territory and burned and robbed as they went. A report came that morning that my brother, Will, had been taken prisoner and was being held at Union headquarters.

Mother had gone down there that morning to see about it and I was left alone with the little children, when a detachment of Negro soldiers from Colonel Phillips' division swooped down and took possession of the house. The big insolent negro men went through the house, taking everything they wanted and destroying the things they couldn't take; they ripped open the feather beds and let the feathers blow away. The men would try to put on my mother's dresses and would tear them to pieces; they took all the groceries and food in the house and left us nothing. The little children were so frightened that they clung to me in terror but didn't say a word. I was no less frightened myself. Our overseer, Mr. Allen, was away too, that morning having gone to see if he could get some news of the men in the army. When mother returned she was panic-stricken but there was no place to go or anything to do. Late that same evening another detachment of Union soldiers came with Colonel Phillips himself in charge and set fire to the house and burned it to the ground. They went through and kindled a fire in every room. Mother pleaded with him to allow her to remove a few prized pieces of furniture, (her bed was one.) He refused and said, "Madam, it's entirely too fine." Mother replied, "Well, it's mine and paid for." They went through the house with an axe and broke every mirror and marble slab on the furniture. Mr. Allen was there and in the confusion managed to get two or three mattresses, a few quilts and one or two pieces of furniture out. One was a little table of my mother's which I still have. The negroes had gone crazy and were no help. There happened to be one or two vacant negro cabins on the place and the bedding was taken to them and that is where we slept, or rather stayed, for no one slept except the babies. That night all the negroes ran away, taking all the best horses, including Mr. Vann's race horses.

The Negro men who took the horses made their way

to Kansas, and the women went to Union headquarters at Webber's Falls. The next morning Mr. Allen went out to Colonel Brewer's headquarters and reported the trouble and secured some food. Late that evening he came back and mother prepared supper, the first meal we had had since breakfast the day before. Mr. Vann got word about what had happened and came home. There was a vacant house of two or three rooms on the Vore place and we moved up there. Some of our neighbors who had not been burned out gave us a few things but in a few days Union troops set fire to the little village, and burned the whole place out. During the thirty-six hours we were without food the little children who were accustomed to three good meals a day did not ask once for anything to eat. We stayed there until August when everyone left and made their way across the line into Texas. We did not have very much to move after having been robbed and burned out. All the best horses had been stolen by the Negroes and Kansas Jay Hawkers so we had only light teams left. Rumors were everywhere that young girls were in danger and one day an authentic report came that some had been insulted by the Union soldiers. My mother and the mothers of several girls became alarmed and at midnight got us out of bed and started us with some companions to Colonel Perry Brewer's headquarters, eight miles out on Dirdy Creek. I had only thin shoes and when I got there about daylight the soles were worn through. Mr. Brewer (Uncle Perry as we called him) took us in and gave us protection for several days. He then sent us with a guard down on Canadian River where his wife (Aunt Dee) and children were. We stayed there until my family started South. Mother came by and took me on with her and I never went back to Webber's Falls.

We traveled slowly as it was hot and Mother was not well. There had been no fighting in the lower part of the Territory, but almost all of the Choctaws and Chickasaws had already left their homes and gone to Texas. We could find vacant cabins to camp in and would stop to rest and cook. We found plenty of late vegetables, turnips, pumpkins, sweet potatoes and late corn in the gardens. What we missed so much was sugar, coffee, white flour, milk and butter. I learned to drink coffee from a tin cup without sugar or cream. I could take a quilt and lie down by a tree and sleep all night. Occasionally the boys found somebody's hog and killed it and divided it among the families traveling together.

There was no regular company traveling together. Some would stop to rest and some would hurry on, but we were never alone. I had a pony that I rode almost all the way, preferring that to riding in the wagons. We finally reached San Bois Creek in the Choctaw Nation where we stopped because my little half brother, Charles, was taken sick with fever. He died after ten days illness and we buried him there. My brother, Will, had been killed by Union soldiers before we left home, and this was a double grief to our family. Mr. Vann had gotten leave from the army to take his family south, and after the death of his little son couldn't bear the thought of leaving us to go on alone. We stayed at San Bois some six weeks to give mother a chance to recover from her grief and loss. The weather had begun to turn cold and Mr. Vann wanted to go on and find a place to spend the winter. While we were on the way and food was such a problem, the Confederate troops captured a wagon train of supplies from the Union Army. I think it was somewhere near Honey Springs that they did that. Our faithful friend, Mr. Allen, was still looking out for us and managed to get a good supply of groceries, including sugar, coffee, rice and flour and tea; also some dry goods of which we were badly in need. I remember I got a pair of shoes which were the same kind but one was a size larger than the other. However, I wore them and was glad to get them.

When the Southern states seceded and a confederacy

of states was formed, they issued their own currency and that was put in general use. It ran from ten cent pieces called "shin plasters" to one hundred dollar bills. It was all paper money. After the defeat of the Southern Army the currency depreciated until it was worth only a few cents on the dollar. I remember paying $120.00 for goods to make one dress; finally it was worth nothing at all.

Mr. Vann applied to his brother-in-law, Major I. G. Vore, for a conveyance to take us on, and he sent an ambulance from his headquarters and a driver.

The first night we stayed at Carriage Point, where the town of Durant [Oklahoma] now is. A public home there was run by the Rider family. The next day we traveled on and went to where Major Vore's family was living, he having sent them with the Negro slaves down there in the spring. We stayed there several days while Mr. Vann looked for a home. He found a two-room cabin some four miles from Bloomfield Academy and rented it, and we stayed there a year and in November after we got there in October, my youngest brother was born; they named him Charles for the little boy who had so recently died. A number of our neighbors from Webbers Falls, who had gone on ahead of us, were living in that vicinity. . . .

Good crops had been raised in that section of the country and we had plenty to eat in the way of vegetables. We were able to get sugar and flour but no tea or coffee, only a little occasionally from the Army. People tried every substitute for coffee, even roasted sweet potato peelings and parched wheat. As all commerce was disrupted, it was hard to get things at the stores. Freight was being captured all the time and it was impossible for those in business to secure goods. There was plenty of wheat raised in Texas and we soon learned to make our hats of wheat straw and they were both comfortable and pretty. We made shoes, something like tennis shoes now worn, of pieces of canvas and leather from the men's boot tops, using the leather for the soles.

They were all right for summer wear. Those who had saved their household goods by going south at the beginning of the war had their looms and wove cloth for themselves and others. We had indigo and copperas and plenty of alum for setting the colors. We boiled oak bark for different shades of brown and made a pretty purple dye of sumac.

Even the dark tragedies of war didn't quite kill the spirit of the young folks. There were parties, dinners and balls. I remember riding horseback to go to a dance twenty miles distant, fording a river, dancing all night and riding home the next morning. Getting party dresses was the problem. One girl took her mother's lace curtains, dyed them and made a beautiful party dress that was the envy of all of us. A friend of Mother's gave me a very full skirt of some soft white material. I took a width out of the skirt and made a waist and wore that one season. The women had gatherings they called "hankings" where everyone would take some wool and go to the home of a friend who had a loom and spin the wool on the spinning wheel. Then the hostess would weave the goods and the cloth was divided among the guests. A fine dinner was served in the middle of the day. The young girls who were not there came early in the afternoon and made preparations for a dance at night. There were several good violinists among the Indians and the music was good. We danced the polka, schottische, waltz and Virginia reel. An old white man of the name McCanaless, who had taught violin at Webber's Falls, went south with the Cherokees and was there at all the parties.

We stayed in the same locality for more than a year, then moved across Red River to a little village called Preston. There I met Lieutenant Joe Robinson and we were married in the spring of 1866. We went to live at the Chickasaw Academy where my father-in-law had had charge of the school since 1850. The school was closed at the beginning of the war and was not in operation while we lived there. The Reverend J. C. Robinson (Joe's father) and his wife were left in charge of the school during the time it was closed. We occupied three large rooms on the ground floor that were a part of the original building erected [in] 1848. A large three-story brick building was attached. My father-in-law had been there for so long and had become such a good friend to the Indians on the western reservations that they regarded him as their best friend and advisor. They would come there in companies, riding their little spotted ponies and carrying their little tepees. They always camped down on the creek, and the first they wanted of Mr. Robinson was a beef to kill. He always had one to give them. Then the men in the party, including one or two chiefs, would come up to the house for a conference. These were Comanche and Kiowa Indians. Before Mr. Robinson was sent to the school, these same tribes had been in the habit of making raids into the Chickasaw Nation and driving off cattle and horses. With the help of the United States Agent he had been able to stop that.

My mother and her family moved from Preston, Texas, where we had been living, to the Academy the first year I lived there. . . . While I lived at the Chickasaw Academy, my oldest child, Cornelia Ann, was born. When she was two years old Joe and I came back to the Cherokee Nation. I boarded that winter with my aunt, Mrs. Louisa Kerr, in Fort Gibson [in what is now Oklahoma] and my second child was born, a son.

My husband had left college in Virginia (Emory and Henry) to enlist in the Army and had no training for any work or profession. He rented a farm about six or eight miles from Fort Gibson on the west side of Grand River and farmed that year. We had a double log house to live in and I cooked on the fireplace in the kitchen. It had only a dirt floor and often when the hired boy went in to make the fire in the morning a big black snake would be curled up in the corner. The farm lay between the mountains on the west and the river on the east. It was a very rich, productive strip of land and we raised fine crops, but snakes were our greatest menace. One warm morning I put my baby outside on a blanket near the kitchen door to play around a large box while I prepared breakfast. I heard him laughing and the dog that always stayed near him growling. I went to the door and within a few feet of the baby was a rattlesnake ready to strike. I grabbed the baby and screamed for the men at the barn. The snake measured 6½ feet with 27 rattles, which indicated that it was 27 years old.

The old settlers told marvelous tales about snakes in the mountain caves. One was that one had lived there as long as they had and no one had been able to kill it. One day as the men were going from the field at noon they saw a huge thing across the road that they took to be a dead log. The horses became alarmed and stopped. When the thing began to crawl[,] all the weapon they had was an ax and one man stuck it into the back of the snake's head, and the men all declared it traveled some distance with the ax in its head. When they finally succeeded in killing it, they told that it was twelve feet long and as large as a twelve-inch tree.

I was glad to leave that place; an Indian boy, Bill Mott, stayed with us and looked after the baby and me when my husband was away. We moved into Fort Gibson from there and Mr. Robinson operated a string of freight wagons from Fort Gibson to Saint Jo, Missouri, the nearest railroad point. His father had retired from active work in the Methodist Church and was living at Paris, Texas. We made numerous trips overland to visit him. We traveled in a carriage with two horses; it was rather slow traveling with two babies, my oldest little girl had died, and we had our third child, a little girl born at Fort Gibson. We would start at noon and drive to Honey Springs (near the town of Checotah) and stay all night at a public house kept by Mrs. Hagerty, a sister of Colonel McIntosh. About the third day we would get to Boggy Depot and spend the night with Mrs. G. B. Hester, the Hesters being long time friends of ours. Every trip we made my father-in-law would urge us to come down there to live. Joe wanted to move to be near his father as he was getting old. I was reluctant to go as I felt that I belonged in the Cherokee Nation and I wanted to stay near my mother. Business opportunities were good in Texas at that time so I finally gave my consent to move.

We lived in the house with Mr. Robinson for a time and my husband was engaged in the lumber business. He bought the lumber standing, had the trees felled and taken to the mills. That section of Texas was malarial and I had such poor health that my husband was forced to let me come back to the Cherokee Nation to my mother's. She and Mr. Vann had moved to "Spring Place," his mother's old home, ten miles east of the present site of Muskogee. In the settlement of the Vann Estate he had gotten the home. The same trees I had played under and the same fruit trees from which I had gathered fruit as a little child were still there for my own children to enjoy. I never returned to Texas, as my husband died. With the exception of the four years I spent in Texas, I have spent the entire 91 years of my life in the Cherokee Nation.[1]

ENDNOTES

[1] Ella Coody Robinson, Interview 13833, vol. 77, Muskogee, Okla., May 6, 1938, 94–127, Indian Pioneer Papers, Western History Collections, University of Oklahoma, Norman, Okla.

Letters between
~ Mary Bryan Stapler Ross ~
and John Ross

The following letters between Mary Bryan Stapler Ross (1826–1865) and John Ross (1790–1866) illuminate their lives and relationship during the Civil War. John Ross's first wife, Elizabeth "Quatie" Brown Henley, a full-blood Cherokee, died on the Trail of Tears in 1839 near Little Rock, Arkansas, from pneumonia after she gave her blanket to a sick child and developed a cold.[1] Ross met Mary Stapler, a young Quaker, and her family in Brandywine Springs, Delaware, when he was in the East in 1841. He wrote to Mary in June and July 1844 from Washington City. Although he was fifty-four years old—thirty-six years older than she—he conveyed the nervousness and insecurities of a teenager. In their correspondence during their courtship, John Ross delicately broached the subject of his love for Mary and, in Victorian language, struggled to communicate his feelings. He desperately wanted reassurance that she felt the same for him. After Mary declared her love, they were engaged.

Ross wrote the following to her on August 2, 1844:

Alas! You are at last willing to tie that sacred knot that fall! But you "would like as long a time as possible"—and if you "had not given me *your whole heart*, and *did not love me*—you would never have consented to unite your fate with mine so soon." My dearest Mary! There is something in these remarks that touch and incites the tender feelings of my heart which cannot be described! Confiding love, innocence and timidity seem to unite in thought as regards

Chief John Ross and wife Mary Bryan Stapler Ross
COURTESY OF RESEARCH DIVISION OF THE OKLAHOMA HISTORICAL SOCIETY

the step you are about to take from the present, to a future
relation in life. It is indeed a very important movement,
one that, may be blessed with peace and happiness, or, be
filled of adversity and sorrow! But, such are the mysterious ways allotted for us by a kind providence through the
career of this life! And it is my most sincere wish that, you
should decide upon all things in connection with our proposed union understandingly—as my whole desire shall
be to render you as happy as may be in my power. And
unless you could be made contented and happy with me,
I should myself indeed become also unhappy. Let me then
beg you to make notes of such points as you may wish to be
informed upon—and when we meet, I will most promptly

respond to answer them in truth and sincerity. Perchance the monitor within should tell you that your heart remains unalterably fixed upon me as you have more than once already intimated. And the consent of your friends being had—we may then unite our hearts in wedlock.

Mary married John Ross in Philadelphia on September 2, 1844. She accompanied him to Indian Territory and became a citizen of the Cherokee Nation. Although she was a white woman, Mary became deeply involved in Cherokee life and culture. The couple had two children—a daughter, Anne, and a son, John.

Mary Stapler Ross adamantly opposed slavery and urged John Ross to emancipate his and the Cherokee Nation's slaves. She had a profound impact on her husband and was likely a major influence in his freeing his slaves and siding with the Union.

During the Civil War, John Ross tried to negotiate with the federal government for the Cherokee Nation. Mary Stapler Ross did not experience physical deprivation, but she did endure the loss of her beautiful home, Rose Cottage, which was burned. She also lost a stepson, nephew, and other relatives in the war. John Ross's sons from his first marriage—James, Allen, Silas, and George—served in the Union army. Three of his grandsons and three of his nephews also fought. His son James was captured and died in 1864.

Mary remained in Philadelphia during the course of the war. She had to expand her traditional role but did not have to step outside her sphere. She helped care for thirty-six people, including ten in her immediate family. Eventually, the entire family except for those fighting in the war moved to Philadelphia. Mary's physical labor increased, even though several house slaves had accompanied the Ross family east. Before the war, the Rosses were accustomed to having fifty to one hundred slaves and enjoying considerable affluence.

The Civil War ended on April 9, 1865. Mary died on July 20 of that year. After serving the Cherokee Nation as chief for thirty-eight years, John Ross was still negotiating with the United States government to the moment of his death in 1866.

> ### [708] Washington Place [Philadelphia],
> ### Dec 4th, 1863

My beloved husband,

I wrote these and sent my letter [of December 3] this morning, although I have nothing new to communicate this evening yet—my thoughts are with thee my dear husband and as I cannot have a personal talk I will take this silent mode of converse with thee and thank thee my loved husband for thy welcome favor which came to hand this morning. O! how sad the intelligence from our dear home and our poor people, may our ever merciful Father be with them and in this dark hour cause light to break upon them. Dear [Eliza] Jane [Ross] and her mother [Elizabeth Ross] must have suffered and do still endure more anguish than can be imagined, and dear Jane Nave none but her Heavenly Father can comfort under the great trials she has been called to endure, but His Everlasting arms have been around her to support her. All looks dark now, but we can trust Him for ["]behind a frowning Providence He hides a smiling face." We short sighted mortals cannot comprehend it now. I enclose thee a letter from dear Jane Ross which came today[. T]he scenes of horror through which she has passed it seems almost impossible to think of. *Home*, my dear husband we have no home [Rose Cottage] there now, one we cherished so long and took so much trouble to beautify is now in ashes, and all is ruin around. I do not think it safe for our loved ones to remain there any longer. I wish some account of what has occurred in our nation could be published in the paper. Lizzie [Elizabeth G. Meigs] wrote thee this afternoon. She has been very much afflicted by the sad news but this evening seems calmer. . . . It is after supper, the little ones have kissed me good night. . . . Now may every blessing be thine, my loved husband. Thee has the great consolation of having faithfully labored for the good of thy poor people and now we must leave all in the hands of God the great Ruler of the Universe. May thee be strengthened and sustained for all that is still before thee is the prayer of thy devoted wife.

M. B. Ross

Washington City 297 Penna. Avenue,
Febry. 13th 1864

My Dear Mary!

I received yours this morning without date, but post-marked 11th inst. I mailed a hasty note [February 12] to Sister Sarah [F. Stapler] last night, enclosing extracts from the reports of the U.S. Agent [Justin] Harlan and Special Agent [John T.] Cox, to Supt. Coffin for the information of the Govt. Which together with the copy of a letter from Wm. P. Ross I sent you respecting the debilitation and suffering condition of the Cherokees. I requested her to lay before Doct. [Thomas] Brainerd as containing facts from sources of unquestionable reliability! I have been so engaged today, as to prevent me from writing you until now.

And I can only say in this hasty note we are all well! Brother [Lewis Ross] and his Cherokee boy Henry [C. Ross], are at Willards. We intend to see the President [Abraham Lincoln] on Monday [February 15], or as soon as he can give us an audience on the present state of Cherokee affairs. And I hope to be able thereafter to progress more rapidly with our business—also to finish the statement I prescribed for the general formation of the good people of this country—of our unfortunate condition. . . .

Your affectionate Husband,

John Ross

[708] Washington Place [Philadelphia],
March 19th, 1864

My beloved husband,

I take my seat this eve at the table where my dear husband has been so often seated writing for the last week, now I am all alone and my loved one is again far away and I am left to fill the void created by thy absence and although but a few hours have passed away I am sad and lonely so I feel like holding a silent talk with thee. A short time after you bade farewell this morning, two gentlemen called and wished to see thee. Upon making myself known, they introduced themselves as Rev. Mr. [Joel T.?] Headly and Mr. Rice. Mr. H is about writing a history of the Cherokees and wishes to get statements from thee. Says thy life will form the basis of all. He is a pleasant gentleman and quite a distinguished historian, he requested me to ask thee, if he had better come down to Washington to see thee or wait until thee comes up. He wishes to get the book out soon and will do thee justice, for he has an exalted opinion of my noble husband.

He wishes a copy of the large photograph in the parlor and also a small one, and a picture of our house. It will be an interesting work. . . . Now my dear husband, good night. I trust thy cold will be better. May every blessing be thine is the prayer of thy devoted wife,

M. B. Ross

[708] Washington Place [Philadelphia], March 22nd, 1864

My beloved husband,

Thy telegraph bearing the sad intelligence of the death of little Henry [Ross] came to hand last eve about half past six o'clock. Poor James [M. Ross], how painful it will be to him to hear that the youngling of his little flock has been taken from him. Truly he has been called to pass through deep waters and where is he now himself, it is mournful to think, what may be his condition. We can truly say "God moves in a mysterious way His wonders to perform," and think "behind a frowning providence He hides a smiling face." I too have to tell of another soul that has passed away. Sally [Mannion Ross] died Sunday night [March 20] about two o'clock. Her spirit is at rest, her last End was Peace. She wished to die and was perfectly conscious until she breathed her last. Sister [Sarah F. Stapler] spent most of Sabbath with her. I went in the afternoon. She knew me and told me she had thought a short time before that she was going. I asked her if she felt she was going *home.* [She] said yes. I told her I hoped we would meet in heaven. She said she hoped so. She had suffered a great trial. She is to be buried tomorrow. So one after another are passing away. . . . [T]he children send kisses. Thy devoted wife,

M. B. Ross

[708] Washington Place [Philadelphia],
June 4th, 1864

My beloved husband,

Thy *very, very* welcome letter of the 1st was received yesterday and its cheering words cast sunshine around my heart and dispelled the clouds that had gathered there. It is certainly very trying for thee to be kept in a state of suspense especially in such a place as Washington is at this time, and I do hope a speedy and satisfactory conclusion will ere long come, then as thee says with the blessing of our Heavenly Father we can enjoy *our Home together* which if adorned with true Christian love and thankfulness we can be happy, be it an elegant mansion or a simple, little cottage, it will be "Home sweet Home." It is too true that some of that needful article *money* is very necessary to enable one to get along in this world without perplexity but not as much is required for happiness as some think, it is the heart, and as our bishop said in his sermon last Sunday [May 29], "it may be heaven in a hut and hell in a palace, but if we have Witness with us, peace and happiness may be ours under all circumstances.["] I feel I ought to be very thankful for the many blessings of which I am surrounded, when I think of our wonderful and providential escape from danger and that I am permitted to have a home in this peaceful location. With thee my dear husband, in safety even if we have to be a short time apart I cannot be too grateful. It is delightful here now, the square looks beautiful and the little birds sing sweetly in the trees, notwithstanding the squirrels. Truly God has been good, and I feel He ever will be if we only trust in him. . . . Well I do recollect the first night I spent on the soil in the land I was to find my new western home at his house, the land over which my dear husband ruled. My feelings were peculiar and never can be forgotten, the warm welcome I the lonely *white stranger* received,

far from my childhood's home. Dear[,] very dear did my
sweet prairie home become to me, but I must stop or memory may have too much of sadness in it, but there are bright,
beautiful spots that can never fade away. . . . [W]ith a heart
full of love I am thy devoted wife,

M. B. Ross

Washington City Willard's Hotel
June 6th, 1864

You see my dear Mary, that, altho, I am in person still
sitting in this wearisome city, yet, my thoughts and heart
wander away off to thee and our loved ones of 708 [Wash-
ington Place, Philadelphia]! I will remember the first words
uttered by our darling child [Annie B. Ross] in this place,
years ago, that have passed away and never again return.
When looking up with eyes of celestial blue into my face
[she] sweetly said "Papa's baby"! As I cannot be with you
kiss our beloved "Annie Brian Ross" for her dear father—
and present her with the small token of remembrance for
her [June 7] birthday gift! . . . In much haste I am, yr affectionate husband,

John Ross

[708] Washington Place [Philadelphia],
Jan 10th, 1865

My Beloved Husband,

Thank thee for thy welcome letter which came at three O'clock to cheer thy Mary's heart this dark, rainy day, but my thoughts have been with thee and I have imagined thee enjoying the company of our dear daughter Jane [Ross Meigs Nave] and other friends. After thee parted from me yesterday I felt so sad and lonely, I came to my room and took a good cry[. A]fter that I felt a little better but not much. I kept close [to the] house, today has been stormy all the time. I expect Katie will think we have more clouds than sunshine in this part of the country. Certainly I do not remember such a wet season for sometime, indeed I do not know when before. . . . [H]oping to see thee soon. Thy devoted wife,

Mary B. Ross[2]

ENDNOTES

[1] Zella Armstrong, *History of Hamilton County and Chattanooga, Tennessee*, vol. 1 (Chattanooga, Tenn.: Lookout Publishing, 1931). See also James Corn Collection, box 1, folder 8, History Branch and Archives, Cleveland Public Library, Cleveland, Tenn.

[2] John Ross Papers, Thomas Gilcrease Institute of American History and Art, Tulsa, Okla., for all letters except those dated Feb. 13, 1864, March 19, 1864, and June 6, 1864, which were accessed at the J. L. Hargett Collection, Western History Collections, University of Oklahoma, Norman, Okla., in 1995; materials no longer available there. For biographical information on John Ross and Mary Stapler Ross, see Gary E. Moulton, *John Ross: Cherokee Chief* (Athens: University of Georgia Press, 1978) and Moulton's *The Papers of Chief John Ross*, vols. I and II (Norman: University of Oklahoma, 1985). Moulton's two-volume collection of the Ross papers provides excellent annotations.

Letters between
~ Sarah and Stand Watie ~

The following letters between Sarah and Stand Watie reflect the hardships they experienced during the Civil War.

Stand Watie (1806–1871) was a member of the Ridge Party, which opposed the Ross Party for decades. Although they did not have authorization, John Ridge, Elias Boudinot, The Ridge, and others endorsed the Treaty of New Echota, which ceded Cherokee land to the United States government in exchange for land in Indian Territory. With that action, they essentially sealed their own death warrants, since the tribe had a law that forbade such actions. The large majority of tribal members opposed removal and the treaty. The United States government used the Treaty of New Echota to force removal of the Cherokees from the East. Shortly after the Ridge Party arrived in Indian Territory, John Ridge, Elias Boudinot, and Major Ridge were murdered. Stand Watie survived.

Watie continued to oppose Ross and his party. He also became a Confederate general. Therefore, Watie and Ross were on opposite sides of the Civil War, just as they had been on different sides since 1835. Both families lost children and other relatives in the war.

Sarah Watie (1820–1882) experienced physical and psychological trauma throughout the war. Like her husband, her son Saladin fought for the Confederate cause. Their son Cumiskey died at age fifteen in 1863. He was not in battle but rather at home with his mother. The Waties had five children.

When the war broke out, Sarah fled with her children first

to the Red River, then to Texas to live with relatives. She was accustomed to relying on slaves to perform the most arduous labor, especially agricultural chores. Female slaves milked cows; made butter, cheese, candles, and soap; and did the spinning, weaving, and sewing. They cooked, gathered wood, hauled water, and washed clothes. In her extensive correspondence with her husband, Sarah wrote that she had to spin every day in order to keep her children clothed. Because manufactured goods were generally unavailable, women's domestic drudgery increased dramatically. Sarah spent much of her time trying to secure food and provisions and even had to plant crops herself. Because traditional Cherokee women were accustomed to this sort of labor, they did not experience the psychological anguish Sarah did when she performed duties she believed were not properly her responsibility.

At times, Sarah Watie felt such despair that she even urged Stand to desert. Finally, she received her husband's letter of June 23, 1865, stating, "Have agreed upon cessation of hostilities." Near Doaksville, the capital of the Choctaw Nation, on a blazing hot day, June 23, 1865, General Stand Watie surrendered to Lieutenant Colonel A. C. Mathews. He was the last Confederate general to surrender his command in the Civil War.[1]

Bust of Stand Watie

Sarah Watie

My Dear Husband,

I do not know what to say first[. T]here is many things to say. I never could begin to tell you half as everything seems to go wrong. I have been here at sister N [Nancy Starr's] one week. I find her very low yet she gains very slowly[.] I do not find her as well as I thought she would be. I heard from her before I left home. I thought she would be able to walk when I got here but now I don't believe she will ever get well. I find much discord here. . . .

We have no news here about the army. We hear of several fights in Tennessee but I do not know as to the truth of them. This state is just like all the rest. . . . I want you to write to me and tell me what I must do if they get in here, must I sell the boys or not? I do not want to be so near the Choctaw line as [I] am now. Nancy wants to buy a place here or near here, there is one here for sale at three thousand in Confederate money. Lucian Bell knows the place. I want to get near the school so the children can go all the time but you can guess better than I can how long we will have to stay. There is a good school near here and I would like to get a place and send [the children] to it. The new session begins in September. I will try and get paper so as to write you a good long letter. I wish I could just see you an hour or two. I know you would laugh at some of the experiences of these white folks. I saw Carlott Ivy; you know that she knows all. I will go to see you as soon as I can get the Children to school and some clothes for you. I can't live through the year and not go, you can write and tell me whether there will be danger or not. I will not go till I know that there will be no danger, you know too that, I can't stay away so long from you. It grieves me to think that we are so far from each other[. I]f anything should happen we are too far off for to help each other. Be a good man as you always have been. At the end a clear conscience before God and man is the advice of your wife.

S. Watie

Burn this for it is nonsense. All the children send love. All well.

June 8th, 1863

My Dear Half,

I have just got home from Rusk and found Grady here and a letter from you dated the 27th of April. It gave me a great deal of pleasure to know that you still have time to write and cast a thought on home and home folks. Mr. Kelly and W. Fields will start as soon as I finish my letters. I have not had a chance to write you a long letter since you left. Grady tells me that Charles [Webber] and Saladin have killed a prisoner. Write and tell me who it was and how it was. Tell my boys to always show mercy as they expect to find God merciful to them. I do hate to hear such things[. I]t almost runs me crazy to hear such things. I find myself almost dead sometimes thinking about it. I am afraid that Saladin never will value human life as he ought. If you should ever catch William Ross, don't have him killed. I know how bad his mother would feel but keep him till the war is over. I know they all deserve death but I do feel for his old mother and then I want them to know that you do not want to kill them[,] just to get them out of your way. I want them to know you are not afraid of their influence. Always do as near right as you can. I feel sorry that you have such a bad chance and so much to do; be careful of yourself. We have not a bit of water here, we almost starve for water. . . . It looks like I can't live and not hear from you. You must write and tell me when it will be safe to come. I send the bay horse; the black was too poor to go. I will bring him. You can either send that back or keep him till I come. I can sell him for six hundred here. I have not time to say goodbye. Yours,

Write soon,

S. C. [Sarah] Watie

Camp near North Fork
Nov. 12th, 1863

My Dear Sally:

I have not heard from you since your letter brought in by Anderson. When Medlock went away I was out on a scout. I went to Tahlequah and Park Hill. Took Dannie Hicks and John Ross. Would not allow them killed because you said Wm. Ross must not be killed on old Mrs. Jack Ross's account. Killed a few Pins in Tahlequah. They had been holding council. I had the old council house set on fire and burnt down, also John Ross' house [Rose Cottage]. Poor Andy Nave was killed. He refused to surrender and was shot by Dick Fields. I felt sorry as he used to be quite friendly towards me before the war, but it could not be helped. I would [a] great deal rather have taken him prisoner. Since my return I have been sick but now [am a] good deal better. . . . Since [Confederate general William] Steele's and [Confederate general Douglas H.] Cooper's retreat from Fort Smith, I have been placed in command of the Indian Troops[, all] but Choctaws.

When I first sat down to write I thought I would send you a long letter but I am annoyed almost to death by people calling on me on business of various kinds, this and that.

I will send you pork enough to do you in a few days. I have concluded to have the hogs killed here and the meat hauled to you. You need not try to buy any. I can get it here. . . .

Let me hear from you often and let me know how you are doing. Whenever the troops go into winter quarters I will go home to you. I have not been as well this fall as I used to. I can't get rid of this bad cough. Saladin is well. . . . Love to the little ones and everybody else.

Your husband,

Stand Watie

Near or at the same place
Dec 12th, 1863

My Dear Stand,

I have not been in a right good [spirit since] you left for several [reasons,] none [of which] I shall name here. We are getting along as well as we can under the circumstances. We always [go] about under more disadvantages than anyone else. We always feed more folks than anybody else and get less thanks. We have our troubles here as well as other places. . . . Send us all that you can in the way of work tools, ploughs and other things. We have no such things—send me a loom if you can without too much trouble—don't risk too much for it[. I]f I had one I could do better.

I have been busy ever since you left but it looks like we can't keep ahead or even. I have spun every day since you left and still all are bare for clothing except Jack and Ninny, but all are well now and we can do better. Charlotte has a bad cough, I fear she will not last long—that is[,] many years. I am sorry you are not so well as you were at the beginning [of the] war. So many of our friends have died. . . . We have had such bad luck with our children that it keeps me always uneasy about them. Bring Charles Watie with you and Saladin for I do not like for him to be there when you are not there. . . . Send all you can and come soon. . . .

Yours,

S. C. [Sarah] Watie

My Dear Sallie,

Camp Watie on Middle Boggy
April 24th, 1864

. . . The wild Indians from Kansas are getting to be very troublesome on the western border. [Confederate] Col. [William] Adair crossed Arkansas River below Gibson but I have not heard from him since; a few men left off from him and returned; they fell in with some Pins[. O]ne of their number[,] young Bent[,] is supposed to be killed. Adair has stirred up the Pins no doubt before now. None but Creeks are at Gibson, part of the Pin Regts have gone to Scullyville.

Two men and two women came out from Fort Smith a few days since they reported the Feds there, about 800. A few days after, two young boys came out, they reported the same story. All agree that the Feds are short of provisions since the failure of the enemy to occupy Texas. Troops at Fort Smith and Gibson, I think I will act on the defensive. We are now ready to move, only waiting for orders. . . . I have always been opposed to killing women and children although our enemies have done it, yet I shall always protest against any acts of that kind. . . . No property is safe anywhere; stealing and open robbery is of every day's occurrence.

I am very tired of this camp; we have bad water.

After Parks' [Lieutenant Colonel Robert C. Parks of Watie's unit] death all sorts of lies were told that I had planned everything. I am sorry that I should be charged in public of an act of that kind but it seems that is my doom. Let me act as I will, my conduct is always considered wrong. No charity was ever shown me yet, I have lived through it and I trust and hope that justice and right will be meted out to me some day. Although these things have been heaped upon me and [it] would be supposed that I became hardened and would be reckless but it still hurts my feelings. I am not a murderer.

Sometimes I examine myself thoroughly and I will always come to the conclusion that I am not such a bad man at last as I am looked upon. God will give me justice. If I am to be punished for the opinions of other people who do not know my heart, I can't help it. If I commit an error I do it without bad intention. My great crime in the world is blunder; I will get into scrapes without intention or any bad motive. I call upon my God to judge me, he knows that I love my friends and above all others, my wife and children; the opinion of the world to contrary notwithstanding. Love to the little ones, and my friends. . . .

Your affectionate husband,

Stand

My Dear Husband,   *July 2nd, 1864*

. . . I wish you would resign and let them all go all they

want to. I can always hear something said that makes me mad. I never go anywhere but I hear something said about that order you sent down here by Lucien Bell for them to go back to camp by the 25 of March. They all pretend that they did not believe you sent it. I want you to call them all up and tell them for I don't look for anything else but for Hooley to be killed about it. You can ask Hooley about it when he gets there. You have no idea how much talk and fuss that has made among them here. The men write and throw out hints and then the women do it. . . .

. . . I do wish one could have peace once more but I fear that is not for me to see in my day. There is a great many things I would put in this letter but I have heard that my letters were opened sometimes so it would not do to trust every little foolishness in here. Keep your eye on Saladin and guide him in the right way and don't let him go astray. I will go see Charlotte before long. Next week I will be at her home for a short time. When you write, send [the letter] by her house. I want to stay at her house in grape time for I never saw so many in my life. I want to make a barrel of wine for you against [when] you come to see me. I can gather bushels of them [with]in a quarter of a mile of the house. Do write. Don't wait so long and tell me if I must go back or not. I would not have come if Saladin had not wanted me to. Love to all.

S. C. [Sarah] Watie

Wood County [Texas]
My dear husband,   *Sept 4, 1864*

. . . When I see you I will tell you a good many things that I do not want to put on paper. I hope you will come as soon as you can. I will be somewhere in my old neighborhood ready to see you all. I hope the war will close soon and we will get time to sit down in peace but it does look to me as if I could not contain myself anywhere. I am all out of sorts. This war, it will ruin a great many good people, they will not only lose all their property but a great many will lose their character which is more value than all their property. You can hardly hear people speak of any of our people but something said that is against their character. I am almost ashamed of my tribe. It has got to be such a common talk that they all follow the army and that for bad purposes. I have long since lost all interest in my people. I sometimes feel that I will never be with them anymore and it does not make any odds whether or not. I could not do them any good. I want to see the end of this war and then I will be willing to give up the ghost. You will think that I got in the dumps before I got done [with] my letter, well I do get that way when I think what they are and what they might be. . . . Love to all. They all send love. Ninny [the Waties' daughter] has written you.

Yours affectionately,

S. C. [Sarah] Watie

Lamar [County, Texas]
My Dear,   *Oct. 9, 1864*

. . . I intend to sow wheat as soon as I can. I do think it is not worth my time to try to do much these times. If you were [only] out just to look around and see how we are to do. I thought I would send you some clothes but I hear that you have done better than to wait on me for them. Well, I don't feel a bit like writing because I cannot write what I want to say. I have been looking for you to send me some brown domestic and some calico. I have not a sheet till I make it, it is all I can do to keep clothes on the children. I wanted to send them to school but the board is 200 a month, apiece and 12 in provision, what must I do? I want to have your advice on it. . . . I want you to come as soon as you can. I am so tired of this world I can't write, it is too cold to sit outdoors and the children talk so much that it pesters me to death. . . . If you can come this fall do so.

You[rs] as ever,

S. C. [Sarah] Watie

Boggy Depot
Dear Sallie: *Jany. 20, 1865*

. . . I find that I can't get along well here without help. I have a house without anything. Send Marye Andrews, my box with what clothes you may judge to be sufficient, [and a] few cooking things if you have any which you can do without, don't forget my big tin cup and whatever you may be able to send me which you do not particularly need at home. Send the Federal Order Books, I find I shall need them. I will not need the tent for a while yet. . . . [E]ither of the wagons will do, it can be taken back. If you can get it, send about 400 lbs of flour. I can trade it for pork 1 lb for three. . . . Try to come and stay with me a few days, stay long as you can as we live in a house without sponging on any of our friends.

Yours as ever,

Stand

[Sarah to Stand]

Lamar Co.
My —   *May 21, 1865*

We all feel disappointed at not hearing from you as one week has passed and no word yet. We hear all kinds of rumors and none satisfactory to us. We heard you was captured and have not heard anything to the contrary. We hear that Gen K. Smith [Confederate general Edmund Kirby Smith] has surrendered and then we hear that he has not. So we don't know what to believe and do let us know all that you know for certain. If it [is] for the worst, let us know it so that we can be prepared for it. If I have to fall among the feds I do not want to be among old Blunts [Union general James G. Blunt's] set[,] for the pins will be mean enough and what is your prospect? I hear that they have set a price on several of their heads and you are included. That is the rumor. I do not want people to believe it for some of them would be after it. I hear that [Confederate general Douglas H.] Cooper will not give you anything. If he does not I believe they all are speculating of it and I hope that the last of them will sink. I do not want you to do anything of that kind. I would live on bread and water rather than to have it said you had speculated of your people. I believe you have always done what you thought best for your people and I want to die with that last belief. If [I] thought you was working for nothing but fill[ing] your pockets it would trouble me a great deal but I know it is not, else it would have been filled before this time. I know that you are capable of making a living anywhere if we are let alone after the war is over.

S. C. W.

Write soon and send it. I do not know what to believe. If you can get any specie get it for we can't get anything for Confederate money here and if we have to get away from here which I fear we will, I don't know what we will do. My notion is that we cannot stay here for the robbers. My black Horse is not found yet. I am all the time afraid the mules will be gone. Write all. We are sold out I believe.

Boggy Depot
May 27th, 1865

Dear Sallie:

No definite news yet, great deal of confusion amongst the troops, more particularly with white portion. I have thought best to send off the majority of them home on furloughs, hints have been thrown out that they would help themselves to the public property. I have sent off enough of them so that I think I can manage the rest. . . . I only write to let you know that I am still in the land of the living—love to all. . . .

Yours as ever—S[2]

ENDNOTES

[1]Dale and Litton, eds., *Cherokee Cavalier*, xxi. Dale and Litton provide informative annotations throughout the collection of Watie letters. McLoughlin, *After the Trail of Tears*, 122.

[2]For all of the letters, see Cherokee Nation Papers, Western History Collections, University of Oklahoma, Norman, Okla., record group 2, Personal Papers of the Bell, Boudinot, Ridge and Watie Families, Stand Watie and Sarah Watie Papers, boxes 115–28, folders 3885–4717, rolls 38–41. Sarah C. Watie to Stand Watie, July 2, 1864, Watie Papers, box 115, folder 3900, roll 38.

~ Hannah Worcester Hicks Diary ~

Hannah Worcester Hicks was the daughter of missionaries Samuel and Ann Orr Worcester. She became a member of the Cherokee Nation in 1852 by marrying Abijah Hicks, the son of an early Eastern Cherokee chief. On July 4, 1862, her husband was murdered near Lee's Creek in what is now Oklahoma on his way back from buying supplies for his store, presumably by Pin Indians whose target was another man but who killed Hicks by mistake. The Pin Indians were supporters of the Union and opposed slavery.

Hicks began her diary on August 17, 1862, about a month after her husband's death. From her entries, it is clear that she was unaccustomed to physical labor. When she went to get a load of wood, she "remembered her husband with renewed sadness" because he would never have allowed her to do such work. Yet women's traditional work remained crucial to survival. She had to fend for herself.

Hicks's diary offers a rare glimpse into a traumatic period. It also provides a counterpoint on the actions of Stand Watie and his men.

Sabbath, August 17th, 1862. Oh! What a year to remember will this year ever be to me and to us all. We thought we had some trouble *last* year, but how happy was that compared with this. Then, we saw our dear friends depart, to go where we have every reason to think they are living in peace and quietness. 'Twas hard to part with them, yet we knew they were better off than we if they could only get safe through. But this year! On the 4th of July my beloved husband was *murdered*, killed, away from home, and I could not see him. So far from it—he had been buried twenty-four hours before I even heard of it. Buried without a coffin, all alone, forty miles from home. Alas, alas, my husband. Still the cry of my heart every day, and every hour, is, oh, my husband.

On the 15th of this month my brother D. D. H. was taken prisoner by the Texas soldiers and today they have sent him off to headquarters at [Fort] Gibson.

God alone knows what next will become of him. But God *is* able to preserve him, and we will pray continually that he may be mercifully dealt with, and permitted very soon to return. I wrote to the Colonel asking his release, having no hope of gaining anything, but feeling that I could not have him taken off without my trying.

Oh God, preserve him. Another cause for trouble is that my darling little Herbert is failing; I fear he cannot be spared to me much longer. *How can* I give him up? But I must subdue my heart to meet this trial also. If he should grow worse fast, how terrible to have no kind physician to tell me what to do to relieve him. He has been worse today. My poor, poor baby. My house has been burnt down, my horses taken but I think nothing of that. How gladly would I have given up *everything*, if they would only have spared my husband and my brother. Truly *now* the Lord of Hosts is our only refuge. Oh that we may have grace to put our trust in Him, and calmly wait for the end. . . . His poor mother and father—I don't know what they will do if he is kept long. They cannot live without him. But we *must* trust in God.

18th. Let me record tonight with heartfelt gratitude, that we have heard some encouraging word from my brother. One of the soldiers, who went with him to [Confederate]

Leonard Worcester, Ann Eliza Robertson, Mary Eleanor Williams, Hannah Hicks (later Hitchcock), children of Samuel A. and Ann Orr Worcester circa 1897. Photograph by Robertson Studio, Muskogee, Indian Territory.

Gen. [Douglas H.] Cooper, came by this evening to let us know that he saw him safely ushered into his (Gen. C's) presence, and that he was very kindly received. From what the soldier says, we may hope that he will be easily dealt with and not detained long. Oh God, grant that it may be so. Mrs. H. is very much relieved, for which I am truly thankful. My baby-boy is still sick, oh that I may be prepared for anything that awaits me concerning him. I *know* that God is merciful.

19th . . . Today the soldiers went to the house where Mrs. Vann's things were, and turned them up at a great rate, took what they could and promised to come back for more. As they have gone with the *Federals*, they (the Ses) [Secesh] will not spare their property. . . .

21st. This evening we have heard that my brother has been released. I hope I am thankful, but I don't know whether to wish him to come home or not. I fear for him here, but my children are so sick. Herbert is worse still and Clara is very sick this evening. What *shall I do* for them? . . . They have sent to take Sally from me. I can do nothing to keep her. She will have to go. A great many of the medicines were taken from my brother's office today, but if they have released him perhaps they will restore his property. . . . I must try to go to Gibson tomorrow. I am so distressed for my little Herbert. Must he be taken from me? . . .

Sabbath, 24th. What a Sabbath has this been. I was very tired and Herbert so very fretful that I could do nothing but fuss with him all day. My other children have been almost wholly neglected. Oh that I could do them some good. I went to Gibson, saw my poor brother, and it makes me so sad, *so sad*, to think of him there, along with such a herd of wretches, guarded like a criminal, with no comfort at all. Oh I am afraid he can't stand it long so, and yet there seems no hope of relief. The report that he was set free was not true, nor likely to be. I went to see Col. Cooper myself, across the Arkansas in Rolly McIntosh's house, and he told me he could not answer for his life, if he should set him free because of the state of feeling in the country. Yet they all say they can find no charge against him, *only* that he has confessed that his *preference* of opinion is for the North. There is no charge on which they can even found a trial, (Oh this *free* and *happy* country). . . . A soldier told me today, that the chief's daughter *declares* that her father was taken off by the federals, by force—against his will entirely. A Lieutenant died, down where the soldiers are camped (near Mr. Murrell's) and was buried in our graveyard yesterday. A brother was since laid by his side. They say that the Southern Army will very soon be compelled to go on Northern soil to get anything to eat. Stand Watie has been elected (by whom?)[.] *Chief* Sam Taylor, second chief, S. Foreman, Treasurer, are now making new *laws*.

31st. It is very hard to believe that it is only two weeks since the Army was established here. The troops have moved to Tahlequah now to guard the *Council* in its deliberation. I hear of only one Law, as yet which is a Conscript law—compelling boys and men from 16–35, into the army. Oh the Cherokee people are *ruined*. I have been to Gibson again—had the pleasure of seeing my dear brother in a comfortable pleasant place. He is on parole—staying at Mr. Kerr's. I hope I am truly thankful, that in the midst of affliction and distress there is still mercy. They visited the office again and carried off *all* the medicines, everything valuable. So now if we are sick we must suffer for want of medicine as well as for attendance. . . . Five Cherokees were condemned for desertion, and shot at Tahlequah, "before the command" Friday evening. . . . A great many soldiers are sick about here and a disease like Small Pox is spreading among the Choctaws across the Arkansas. . . . My little Herbert has been better the week past; I begin to hope again that he may recover.

September 1st.We have had such very quiet times today, it makes one dread what may be to come. It seems like the calm before a storm. Oh how I long to know what next will happen here and what is going on in other parts of the Country. But I try to *believe* that all will yet come out right. I know that it must be right whatever the result. But it seems long to wait in such suspense. I am so cast down, so discouraged, I don't see how we are to live,—and my children—I am not training them up as I should. I do not pray half enough for that grace which alone can help me, and I fail every day and every hour. Oh for *strength* of *mind*, and of body too.

5th. I have had a hard turn of sick-headache which has made me useless for two whole days. Oh what a worthless life I do live. I do not make the effort that I might, to *do something*. *Teasle* (the Dr.'s horse) came home the other morning, was allowed to stay and be petted two days & nights & then, today, they sent and took him off *again*. . . . They decided that the horse *was* confiscated—anyhow, "they wanted him to haul cannon and couldn't give him up." Poor Teasle.

7th. This is the ninth Sabbath that I have been a *widow*. Two sad, weary months. How many times in past days have I wondered what my future would be—wished that I could have some idea. But oh I did not think it would be as it is. Left a widow, at twenty-eight, with five children growing up around me, and oh, most dreadful of all, my dear husband *murdered*. Oh the bitter, bitter repentance for my unkindness to him. I might have done better, have grieved him less. But the only comfort is, he is happy now, he sorrows not *now* for anything I have done, nothing *can* dim the brightness of his crown of rejoicing, in the presence of that glorious Redeemer whom he loved here and now loves in perfection. Oh may I be forgiven and enabled so to live and so to train our precious children that we shall at last join him there. He loved his children so, never a father better loved his children, I love to think of it, but oh how we miss him. God be merciful to us, and help us.

This weary, weary time of war. Will the suspense *never* end? I know not what is to become of us. Famine and Pestilence seem to await us. We can only stand and tremble, and dread what next may befall us.

On the night of the 31st of July, rather, the morning of the 1st of August, our house was burnt down, that was the first great trial that my husband was not here to share with me. But truly I hardly felt it a trial, so very little did it seem compared with what I suffered in *losing him* in such a terrible way. Oh for grace to submit in a right spirit to every trial. I believe my heart is almost dead within me.

10th . . . Today I went to the printing office. I did not know before how completely it had been cleared out. The Press types, paper & all carried off. By Watie's men, with the help of the Texans. We hear today that the "Pins" are committing outrages on Hungry Mountain and in Flint, robbing, destroying property & killing. It is so dreadful that they will do so. Last week, some of Watie's men went and robbed Ross' place up at the mill; completely ruined them. Alas, alas, for this miserable people, destroying each other as fast as they can. . . .The troops have mostly left Tahlequah, for Maysville, and Grand Saline. We have now only to wait as calmly as we can, and see what will happen next. I do hope the suspense will not last much longer.

14th. Sabbath once more. I have worried through the day with my children, trying to keep them from evil and to teach them some good. But oh how poorly do I succeed. It seems almost impossible to make any impressions on their minds. Only, for my oldest daughter I must have some hope. She seems to be conscientious, anxious to do right, and usually gentle and obedient. Oh that she may be indeed a lamb of the Savior's flock. . . .William Spears was killed some weeks ago. His wife has been searching, until yesterday she succeeded in finding part of the bones and the remnants of his clothing. It is said that they told him to pray, and that he did so, and was kneeling in prayer the second time when he was shot. Perhaps in that last hour he found mercy for his soul. . . .

Friday 19th. To Gibson yesterday and back today. It seems that I can go for company better than anyone else and I am far from unwilling, more especially as I think it is a great help to Herbert to take the rides. He has improved very much. We found br. D. D. well and certainly in very good spirits considering the circumstances. . . .

20th. A company of soldiers with Johnson Foreman for guide (I suppose) went down to Alex Ballard's and took his wheat, yesterday. Leaving none for his family to live on except one barrel of "seed-wheat." . . . I went today to help get a load of wood, which makes me remember my husband with renewed sadness as . . . I know that he would never consent while he lived that I should do such work. Oh the sad, sad changes that this year's course has brought to pass.

24th. Hauling wheat and bolting flour, this week. I begin to find out what it is possible for me to do. Mrs. W.

Chamberlin was here today. She had heard that we were going away and hoped to send some word to her relatives. So she had a long hard ride for nothing. On horseback carrying a baby four weeks old. She said that at home and on the way she heard that a Battle was in progress, and "the Federals were whipping the Southerners all to pieces," but when she got to this neighborhood, she heard that the *Southerners* were whipping . . .

Sabbath, 28th. Oh how my heart has *longed* for my husband today. It is terrible, this bitter longing. I have been sick for several days and today, when Sabbath came felt utterly unable to attend to my children. Poor children, *his* children that he loved so much and now he is not here to attend to them when I am sick. I don't know what I should do if it were not for the love and sympathy of his sister Sarah. I feel that *I have* her love, and look to her for sympathy and never fail to receive it. She is far kinder to me than I deserve. Oh my precious husband, are you allowed to know how it is with us, to see how all these trials shall end in good at last? May the Lord grant that he may still watch around us, and be to us a "ministering spirit." Mr. Daniel Ross' little boy died two nights since at Gibson, & was buried here, yesterday. Sometimes I think it would be better that mine should be taken now. I do *so fear* that some of them may fail of being saved at last. Oh God will Thou have respect unto Thy covenant, deal not with them according to my unfaithfulness, but according to Thine infinite mercy through thy dear Son our Savior. . . .

Mon. October 6th . . . I have begun today to wean Herbert hoping it may do him good, as he has been much worse again for several days.

Oct. 22nd. I have been sick, so I have written nothing

for a long time. . . . Oh may a merciful God direct all aright. I know that he will, but oh for *trust* in Him. I hope we will soon know what our fate is to be. May God preserve us all.

27th. No relief yet, but tonight we hear by a "Pin woman" who has come in, that the Federals are at Beattie's Prairie, preparing to come. She says she was run away from here at the time they came shooting the "Pins," & has been out ever since. She is just now trying to get home, as she says they are getting cattle together, and when they are ready they will come quick. Repeating several times, "There are *so many* and they will come *quick*." . . . Teasle has come home once more. I hope they will let him alone this time, but the poor fellow has been branded for the Confederate service. I do hope the next I have to write here will be something decidedly *good*. Oh my husband, why could you not have been spared to see this country settled in peace. It is supposed that Mr. Bishop was killed. Truly the ways of God *are past finding out*. We *cannot* see *why* two such *good* men as my husband and Mr. B. should have been allowed to be murdered and have their poor wives and little ones left helpless. For myself, I do feel that it is a judgment for my many repining thoughts. Oh may I lay it to heart and never cease to *repent* in dust and ashes, never cease to feel *humbled* that perhaps I may not have to suffer further chastisement. Oh if I did not *know* that *he* is perfectly happy, that no shadow of trouble can reach him now there would be no comfort for me. Alas this dreary, dreary winter that I am to struggle through *alone*. Oh! God be merciful.

November 7th. After all our expectations we are still in doubt and fear and suspense. Though the Federal scouts have been about here, & though an Army has been within 18 miles, they have all gone back to Bentonville [Arkansas] and we are left again. We are having bitter experience of that "hope deferred that maketh the heart sick." Sick indeed our hearts are. How dreadfully we felt yesterday as we watched Col. Watie go by with a body of men & we didn't know what they might be intending to do. . . . "The good hand of our God" was with us, and we were once more preserved in the midst of danger. Let me still trust in Him. . . .

8th. Today we hear that Watie's men declared their intention to come back and *rob* every woman whose husband has gone to the Federals, and every woman who has Northern principles, which would include us of course. Our only hope is in the Great Jehovah.

9th, Sabbath. Oh how little like the Sabbath it is, when instead of going quietly to the house of God, the country is full of bodies of soldiers passing along. Yet today we almost forgot the day in *rejoicing* that at last *friends* have come again. [Union] Col. [William A.] Phillips' Brigade, mostly Cherokees, have come. . . . If they now succeed in holding the Country, as no doubt they will we may hope for more quiet times. Oh if we can only have protection.

11th. Col. Phillips got some information which caused him to change his route and go from here to Webber's Falls. So they have not yet visited Gibson. We had an exciting time when they passed here, 2,500 of them, all mounted. It was indeed a *glorious* sight to us who had been so long looking in vain for friends to come. . . . My brother has been most faithfully taking care of Capt. Miner and his reward was, partly, in being preserved. Oh what cause we have for gratitude and praise. So many deliverances, so many mercies.

16th, Sabbath again . . . As we heard the other day of Southern men in Federal disguise coming down Grand River, the Dr.'s mother went in haste after him, and brought him home, so now we feel that he is again in extreme peril. I can only write once more, may God in mercy preserve him. How different—*how different* our feelings tonight from what they were a week ago. Our friends come and make us glad, then leave us again to misery & despair. *Why is it so?* . . . They travelled very fast, are without a provision train, and are killing cattle[,] hogs & sheep at a great rate. I expect many of my cattle will go. But oh I will be so thankful, if only they will not molest my brother again, or rob our houses. How shall we escape, "Sufficient is *Thine* arm alone, and our defense is sure."

I did not write that I received (by Major Martin) a letter from sister Ann Eliza. It was sweet indeed to see her handwriting once more, and to read such warm expressions of love & sympathy. She knew my husband for *what he was*; a humble, trusting disciple of Jesus, and it was sweet to read what she said of him. She had just heard of his death. We heard also that *Mr. Bishop* was not killed, but after being abused a great deal & kept prisoner awhile, was released and has gone with his family. I am thankful to know that the "Pin Cherokees" are not guilty of *that one* sin. For oh how much they *have* done. They have utterly ruined many, many families. I don't know what can become of them this winter. It is pitiful, pitiful to see the desolation & distress in this nation. Poor ruined Cherokees.

17th. Today we have had experience in being robbed, as I expected. As soon as it was light they came and began. They took many valuable things, and overhauled every closet, trunk, box, & drawer they could find. The leaders were Cherokees, those who have often eaten in my house, some of them. When sister N. went and reported to the Gen. (Gen. Marmaduke) he sent a guard at once, ordered them all away, & made them return what they saw. But the most valuable things are gone "for good." Still I can rejoice[,] oh,

I am so thankful, that *life* is still spared, that they did not find my brother. The hand of the Lord was in it, and officers were sent there *by Him* in time to make the robbers keep away, so they did not search the house as they did here. Still one of *Watie's* men, a white man, lagged behind, and swore that he would "knock them all to pieces," unless they gave three blankets, to himself and two others. Poor Teasle had to go again. The *Confederate brand* sealed his fate. I begin to think that we have no true friends at all. The Federals come and give us good *words*, then pass right on & leave us to a *far worse* fate than would have been ours if they had not come. When shall we be delivered? Yet tonight I feel that I can still say, "Praise the Lord oh my soul," for in the midst of trouble & distress there is still such great mercy. . . .

December 9th. We heard yesterday that five of "Livingstone's [Confederate major Thomas R. Livingston's] men," with two or three of Watie's, were at Gibson, professing to have orders from Watie & Cooper to rob the wives of all union men and to arrest for the Confederate service all boys and men between the ages of 14 and 50. The order for robbing union women of *all* their property, they said they were going to execute yesterday at Gibson. . . .

10th. Poor old Teasle has come home *again*. He was taken by one of the Federals on the battle-field at Cane Hill, and when his master went with them he got them to let him go, as he was very poor and lame. He has gone through many adventures. . . .

11th . . . We hear also that Watie's men have begun to kill women and children, that four women & some children have been killed near Ft. Smith. Oh I hope it is not true. Mr. Palmer does not appear again yet. Perhaps he has gone to the Federal camp. . . .

20th. Yesterday (19th) we heard—first, that Watie's men were coming, to rob, they were starving & were coming to rob *something to eat*. Next, that they were at Mrs. Patrick's robbing her, and would be here that evening. That, they had shot at Tom Ore six times & he had been seen running from them with all his might. Then when we were just beginning to hope that they might not come here at last, we heard that they had taken Mr. Kerr & his son, and that a company had passed Mrs. Nave's. So we expected them every minute & busied ourselves in trying to save a *few* things, that we would suffer most to lose. But they did not come. We spent a restless night, most of us not undressing at all. Mother and Mrs. H. will not get over it for a month. . . .

25th. Foes and Friends! Yesterday Col. Phillips passed again, with a large force. I spent last night in the camp, six miles from here on the road to Gibson, having gone there to see Col. Phillips, to beg him [to] find some way of deliverance from the danger that surround us when the Federals are not here. They have gone on today, earnestly hoping to come up with the enemy and to capture some wagons. The Col. said he could not tell whether he will even come back this way or not. But he seemed to wish to help us, if he could. Perhaps we will have to leave here in a few days. Oh how hard it will be to leave, and yet how hard to stay here in this way. May we be directed aright. . . .

January 4th, 1863. We have entered upon a New Year, and are so far left in peace. I hope we are thankful.

Last Sabbath morning just after sunrise, Col. Phillips' Army came in sight again. It proved that his negotiations with the Creeks had been very suddenly cut short, by peremptory orders from Gen. Blount [James G. Blunt], to return forthwith to head-quarters. So they hastened by—

only brother Dwight, Col. P., & a few others, stopping for breakfast. They supposed that there was another Battle pending. . . . We have waited a week since they left here, and have heard *not a word* what has become of them. It seems a *month* rather than a week. Sarah Stephens, with her children, went with them. Her husband came with a wagon for her, and she found she must go. It was hard to part with her, but I suppose it is best so. Nancy stays for the present. The black women both started and left us without any help, but "Aunt Edie" lost her horse & had to come back—which I consider as specially ordered by a kind Providence. We have heard nothing the past week except by Capt. Gunter's black man, Dred, who made his escape from the Southerners & was about here a day or two. . . .

   21st. No cheering news from friends yet. But the other day we heard that *Watie's* men were all on this side of the Arkansas, that Jim Butler with a company stayed overnight at Scrimscher's place, a week ago now. That he said, property had been respected, hitherto, but now they should respect *nobody's* property. . . . But of our particular friends, and whether there is any hope of their coming—we know nothing. The women said that part of the Cherokees had gone north to meet a large company of soldiers, of another tribe of Indians. We have had rain, snow, and cold weather a plenty for a week past, which may have helped to prevent both friends and enemies from travelling. Today it is clearing off pleasant and warm again, so we would not be surprised to have a visit from some of Watie's men any time. But I *try* to hope for the best. Have just been making me a pair of cloth shoes to help me along a little. In the cold stormy weather had to chop and carry wood, all that I could endure (which wasn't much.) We had no wood and nobody to get it but Percy, but on *Sabbath*, the black men brought me a little. Oh sad *times*, when [it] comes to hauling wood for me, on the Sabbath.

29th. My birthday—I am 29 today, but it seems as though I had lived many years in the last one. We have come to such *times* as I *never* thought to see—and no prospect for a living ahead. But I must try to *trust* myself and my children in the hands of Him who has preserved us hitherto. We know not what next will become of us. I fear that I shall never even see my husband's grave. Oh I do so long to go there, to see where he is laid, at least, but it is impossible. It is a comfort to know that *he* is not distressed now by anything that we may have to suffer.

Last Saturday, (21st) Lt. Col. [Lewis] Downing, with two or three hundred men—came down to bring flour for the needy. An eager crowd of hungry women and children soon gathered to receive it. They stayed only over one night, and sister N. E. B. went with them. So we separated, perhaps *never* to meet again in this world. Oh this *cruel* War. . . . There has been a terrible reverse to the Federal Army in Virginia, it makes one heart-sick to read of it, (in the papers which the Dr. sent down). We don't know what situation sister Mary may be in now, but it is impossible to communicate with her, Brother Dwight wrote that Blunt's troops plundered almost every house in Van Buren. She may have lost her all.

If the Confederate soldiers have the opportunity, they will most surely revenge themselves on us, for all these things. We hear that Jim Butler is still going about robbing, but they have not yet visited us. They, i.e., *some* of Watie's men, are expected in, to move away Southern (rather, Se-cesh) families from Tahlequah. If they come they will give us a call, no doubt. . . .

Feb. 20th. Since I wrote here—Col. Phillips has twice again sent flour for the suffering people. He is doing much for the Cherokees. A council has been [and] is now going on to decide some questions, on the relations of the people with the Government, I believe. . . . Have you heard that Ann Spears Ross, with one of her children—was killed, by Kechis [Kechi, or Kichai, Indians], some weeks ago. Shot through with an arrow. The same party went to Mr. Archer's and were about to carry off Mary A. One was pulling and another pushing but her mother begged so hard they let her go. It is said they killed Ann because she would not go when they tried to take her prisoner.[1]

ENDNOTES

[1] Manuscript of *Diary of Hannah Hicks*, Hicks Collection, Thomas Gilcrease Institute of American History and Art, Museum Archives, Tulsa, Okla. Included in the manuscript are notes to sister Ann Eliza that amplify Hannah Hicks's entries. I have omitted them here. See the full manuscript for details. See Grant Foreman Collection, box 5, 83–229, Oklahoma Historical Society, Oklahoma City, Okla., for details regarding Hannah Hicks's biography.

~ Mary Cobb Agnew Interview ~

L. W. Wilson interviewed Mary Cobb Agnew in Musk-ogee, Oklahoma, on May 25, 1937. Mrs. Agnew's comments about the Trail of Tears are quoted in Part 4. Here, she talks about her life before, during, and after the Civil War.

Agnew makes reference to "Bread payments" and the Cherokee Strip. Based on the 1880 Cherokee census (called "the Lipe Roll"), a per capita payment was made to citizens of the Cherokee Nation. It was called "bread money" because it was used for a basic family need. Other payments were also made. For example, "grass money" referred to per capita money derived from leasing the Cherokee Outlet, and the 1893 Cherokee census was the basis for a per capita payment derived from funds received from the sale of the Cherokee Strip. The Cherokee Outlet—a 60-mile-wide, 225-mile-long strip of land south of the Oklahoma-Kansas border—was granted to the Cherokee Nation by the Treaty of New Echota. The Cherokee Strip was a 2-mile strip along the northern border of a portion of the Cherokee Outlet.[1]

> In my girlhood days, we lived in log cabins with large fireplaces. Some of the cabins had puncheon floors, some dirt floors. We cooked in fireplaces and on open fires. We had no matches to start our fires. We had to start the fire with a flint and steel, or had to keep the fire continually burning.
>
> Our farming consisted of raising corn in small clearings in the woods. We raised good gardens of beans, pumpkins and common garden vegetables. Of course, we didn't

have all the new farm tools they have now. Almost all the work done on the farm was done with a deer tongue and a hoe.

We raised some cotton, just enough for our clothing. We had no [cotton] gins. We used to lay the cotton around the fireplace and get it good and dry and pick the seeds out by hand.

The corn for our bread was crushed in a mortar with a pestle. Also our hominy grits or "Canahomie" was made with the pestle and mortar. We had hominy too. We called it skinned corn. Later we got a hand grinder to make our meal at Fort Gibson.

We made our soap. We had an ash hopper and saved all the ashes. The water made a lye after going through the ashes and with this water and old fat meat scraps of all kinds, we made soap.

We made our own cloth with the spinning wheel, reel and loom. Many, many days I have carded and spun thread. I have spun wool, but most of my spinning was cotton. After we made the thread, we would dye it different colors from dyes made of oak bark, indigo, walnut hulls, etc. We always put copperas in our dye solutions to keep the cloth from fading.

Before the war, we were all getting along well, had plenty of everything to eat and wear. Had horses, mules, oxen, cows, hogs, sheep, chickens and everything and there were still wild game, berries, fruits, and nuts, so we really wanted for nothing.

Schools and churches improved. They taught and preached in English and sometimes in Cherokee. The best schools and the printing press of the Cherokee Nation were at Park Hill. John Ross was our principal chief and was determined to affiliate the Cherokees with the Northern army but my family and I could not agree with him here. We fell in with Albert Pike for the South.

Army troops occupied Fort Gibson until just before the Civil War. They were there until about 1857 or 1858.

I was married to Mr. Agnew before the Civil War. He was a well-educated man and was a graduate from the Cherokee School at Park Hill. He served on the Cherokee Council at Tahlequah and was also a District Judge and held different positions in the affairs of the Cherokees. . . .

After the Civil War, the Cherokee Nation was in a deplorable condition. Houses and cabins had been burned. Fields had grown up into thickets of underbrush. The hogs and cattle which the soldiers had not killed had gone wild in the woods and canebrakes.

People had to start life anew, build cabins, clear ground, plant crops, and build rail fences, in fact, do as they had done before the Civil War.

The soldiers were still at Fort Gibson and stayed there until 1889 when they left and never returned. These soldiers were to keep down uprisings among the people which usually flared up at elections such as the Green Peach War over there in the Creek Nation. They also would be sent out at times to try and confine wild Indians to reservations on land which the Government had taken from us Cherokees and others of the Five Civilized Tribes.

We Indians got our homes rebuilt and were doing well when the Government took another shot at us and set up the Dawes Commission in 1894. We owned all the land as a whole and could farm all we wanted to as long as we didn't infringe on our friends' land. We had a good government of our own just like we had had back in Georgia, but the white men wanted our land just as they had wanted it in Georgia. Again there was much discussion. The white people called us barbarians, half-wits, said we couldn't run our business, etc. So they sent men out to enroll all the citizens of the Cherokee Tribe. I and all my kin enrolled without any trouble, for I saw and so did Mr. Agnew, that if we were to get anything, it would be necessary to enroll. Many people tried to get enrolled and get a little land that way who were not entitled to it.

I am an old woman who has lived a long time and if there ever was a race of people that was downtrodden it is the Cherokees. The white people came in with the negroes and we had to give them part of our land. I never will know why we owed them anything. We didn't bring negroes here, God knows. . . .

I received my allotments under the Dawes Commission and I am enrolled. Restrictions were raised on my allotments and I sold them to get money to keep me in my old days.

I received Cherokee Strip payments, also Old Settlers payments. I never received any Bread payments. With all the money due the Cherokees for their lands in Georgia and in the Territory, the Government practically has given us nothing.[2]

ENDNOTES

[1] See www.cherokee-strip-museum.org. For more on bread money, see http://files.usgwarchives.net/ok/nations/cherokee/census/cherwest.txt.

[2] Mary Cobb Agnew, Interview 5978, vol. 1, May 25, 1937, Muskogee, Okla., 289–303, Indian Pioneer Papers, Western History Collections, University of Oklahoma, Norman, Okla.

～ Lizzie Wynn Interview ～

As part of the WPA's Indian-Pioneer History Project, field worker Grace Kelley interviewed Lizzie Wynn in Dustin, Oklahoma, on November 29, 1937.

. . . Daddy had two [slave] families, besides three others who worked in the house. I don't know just how many but there were quite a few.

The war was caused by some wanting to free the negroes so daddy said he guessed that we would be safe if he just turned them loose. But he took a notion to do like the rest were doing. He had freed all but the old woman and for some reason she was going with us. We got close to Netuma when he took very sick and had to be put to bed. We had stopped at an Indian house. The Northern soldiers came to the door and I was standing at the head of his bed. They told me to move but I thought that if I stayed there they surely wouldn't shoot him. They shot him and blood and brains spattered all over me. I wasn't scared but I was sad. After they had killed him, they left and the old negro woman said that they would go after some wagons and come back after us. We covered daddy up and shut the doors and left him lying in the bed. There was a hill at the back of the house so we ran to it so that we could get away without being seen. We traveled two days and nights without food or water and were exhausted when we came to a little house where an old woman lived. She had some hominy or rather corn cooked in water. We stayed there two months and were absolutely naked. One morning early, I went down close to the road and was sitting behind a big tree, sunning myself to get warm. I wasn't in the habit of going down there and don't know why I'd want to unless they led me to. I saw a negro coming down the road on a white horse and he looked like our old woman's boy that we called "Siminole." When he got closer I knew that it was and hollered at him. He wanted to know why we were there and all about us. I was crying and trying to answer all his questions at the same time. He said he would go and see mother. He told her that if he could he would get a wagon and get us away that night. The women stayed awake that night but we children went to sleep. He came back and they woke us. He had blankets and quilts to wrap us up in and we started on another and the last part of our journey.[1]

ENDNOTES

[1] Lizzie Wynn, Interview 12286, vol. 101, Nov. 29, 1937, Dustin, Okla., 57–59, Indian Pioneer Papers, Western History Collections, University of Oklahoma, Norman, Okla.

～ Emma J. Sixkiller Interview ～

Field worker Nannie Lee Burns interviewed Emma J. Sixkiller on June 29, 1937.

The first time that our home was robbed, we had been told that the bushwhackers were coming and some of the neighbors, thinking that as there was no man at our home, they would not molest us, had packed and boxed much of their goods and had brought the boxes to our home. My brother, Willie, and Tom Reese were in the timber near, trying to get some wood for the home when we heard a shot and mother said[, "T]hat is the bushwhackers now["]; so she put a new shawl over her head and started to the timber to warn the boys and had reached the door when she saw the men coming, so was afraid to go on and stopped at the door and was standing there when they rode up. They asked her if there were any menfolks there and she said, "No, I am a widow." They started in the house and when they began to pile things up she tried to persuade them not to take the things from her children but they told her that they needed them too; and gathered up the quilts and blankets and were preparing to rip open the feather beds when one of the men opened the door where the boxes were stored and when he saw them he told the others, "Here is all we can take already packed so we will leave the beds till next time." I happened to put on a new pair of shoes that morning so I did have good shoes that winter. It was cold weather and there was a light snow on the ground at this time. One of the men jerked the shawl from mother's head and they took it with them. Not being able to take as much as they found, they poured our sugar in the snow and with their feet rubbed it into the snow and dirt to keep it from being used and all the covers we had left were some of the quilts that they dropped and which we gathered up after they left. I remember watching them load up the things as I stood on the porch and looked over the banisters at them while they were loading up our things.

We were robbed three times, once they took our horse from the plough. This made mother sick for it meant so much to us. On one trip they killed four men in Tahlequah—Nick Hair, Waitie Robinson, (here she paused and studied and finally said, "I can't remember the names of the others now.") The daughter of Robinson came and lived with us and she felt so badly over it and would cry when they talked of it. The third time that they came there were several women in the gang and mother said to them, "I know who you are.["] (They were painted and dressed so as to try to disguise themselves.) ["]I have never done you any harm and I have these children here to feed," etc. But they told her that they needed the things too[, and] so just went about helping themselves to anything that they found that they wanted and destroying what they thought we could use that they did not want.[1]

ENDNOTES

[1] Emma J. Sixkiller, Interview 6468, vol. 84, June 29, 1937, Fairland, Okla., 49–51, Indian Pioneer Papers, Western History Collections, University of Oklahoma, Norman, Okla.

~ Mary Alice Arendell Interview ~

Field worker Dovey P. Heady interviewed Mary Alice Arendell in 1937.

My father was a Southern soldier during the Civil War. I do not remember to what company or regiment he belonged. He could not get a furlough to come home so he deserted the war and came home. I remember we were here living at Parker, Texas, in a one-room log house, the door had fallen down and had been walked over for several months. My mother raised the door and dug a hole just long and wide enough for him to lie in on his back, then the door was lowered and walked over as usual. There she kept him hidden for several weeks. He would be let out each day for a few minutes to exercise. We children were taught that he was just a good man that needed protection from bad men, not until after the war did we know that he was our father. When he came he was badly in need of clothes. My mother carded and spun the cotton and made him some clothes before he returned to the war.[1]

ENDNOTES

[1] Mary Alice Arendell, Interview 5508, vol. 3, 1937, no location noted, 30–31, Indian Pioneer Papers, Western History Collections, University of Oklahoma, Norman, Okla.

~ Mary Scott Gordon Interview ~

Field worker Jennie Selfridge interviewed Mary Scott Gordon in Ardmore, Oklahoma, on March 31, 1937.

When the Civil War started all full-blood Cherokees went north and joined the Union. The white men and half-breeds crossed the South Canadian [River] and came South. The full-bloods would sometimes slip across the river and kill the southern Indians.

We lived just a little ways from Fort Gibson on Bayou-Maynard Creek. One day a man came down the road from toward Tahlequah on horseback. He had been riding his horse so hard that it fell when he reached our gate. This man, I do not remember his name, told Papa he had better leave at once because the full-blood Cherokees were coming in that direction. Papa wanted to take time to get something to eat but the men insisted that they hurry on across the Canadian. Papa was a big cattle owner, and had sold many cattle that year. While he was getting his horse saddled, and a new horse for his friend, I went to the room where he had three trunks full of money stored under the bed. I pulled out the smaller trunk which was full of money sacks. Each sack contained five hundred dollars in twenty-dollar gold pieces. I put it in his wallet and the rest in his overcoat pockets.

After papa went south, it left my stepmother, her children and me at home with the negroes. The negroes all went to Fort Gibson. We only had six or eight of them. After they left, my step-mother did not want to stay there, so we moved over to her mother's home. Her mother was Mrs. Ada Adair. She lived in a sixteen-room house, which had been built by an old woman who was a whiskey-peddler. She died and my grandmother bought the house. Grandmother's negroes carried over about one hundred fifty or two hundred head of hogs that papa had butchered. He killed about that many hogs every fall and sold the meat and lard to the fort. He smoked the hams and shoulders in Hickory smoke and sewed them up in sacks. The negroes were always happy at hog-killing time. They would usually butcher fifty at a time.

The Negroes carried the meat over to grandmother's house and hid it in the basement, which was concealed under the dining-room floor. We put our bed-clothes through a trapdoor in the bedroom. This door had a ring on it and was always kept concealed under a rug. Underneath was a hole that did not connect with the basement. I wanted to bring our money over and hide it here, but my step-mother was afraid we would get caught with it.

We could get our bedding out after ten-o'clock every night because the Cherokees and Creeks never made a raid after that time.

In February father decided to come back across the river; [Arch] Love was with him. They crossed the river and got the horses. Love took three of them and went to his home, and papa brought four and came to us.

Grandmother had a turnip-patch at the side of the house. She also had a yoke of oxen, one of which wore a bell. That night Grandmother's negro boy, eighteen or nineteen years old, heard one of the oxen jump into the turnip-patch. He went out to see about it. It was a bright night. The moon was shining almost as bright as day. When the Negro crossed the turnip-patch, someone began shooting at him from the barn. Of course, we knew it was the Indians after papa.

I helped papa get into his clothes. He wanted to cross the yard and make a run for his horse, but I knew if he did he would be killed. There was a large walnut tree standing at the back of the house, and this was the only safe place I could think of for him to hide. He went out the back door and made for the walnut tree. I gathered up his saddle, saddle-bags and clothes. Grandmother always raised some cotton every year and kept the seed in one room of the house. I took his things and went to this room and began burying them in the cotton-seed. The Indians saw the light and began shooting into this room. I kept working, and had just got the things covered when they broke into the house. They came into the room, sixteen of them, and forced me to take the lamp and go with them to search the house.

I told them papa was not at home. I led the way upstairs and all over the house. They then went into the smoke-house. [Text missing.] They got on their horses and rode off. I stood and watched them to make sure all sixteen of them were leaving.

After they left papa came back into the house. I told him to leave, and I would send his things together with some dry clothes to Little Shelf on the other side of the creek. "Little Shelf" was a rock ledge on the south bank of the creek not far from where we lived. Papa waded the creek and went to Arch Love's house. His clothes were frozen to him before he got there. He and Arch Love got the three horses and went across the river that night. The next morning we counted the holes and found that there were sixteen shots fired into the room where I was that night.

My sister told Arch not to come back home anymore because he would get killed if he did. He told her he would have to come back and cut her some wood. Papa told her to get a Negro by the name of Cicero to cut the wood. A short while after that Arch came back and brought a white man by the name of Jim Goree with him. The Indians attacked the house and killed both of them. Arch got out in the yard before he fell and Jim Goree got a little ways from the house. They cut his head off. After they were gone my sister had a hard time keeping the wolves away from their bodies. They came out of the hills in a large pack, ran the dogs away from the house and made for the bodies. My sister got the gun and killed some of them. As fast as she would shoot one, the others would devour the body. She finally got a pen built around the men and the old Negro, Cicero Riley, got there. We went down the next morning and helped dig their graves. There was no way of getting coffins so we wrapped quilts around them, put some sheets over them and lowered them into the graves.

After the white men came to Fort Gibson, they put guards around our house and wouldn't let anyone in without our permission. There were ten thousand soldiers camped around the fort. We put up all of the milk cows we could find and milked them. I sold the milk to the soldiers for one dollar a pint. We would fill up a canteen for two dollars. My step-mother had always had Negroes do the work for her, and didn't do anything except knit and piece quilts. This left most of the work for me to do. Grandmother was only seventy-five years old but she thought she was old. She had three negro women, one negro girl, one boy and one old Negro man. They all stayed with her during the war.

We stayed at grandmother's almost all of the first three years of the war, then went south under a flag of truce. We went to Warm Springs [Arkansas] and met the southern men. That night we all camped together, both Union and Confederate.[1]

ENDNOTES

[1] Mary Scott Gordon (Mrs. Raymond Gordon), Interview 1162, vol. 35, Ardmore, Okla., March 31, 1937, 30–34, Indian Pioneer Papers, Western History Collections, University of Oklahoma, Norman, Okla.

~ Elinor Boudinot Meigs Interview ~

James S. Buchanan, a field worker for the WPA, interviewed Mrs. Elinor Boudinot Meigs at Fort Gibson, Oklahoma, March 2–4, 1937.

I was the fourth child of William Penn Boudinot and
Caroline Fields Boudinot. Born March 8, 1862 in Illinois
District, Cherokee Nation. Father was the son of Elias
Boudinot, a full-blood Cherokee and Harriet Gold Boudinot, a white woman. My mother was the daughter of Thomas Fields and Nancy Downing Fields, both Cherokees. She
was born in Tennessee, reared in the Cherokee Nation and
educated in Dwight Mission.

I remember my mother telling of a peculiar incident
that happened during the raid that the Pin Indians made
upon our home. She said father had a large amount of gold
hid in an old leather satchel hanging on the wall, and during the search they were making of the house, an Indian
reached up and taken hold of the old satchel, and just as
he did so, his attention was attracted by a beautiful bright
colored blanket that hung near[. H]e left the old satchel
and took the blanket and a side saddle that was hanging by
it and walked out of the house, leaving father's money as
though they were not looking for it.

At the time of the Civil War there yet existed a fac-
tional feeling that originated in Georgia between the Ross
and Ridge[-]Boudinot factions prior to the moving of the
Cherokees from east of the Mississippi River to the Indian
Territory, and caused the assassination of my grandfather,
Elias Boudinot, Major Ridge and his son John Ridge on
June 20, 1839, and as my father was a southern sympathizer
the Civil War furnished an opportunity for renewal of per-
secutions by the opposing faction. For that reason and the

safety of the family was the cause of my father leaving the Cherokee Nation during the Civil War.

When he considered it safe for the family he started on the return trip to the old home in the Cherokee Nation. All of our possessions in a wagon drawn by an ox team. We crossed the Canadian River at the old Tom Starr place where my brother Frank Boudinot was born while there in camp August 20, 1866.

I never attended public schools as my early education was attained at home[,] being taught by my mother until I was fourteen years of age. I was then placed in the Cherokee Female Seminary at Tahlequah, graduating in 1881. I taught in the grade schools and Cherokee schools for about ten years.

I was married to John H. Meigs September 2, 1890 and seven children were born.[1]

ENDNOTES

[1] Elinor Boudinot Meigs, Interview 0000, vol. 62, Fort Gibson, Okla., March 2–4, 1937, 75–77, Indian Pioneer Papers, Western History Collections, University of Oklahoma, Norman, Okla.

~ Elizabeth Watts Interview ~

Field worker L. D. Wilson interviewed Elizabeth Watts in Muskogee, Oklahoma, on April 27, 1937. Excerpts from Watts's interview about the Trail of Tears are included in Part 4.

In this excerpt, she talks about the Civil War.

After much controversy, the war got under way. My father joined the Northern Army and was stationed at Fort Gibson, Indian Territory, under General and Captain Robert Blunt. He held the rank of Sergeant. I cannot locate his discharge papers and I have forgotten the name of the company as well as the numbers.

Albert Pike came back and built Ft. Davis [Oklahoma] across the Arkansas River about four miles west of Fort Gibson for the South. [General Douglas H.] Cooper, Stand Watie and General [William] Steele were in charge.

General Pike also had a fight in Arkansas and they called it Pea Ridge. His Indian troops fought Indian style with bow and arrow and the North whipped them there.

The North burned down Fort Davis and ran them out of there.

They had little skirmishes here and there and did all kinds of meanness.

I remember mother and we children went over close to Fort Gibson during the War, and one day four Southern soldiers came and took the food we had. Took out the feather bed and cut it open, let the feathers fly in the wind and used the tick for a saddle blanket. As they went through the yard they took all our green onions. They simply stripped us of everything. Mother took her best dress and sat on it to hide it. They made her get up and they tore the dress into strings. The reason we moved to Fort Gibson was because father was at the fort and we could draw on our rations like the soldiers.

The big battle was on Elk Creek, they called it the Battle of Honey Springs. That was near the present town of Rentiesville, Oklahoma.

They whipped the South at Honey Springs in July 1863. It was a hard battle. Many men were lost on both sides. They brought lots of prisoners back to Fort Gibson with them. Some of the prisoners were Negroes, some whites, and some Indians. Prisoners consisted of men, women and children of all three of these races.

Most of the Southern men's wives and families took refuge in Texas, and the Red River District, while the men fought. Our family never did leave the Territory and hardly got out of our District. Just from where I live here, over to Fort Gibson, (a distance of 18 miles.)

There were no more battles in the Territory during the War. There were lots of raiding parties. They would go over the country, burning all the houses, cabins, barns and cribs, carrying all the beds and chairs away and killing or driving away the cattle.

The Cherokee Nation was almost wiped out. First, the North would raise havoc and then the South. The war was over in 1865, but it was 1866 before the Indians were let out of the army.[1]

ENDNOTES

[1] Elizabeth Watts, Interview 0000, vol. 95, Muskogee, Okla., Apr. 27, 1937, 536–38, Indian Pioneer Papers, Western History Collections, University of Oklahoma, Norman, Okla.

Part 6
ALLOTMENT AND ASSIMILATION

I
ALLOTMENT

In her book *And Still the Waters Run*, Angie Debo characterizes allotment as an "orgy of plunder and exploitation probably unparalleled in American history."[1] The United States government had assured the Cherokees that if they "removed" from the Southeast and their ancestral lands, they would hold the Western lands in perpetuity without white encroachment. But in the aftermath of the Civil War, the government abrogated its treaties in its desire to acquire more Indian land for white settlements and economic development by railroad and mining companies. Eastern philanthropists joined railroad and mining officials to push for allotment of Indian land and to promote the Dawes Act, which was passed on February 8, 1887. The main provisions of the act were to grant "160 acres to each [male] family head, eighty acres to each single person over eighteen years of age and each orphan under eighteen, and forty acres to each other single person under eighteen." In addition, a "patent in fee would be issued to each allottee," which would be held in trust by the United States government for twenty-five years. Allottees could receive citizenship if they abandoned their tribes. Indian women in tribes covered by the Dawes Act who married white men received allotments.

Although the Dawes Act did not apply to the Cherokees,

Unidentified Cherokee women

the United States government planned the allotment of Cherokee land and the land of all the "Civilized Tribes." The process began with the passage of the Curtis Act in 1898.[2] The legislation codified Indian men as heads of households, which led to profound changes regarding gender identities. Married Indian women eventually were given allotments, but their power was diminished. The policy of designating Indian men as heads of households was a conscious effort to encourage patriarchal family structures and undermine women's power and matrilineal traditions. Under the amendment, married women received the same allotment as single children over eighteen. Therefore, the allotment policies severely destabilized Indian families.[3]

The Report of the Commissioner of Indian Affairs on October 1, 1889, presented the federal government's policy of allotment:

> The Indians must conform to "the white man's way," peaceably if they will, forcibly if they must. They must adjust themselves to their environment, and conform their mode of living substantially to our civilization. This civilization may not be the best possible but it is the best the Indians can get. They cannot escape it, and must either conform to it or be crushed by it. . . . The tribal relations should be broken up, socialism destroyed, and the family and the autonomy of the individual substituted. The allotment of lands in severalty, the establishment of local courts and police, the development of a personal sense of independence, and the universal adoption of the English language are the means to this end.[4]

Powerful interests such as homesteaders, land companies, and railroad companies supported this position, seeing allotment as a means to gain large areas of Indian land by legal means. Much confusion about the Dawes Act existed among the Cherokees. They were not legally required to enroll with the Dawes Commission, and their land was not allotted until after the Curtis Act was passed. However, many believed they had to enroll. Eventually, only those who enrolled or whose descendants could claim a relative on the rolls qualified as members of Indian tribes. The rolls, and not the tribes themselves, came to define who was an Indian.

The allotment policies and the Curtis Act officially abolished tribal governments, disrupted clan and familial relationships and undermined women's traditional association with the land. The enforcement of these policies met with fierce resistance from many Cherokee women and men. Yet a number of females, especially elite Cherokee women, supported allotment and statehood. They thought the Cherokee Nation did not deal effectively with the problems of violence and alcohol.

Because Cherokee women did not assume public roles in the struggle over allotment, it is necessary to look to oral histories to discover their views and actions during that period. They were not passive victims. Many traditional Cherokee women opposed allotment and joined the Keetoowah Society and the Four Mothers Society, both of which struggled against allotting tribal land and supported a return to matriarchal and matrilineal traditions and ceremonies of the Cherokee Nation.

The Cherokees resisted allotment by a variety of means: by stalling and refusing to negotiate with the Dawes Commission, by refusing to enroll in the program, and by revitalizing their traditional ceremonies. Nevertheless, through the Dawes Act, the United States government eventually took almost two-thirds of the Indians' land between 1887 and 1930, even requiring the tribes to pay for surveying and allotment.

The rationale for the policy of allotment was to civilize the Indians; the true motive was greed, and the aim was to dispossess them of their land.[5] The Civil War and allotment of Cherokee land in Indian Territory undermined tribal sovereignty and led to impoverishment and dispossession. Allotment failed to accomplish its stated goal of assimilating Cherokee people into white society. It also destabilized gender and family relationships. The policy aimed to substitute individualism and autonomy for the Cherokees' ethic of harmony and communal land ownership. The abolition of the Cherokees' communal ownership of land and the official termination of tribal government caused profound changes, especially for Cherokee women.

The following selections record the recollections of Cherokee women regarding allotment and their choices to enroll or to oppose the process of allotting their land.

ENDNOTES

¹ Angie Debo, *And Still the Waters Run: The Betrayal of the Five Civilized Tribes* (1940; reprint, Princeton, N.J.: Princeton University Press, 1991), 91, 165, 171.

² D. S. Otis, *The Dawes Act and the Allotment of Indians*, edited by Francis Paul Prucha (Norman: University of Oklahoma Press, 1973), 6–7.

³ Otis, The Dawes Act, 148. For the text of the Dawes Act, see http://www.nebraskastudies.org/0600/stories/0601_0200_01.html. For the Curtis Act, see http://www.accessgenealogy.com/native/laws/at_June_28_1898_curtis_act.htm.

⁴ Report of the Commissioner of Indian Affairs, in Report of the Secretary of the Interior, Oct. 1, 1889, published in 1900, 4; Otis, The Dawes Act, 31.

⁵ D'Arcy McNickle, "Indian and European: Indian-White Relations from Discovery to 1887," in *The Rape of Indian Lands*, edited by Paul Wallace Gates (New York: Arno Press, 1979), 3, 10. See also Wilcomb E. Washburn, *The Assault on Indian Tribalism: The General Allotment Law (Dawes Act) of 1887*, edited by Harold M. Hyman (Philadelphia: J. B. Lippincott, 1975), 9; Francis Paul Prucha, *The Great Father: The United States Government and the American Indians* (Lincoln: University of Nebraska Press, 1984), vols. 1 and 2, 179–81.

～ Josephine Pennington Excerpt ～

L. W. Wilson interviewed Mrs. Josephine Wilson Pennington in Hulbert, Oklahoma, on October 12, 1937. In this excerpt, Wilson uses the third person to paraphrase what Mrs. Pennington said.

In the early nineties the Dawes Commission was formed and by 1896 had started operating.

Arrangements were affected and laws made that the Cherokee Nation was to be owned individually not severally. Headquarters for the Commission in the Cherokee Nation was at Tahlequah. Enrollment parties were organized, to get all qualified Cherokees to enroll so that land could be allotted to them. A great many wanted to enroll, who had hardly ever seen an Indian but they were not allowed to do so in most instances. Some, however, did sneak in and enroll. Many of the Indians did not like the idea and would not enroll but the Government enrolled them anyway, knowing they were entitled to allotments.

The land was appraised at from $.50 to $6.00 per acre. This appraisal accounts for some receiving more acreage than others since the allotment to Cherokees was by value rather than acreage.

Townsites were laid out, section lines run and allotments made. Mrs. Pennington's mother was allotted the old home of her grandfather, Chief John Ross. Many of the Cherokees were allotted the land which they occupied at the time allotment was made.

One of the men who rode the hills trying to get the full bloods to enroll was himself a full blood Cherokee, who talked and wrote Cherokee as well as English. He is a farmer living today in Gooseneck bend, southeast of Muskogee. One of the appraisers was Jim Henderson.

In the office at Tahlequah was Osie Rattlingourd who was the official interpreter or at least one of them for the Commission. Walter Rattlingourd was one of the file clerks, and there was a Mr. Cobb who was a clerk in some capacity. Mrs. Wilson enrolled all of her children and each received an allotment.[1]

ENDNOTES

[1] Josephine Pennington, Interview 7783, vol. 70, Hulbert, Okla., Oct. 12, 1937, 398–99, Indian Pioneer Papers, Western History Collections, University of Oklahoma, Norman, Okla.

~ Lena Barnett Interview ~

Field worker Margaret McGuire interviewed Lena Barnett in Eufaula, Oklahoma, on October 15, 1937.

My mother was a slave of Mr. Lee Stidham's father before the Civil War. When the war began Mr. Stidham moved to Texas and carried all of his slaves with him.

When Mr. Stidham moved to Texas my mother went with him and about the same time Mr. Lee Stidham was born. Mrs. Stidham died when Lee was an infant and my mother nursed him and my brother too, and raised Lee until he was grown. Mr. Stidham moved back to the Territory after the war and my mother came back to the Territory with him. My father was a Cherokee Indian by birth but registered in Muskogee with the Creeks.

He was a relative of James Ross of Muskogee. My father and mother lived near here until they died.

I married a Creek Indian named Barnett. He had an allotment west of Eufaula where we have lived all the time with the Creek Indians.

The Snake Indians were called "Snakes" because they did not want to register or file with the other Indians and one Indian man seemed to be a ruler among a lot of others. They were his followers and would do anything he asked them to do, so he was called "Crazy Snake" and he would never file but he was filed for by the Commissioners.

Crazy Snake was opposed to making the Territory a state. We had rather not have the Territory a state but we filed.

We went to Okmulgee to file; we went in a wagon and crossed the North Canadian River about four or five miles northwest of Eufaula at Burny's Ferry.

It took us two or three days to go and return because the roads were so bad.[1]

ENDNOTES

[1] Lena Barnett, Interview 7838, vol. 5, Eufaula, Okla., Oct. 15, 1937, 386–87, Indian Pioneer Papers, Western History Collections, University of Oklahoma, Norman, Okla.

⟿ Mary J. Baker Interview ⟿

L. W. Wilson interviewed Mrs. Mary J. Baker in Sallisaw, Oklahoma, on February 24, 1938.

My grandparents on my father's side were Western Cherokees and settled in what is now Oklahoma in 1828. My parents were of the Eastern Cherokees, members of the Anti-Treaty Party, and they made the journey from Georgia over the Trail of Tears in 1838. My father's name was Jay Hicks and mother's was Katharine Levy-Hicks. They were both full-blood Cherokees, born and married in the state of Georgia.

I am enrolled as a full-blood Cherokee, having been born April 13, 1853, in the Flint District of the Cherokee Nation, Indian Territory. . . .

The Civil War had left the Indians in the Indian country in a deplorable condition. Many of them had been killed and many had died from cold and exposure and many children had found their way to the Cherokee Orphan Schools.

My parents died of natural causes in 1871 and I, too found my way to one of these schools though I had attained the age of sixteen years.

Immediately after the War, the Cherokees began to clear ground once again for cultivation, all the fields having grown up with brush, briars, and sprouts. Log cabins were built and rails split for fences to enclose their little clearings. In due time, the Cherokees had again established themselves.

They raised corn and some cotton. Many nights I sat around the fire picking seeds out of cotton for there were no cotton gins. Few sheep were raised and the sheep were sheared, the wool washed and hung on rocks to dry.

I have helped to card both cotton and wool, spin it into thread and yarn on the spinning wheel and then into cloth with the loom. Our clothing was mostly home spun.

Pretty red hunting coats with fringe on the bottom were made for the men and in most instances these coats were made of wool and shirts were made of cotton cloth. The trousers were made of a material which we called cotton jeans. Women wore no hats, but wore large shawls and blankets. The shawls were made at home. The blankets in nearly every case were purchased or traded for from peddlers coming through the country in wagons laden with blankets, beads and jewelry of all kinds. Hides and furs were traded for the wares of this peddler. Fort Gibson [Oklahoma], Webbers Falls [Oklahoma] and Fort Smith [Arkansas] were trading places. Hides and furs came near being a medium of exchange for all kinds of merchandise.

Besides raising corn, nearly all Indians raised beans, pumpkins and other vegetables and melons. . . .

I could dwell at considerable length on the act that caused the Dawes Commission to be formed, upon the acts of the Dawes Commission; its manner of enrollment and making of allotments. I wish to say that some Indians received lands who should not and some who should have received lands never did. Many times this was the fault of the Full-bloods because they did not enroll, but they did not approve of the enrollment and could not be made to understand it and did not believe it would ever be done. I blame a great part of this trouble on the Principal Chief for not leading the Full-bloods to know and understand about the enrollment.

As to myself, I enrolled and received my allotment of eighty acres of land here in Sequoyah County. I have received a few dollars at times which came from pasture fees, called by some "bread money." I secured, by sale of the

Cherokee Strip to the Government of the United States, my pro rata part of this money. I also received what was called Emigrant money from annuities due my parents long before they ever left the state of Georgia.

All in all, besides the payments such as I received, the Cherokees never got anything except money to build the Female Seminary and the Boys Seminary at Park Hill [Oklahoma].[1]

ENDNOTES

[1]Mary J. Baker, Interview 13113, vol. 4, Sallisaw, Okla., Feb. 24, 1938, 241–43, 248–49, Indian Pioneer Papers, Western History Collections, University of Oklahoma, Norman, Okla.

⌁ Minnie L. Miller Interview ⌁

L. W. Wilson interviewed Minnie L. Miller on April 11, 1938, in Tahlequah, Oklahoma.

Many Cherokees were grieved, many never enrolled, and many did enroll who were not entitled to do so. This was another time in the history of the Cherokees where the white man laid the foundation to take from them their lands, their homes and all that they held dear and their tribal laws under which they had lived for a century.[1]

ENDNOTES

[1] Minnie L. Miller, Interview 13626, vol. 63, Apr. 11, 1938, Tahlequah, Okla., 216, Indian Pioneer Papers, Western History Collections, University of Oklahoma, Norman, Okla.

~ Rose Stremlau Excerpt ~

In *Sustaining the Cherokee Family*, published in 2011, Rose Stremlau made the following observations about allotment.

When I remember it, I see the handful of small children following the adults around the fire. Some wore the glow necklaces and bracelets that I once loved to wear as a child at Fourth of July celebrations. The smallest ones wore the sneakers that light up with each step. I like this memory because when it was hard to read through the records of the Dawes Commission or write about this egregious mistake in the U.S. government's relationship with indigenous nations, I thought about those Cherokee kids in their light-up shoes taking the fire with them wherever they go in their everyday lives. I envisioned them sparking their way through the hallways of schools in which the Cherokee language is taught once again. Or perhaps they spark down the aisles of the big Wal-Mart in Tahlequah with their grandmas, who remain powerful forces in Cherokee families. In trying to quantify, codify, and reduce what it meant to be Cherokee, the Dawes Commission tried to smother these bonds of family, identity, and community that had brought these children to that ceremonial fire. Allotment wrought unspeakable damage, but, ultimately, it failed. A century after the presumed dissolution of their republic and their proclaimed assimilation into American society, Cherokees survive as families, communities, and sovereign governments. That they have embraced elements of mainstream American life, including even big-box stores, should not be surprising because this is what Cherokee families do—they change in order to persist.[1]

ENDNOTES

[1]Rose Stremlau, *Sustaining the Cherokee Family: Kinship and the Allotment of an Indigenous Nation* (Chapel Hill: University of North Carolina Press, 2011), 246–47.

II
ASSIMILATION

Cherokee women in the West faced the daunting challenge of rebuilding their lives after the Civil War. Their experiences varied depending on class, race, and educational opportunity. Traditional Cherokee women were in the majority but were generally poor and increasingly viewed as backward because of their resistance to civilization.

The Cherokee Male and Female seminaries, established in 1850, reopened after the Civil War to train the future leaders of the nation. English was the official language of the schools. Assimilation was not strictly imposed on the Cherokees,[1] but women who attended the Cherokee National Female Seminary saw the adoption of white American values as necessary for survival. In federal boarding schools such as Chilocco and Carlisle, as well as in the Cherokee seminaries, American Indians took what they needed but did not abandon their traditional cultures. Some used their knowledge to defend tribal interests and identity. Like African-American women in the late nineteenth century who aspired to middle-class gentility and respectability, Cherokee women saw education as a vehicle of mobility and considered white values something to be learned and then used to benefit their interests.

Cherokee women's power declined in the eighteenth and nineteenth centuries, but those women who attended the Cherokee National Female Seminary helped prepare the way for a resurgence in the twentieth century. The Cherokee National Female Seminary enabled many of its students to become physicians, businesswomen, educators, and prominent social workers. Some who attended the seminary genuinely embraced white values, abandoned speaking Cherokee, and adopted Christianity. Most of these women were from families who were already highly assimilated. Educated women contributed tremendously to the survival of the Cherokee Nation. At the same time, the social atmosphere at the school contributed to tensions between progressive Cherokee girls of mixed heritage and those from more traditional, uneducated backgrounds. Traditional, full-blooded women did not attend the seminary in large numbers. Only 2 full-bloods attended the Cherokee National Female Seminary the year it opened, in 1851. Only 160 full-bloods eventually enrolled in the seminary, about 9.6 percent of the total.[2]

Isabel Cobb, perhaps the first Cherokee woman trained as a physician, attended the seminary. Her life revealed the ways in which students there went on to become professional women and community leaders. The curriculum at the seminary was modeled on that of Mount Holyoke, and a number of the teachers were from the East. The students rose at five-thirty and studied subjects including the English language, Latin and

Latin mythology, philosophy, ancient languages, Roman history, *Paradise Lost*, Ovid, Cicero, Goethe, Livy, moral science, chemistry, algebra, and geometry. Their catalog and newspaper articles reveal a lively intellectual atmosphere.

Cherokee women who were in the upper class increasingly viewed education as a vehicle of success. They adopted many of white society's Victorian values of morality, culture, and progress. They also cultivated the domestic arts and adopted outward symbols of gentility and respectability, from their style of dress to the ways in which they furnished their houses.

However, just as the earlier adoption of spinning wheels and calico dresses had not led Cherokees to stop strongly identifying with their own culture, so, too, this later acculturation did not eradicate the traditional ways. African-American women fought for their share in the Cherokee Nation's land and treasury and endured discrimination and destitution. In the post–Civil War period, no consensus emerged within the Cherokee Nation regarding meanings of gender. Many Cherokee women in Indian Territory and in North Carolina continued to participate in traditional ceremonies and resisted assimilation as they faced new pressures. Meanwhile, the United States government's concerted campaign to dispossess the Cherokees of their land and tribal sovereignty continued relentlessly.

The following selections introduce the "new" women who attended the Cherokee National Female Seminary and published their own newspaper. In a time when few American women had access to an education, the Cherokee policies were quite advanced.

ENDNOTES

[1] Commissioner of Indian Affairs to Secretary of the Interior, Reports of Superintendent of Schools (Washington: GPO, 1900), 112–13.

[2] Devon A. Mihesuah, *Cultivating the Rosebuds: The Education of Women at the Cherokee Female Seminary, 1851–1909* (Urbana: University of Illinois Press, 1993), 2, 3, 5, 30, 69, 81, 83.

~ Ella Robinson Excerpt ~

The following excerpt is from Ella Robinson's research paper on Cherokee seminaries, which she wrote for the Indian-Pioneer History Project on April 12, 1938.

When the Seminary at Park Hill opened, Miss Ellen Whitmore came out as Principal teacher and Miss Sarah Worcester came as her assistant. Working among the Cherokees was not a new thing for Miss Worcester as her parents were missionaries among them in the East and she had been born and reared among them. Mr. William Ross went north to accompany the young ladies on their western journey, which was a great undertaking and took some three weeks time.

The school opened with twenty-five young lady pupils. Opening day was a grand occasion. The rooms and halls were decorated with wild azaleas, honey suckle and roses. The military band from Fort Gibson was on hand, through the courtesy of General [William W.] Belknap.

Miss Whitmore's stay was short. In response to her earnest plea, Miss Chapin filled the vacancy she left with Miss Pauline Avery, whom she sent as our principal teacher. She, too, belonged to the teaching staff of Mt. Holyoke. The salary of the teachers had been fixed at thirty dollars per month, including all expenses, which was considered a fair salary.

It was the policy of the Board of Education that they follow the working plans of Mount Holyoke as nearly as possible. Truly the Female Seminary could be called the Cherokee daughter of Mt. Holyoke.

The religious life of the student body was by no means

a secondary matter. From the beginning, church services for every Sunday were provided. Sunday school was in regular order each Sunday and each pupil was required to attend unless prevented by illness. Different ministers were invited to preach. In 1854 Miss Eliza Ross; niece of Chief John Ross, joined the faculty. The teachers from Mt. Holyoke fitted themselves into the life, not only of the schools but into the community life as well, and formed lasting friendships among the Cherokees. Miss Avery proved to be just the one to fill the place of principal teacher and in a letter to her friends at Mt. Holyoke expressed herself as being highly pleased with her work and at the end of the second year reported the school in a flourishing condition.

In 1854 Miss Charlotte Raymond came out from Mt. Holyoke to fill the place of Assistant Teacher. As the student body increased each year, additional teachers were employed. One of the common features of all educational work at that time were the public examinations held at the close of each term, and as the result of these examinations, the student's grades were regulated. Visitors were invited and welcomed, as all instructors were glad to show the progress of their students. During Miss Avery's principalship a publication was begun at the Female Seminary called "Cherokee Rose Buds," devoted to "The Good, the Beautiful, the Fine." The second number was dated August, 1854. The year prior to that the young men at the Male Seminary had started a publication, "The Sequoyah Memorial," embodying the principles of "Truth, Justice, Freedom of Speech, and Cherokee Improvement."

Both Seminaries had an advantage over many institutions of their kind in that the teachers and students lived in the same building and were associated together, which was advantageous to the students. The teachers also had direction of the outside reading courses, and one teacher was detailed for duty each Saturday in the Library. Students were admitted at the age of fourteen, provided they had passed a satisfactory examination given by the public school teachers.

The daily program for each school was as follows:

Students' Rising Bell	5:30 A.M.
Study Hall	6:00–7:00
Breakfast and detail	7:00–8:30
Chapel Exercises	8:30–9:00
Recitations	9:00–12:00
Noon Hour	12–2:00 P.M.
Military Drill	4:00–4:50
Supper	5:00–6:45
Study Hall	6:45–8:45
First Retiring Bell	9:00 P.M.
Second Retiring Bell	9:15 P.M.

The schools were thoroughly graded, and a three years preparatory course was required before entering the Seminary work proper. The first year work consisted of Penmanship, Phonetics, Reading, Arithmetic, Geography, English Composition, History and Spelling. Advanced work in each subject was given in second and third years. The first year of the Academic Department work consisted of Latin, English Grammar, Geography, Ancient History, United States History, Higher Arithmetic, Algebra, Physical Geography, and Philosophy. In the sophomore year the following subjects were given: Ancient Languages, Analysis, English Rhetoric, Caesar, English History, Algebra, Geometry, Chemistry and Natural Philosophy. In the third year or Junior year, the subjects given were ancient languages, Cicero, Ovid, Thucydides, Modern Language, French, German, English Literature, American Literature, Mental Science, Political Economy, Moral Philosophy, Trigonometry, Geometry, Botany and Geology. The fourth or senior year offered ancient languages, Virgil, Livy, Modern Languages, Moliere, Goethe, English Literature, Mental Science, Mental Philosophy, Theology, Arithmetic, Surveying, Calculus, . . . Zoology. . . .

After having been in operation for some five years, both Seminaries were forced to close in 1856, on account of lack of funds. The Male Seminary closed October 20, 1856, and the Female Seminary at the end of the regular fall term.

During the time the schools were in operation, no time was lost in preparing classes for graduation. The first class was ready in 1855, showing that the regular four years courses had been completed.

The Seminaries were not reopened until in the early seventies and it was not until 1879 that a class was ready for graduation again. When the Cherokees returned to their operation after the close of the war, they found the country in a pitiful condition. Their dwellings for the most part, had been destroyed or burned, stock driven off by the invading army . . . and the fields overgrown with weeds and underbrush. However, even in their poverty they did not forget the most important thing in their nation—that of schools, and they set about to reorganize the two seminaries. Again they appealed to Mt. Holyoke to send them teachers. Among those who responded in 1875 to the call was Miss Florence Wilson, a young graduate from that institution. She served as principal teacher until 1901, then she retired. Another who came in 1873 was Miss Addie Noyse, who remained for some two years.

The first graduating class of the Female Seminary after it was reopened was January 27, 1879, and was composed of Isabelle [sic] Cobb, a medical doctor now living in Tennessee, and Vann Steele, deceased.

In 1887, on April 10, the Female Seminary building was totally destroyed by fire. Plans for the erection of a new building to be located in the north section of Tahlequah were begun and a new substantial three story brick building was started November 3, 1887, and completed April 18, 1889, being dedicated May 5, 1889.

The Cherokees were justly proud of their educational institutions; as well as other things belonging to the nation and were a happy, prosperous people. But the insatiable greed of the white people prevailed and sections of land were opened to white settlement and finally the Indian Territory proper, with Oklahoma Territory, was admitted to Statehood in 1907. It had been the proud boast of the Cherokees that they were able to maintain their educational system "which was their own" without advice or interference from the United States Government through the Indian Department in Washington. No work of the Female Seminary went on in their new home until statehood, when the property was sold to the state of Oklahoma. It had always been in the minds of the leaders of the nation to train and educate their young generation so when those in positions of trust retired there would be others to fill the places. . . . With the closing of the tribal affairs of the Cherokees and the abolishment of their school system, was brought to a close the existence of a government of the happiest, most contented and prosperous people ever in existence.[1]

ENDNOTES

[1] Ella Robinson, "Cherokee Seminaries," vol. 108, no. 13812, Apr. 12, 1938, 9–18, Indian Pioneer Papers, Western History Collections, University of Oklahoma, Norman, Okla.

~ Annie Williams Armor ~
Interview

W. T. Holland interviewed Mrs. Annie Williams Armor at her home at 440 North Cincinnati Street in Tulsa, Oklahoma, on January 10, 1938.

I was born at Thomasville, Georgia, March 17, 1864. Although we were Cherokee Indians, we didn't come into the Territory until 1882. My father, Mat Williams, had come out and gone into the cattle business, his ranch being on Coody Creek, east of Muskogee, where he had a big ranch and grazed a big herd of cattle. He wanted us to come West, so my mother bundled us up and we came out to Muskogee. This was in 1882. We lived in Muskogee, never living out on the ranch. While we were Cherokee Indians, we had been used to a quiet and secure existence so the wild new country frightened my mother and she preferred to live in town.

My sister and I attended school at the Female Seminary at Tahlequah for the years 1882 and 1883. We were boarding students. At that time there were about 300 girls there. The cost of board and tuition was $25.00 per month. We paid one half of this and the Cherokee Nation paid one half. Miss Allen was my main teacher and Miss Wilson was the principal.

After two years of schooling at Tahlequah, my mother decided that the West didn't provide the proper environment for the rearing of a family, especially for girls, as it was entirely too wild. So we decided to return to the East to our old home.

In May, 1885, I was married to James Madison Armor,

a white man, at Chattanooga, Tennessee. In 1892 my husband came out to the Territory in the vicinity of Vinita [in what is now Oklahoma]. He looked about and decided he would select a place near Vinita. He returned East, and in 1893 we all came out. Back East, at Chattanooga, we were married according to the laws of the land, but upon reaching Vinita, in 1893, we were again married, this time in accordance with the Cherokee laws. This was thought best in that my husband was a white man and I an Indian woman. In doing this, he became a member of the tribe, and on equal footing with the other members.

We lived near Vinita on a farm until 1907, when we came to Tulsa. Here, Mr. Armor was engaged in the real estate business, building and owning residence property.

Mr. Armor's ancestors originally spelled their name Armour, same family as the Chicago Armours.[1]

ENDNOTES

[1] Annie Williams Armor, Interview 12635, vol. 3, Tulsa, Okla., Jan. 10, 1938, 60–62, Indian Pioneer Papers, Western History Collections, University of Oklahoma, Norman, Okla.

~ Lucille S. Brannon ~
Interview

In this entry, Lucille (or Lucile) S. Brannon talks about her uncle Spencer Stephens, the first superintendent of the Cherokee National Female Seminary when it reopened in 1889 after a fire destroyed the building on April 10, 1887.

The New Female Seminary was built in north Tahlequah, beginning on Nov. 3rd, 1887. Completed in April 18th, 1889. A modern brick building on a lovely site supplied with water from the "Big Spring" with steam heat and inside toilet. The pride of the Cherokee Nation, where were gathered 250 Cherokee girls, and looking about for the right man, to superintend this beautiful, high-class institution of learning—Spencer Stephens was chosen when given an appropriation to select the proper appointments for the school. Uncle Spencer went to St. Louis, and among other things, selected real linen table cloths and napkins, and silver dish and knives and forks for the 14 long tables in the dining room. Some complained that he was spending the Nation's money needlessly[. H]e told them, that "young ladies of the best families demanded the best." But politics put him out after that 1st term as Superintendent. There is a tablet in the entrance hall perpetuating his memory, and educational efforts.

He was an ideal Superintendent. I remember when passing through the halls, he found pencil marks on the wall, going up the back stairs and he called Miss Bushyhead's attention to it, and told her to find the culprit and make her scrub the marks off. And another time when he went to Aunt Sarah's room on the 2nd floor, he found greasy finger marks around the knob; he called Aunt Sarah, and told her to scrub around the knob. He was so alert that everything was just right; every employee was required to bring in their orders for supplies for the day, to his desk by 9 o'clock in the morning, and he ordered needed supplies for the day.[1]

Endnotes

[1] Lucille S. Brannon, "Cherokee National Female Seminary," Interview 0000, vol. 10, 332, Indian Pioneer Papers, Western History Collections, University of Oklahoma, Norman, Okla.

⁓ T. L. Ballenger Excerpts ⁓

T. L. Ballenger (1882–1987) lived in the area around Tahlequah, Oklahoma, for sixty-eight years and died at the age of 104. He taught for many years at Northeastern State College, where he established the Department of Special Collections, which houses over one thousand documents on the tribal history of the Cherokee Nation.

The Cherokee National Female Seminary eventually became Northeastern State College, then Northeastern State University. In his book *Early History of Northeastern State College*, Ballenger drew on the published catalog of the school, as well as documents composed by teachers and students at the institution. Below are four student selections: a description of a typical week at the seminary, a piece entitled "A School Girl's Complaint," a quotation, and a poem.

⁓

⁓ *A Week at the Female Seminary*

Monday morning, long before daylight, when all are profoundly sleeping, enjoying the most delightful dreams, the loud ringing of the rising bell arouses us from our slumbers to prepare for the duties of the day. The rattling of shovels and tongs, and the rolling of wood, show that the fires in our rooms claim our first attention.

When breakfast is over, and the school bell calls us to our recitations, we find our teacher occupying her usual seat, looking rather dubious, for Monday [is] often a blue

*Group of students at Cherokee Female Seminary
in Tahlequah, Oklahoma after it was rebuilt*

Courtesy of Western History Collections, University of Oklahoma,
Ballenger Collection, #7

day in our school calendar; out by evening if everything goes off pretty well, she appears as serene as any New England lady . . .

Tuesday is washing-day, and some of our most industrious ones are up even before the rising bell. Stumbling over chairs and through the dark halls, they descend to the wash house where a roaring fire scatters the darkness, and reveals tubs, wash-boards and boiling kettles, which are soon put in active use by these early risers, so that their domestic duties may not interfere with more intellectual pursuits.

. . . [Wednesday] is composition day. One third of it is generally done before the wide-ranging, unwilling thoughts can be collected in a speed sufficiently small to compose a dozen lines that will harmonize with the subject selected. The most appropriate name for this dark day would be, I think, the Babble of Sentiments.

By Thursday—every mind has become calm—smiles are displayed on the countenances of both the teachers and pupils; difficult lessons are mastered, and by evening all feel "happy and free." Friday is another pleasant seventh part of a week though mingled with more of stir and bustle; besides lessons to review, every room in the house must be put in order; and then when night comes all impatiently wait for the mail, expecting letters from home—from absent friends (or perchance from some strange admirer.) A reading circle closes the day.

Saturday, our recreation day, is highly prized by each one. Its hours speed swiftly away in amusement, visiting, extra study, or in the use of that little, shining implement, the needle.

Then comes the Sabbath and its calm pleasures, its sacred duties and its holy lessons, [to] close up a week in our Seminary Home.

~ A School Girl's Complaint

Oh! What a hard time school girls have! It makes me shiver now, to think of rising before six o'clock those cold, dark mornings, washing our faces in ice water and going down to breakfast before we get our eyes half open.

But I could be patient with those things if we had had not such long lessons to learn. Now just think of studying hour after hour on one of those long demonstrations of Geometry—then when I am sure I can prove to the satisfaction of all that the sum of any two sides of a triangle is greater than the third side, I go to the board and take the A.B.'s for B.C.'s or the B.C.'s for A.C.'s, and finally prove nothing to my teacher and . . . I come very near being a blockhead.

Or perhaps my Latin is to be learned, I study it over and over, and think I have at last got it nicely, but when I go to recitation, behold, my teacher reverses my translation, makes all my nouns verbs, and changes my verbs to participles. Now is it not discouraging? If I complain to my teachers they tell me to study more and my classmates give me only the same advice—I suppose it is all right—but very often I cannot help thinking Geometry ought never to have been made for the school girls to learn, and Latin should be translated by wiser heads than mine.

~ A Quotation

"Some persons mistake their friends, others their foes—some mistake their talents and calling, but the worst of all is, to mistake our moral character, and think we are something, when we are nothing."

⟶ A Poem

> Farewell Sisters—Fare ye well;
> Mid your kindness and your love
> We no longer here may dwell
> May we reach the nest above
> There the chorus glad to swell
> Where there comes no fare ye well.[1]

ENDNOTES

[1] T. L. Ballenger, "A Week at the Female Seminary," in *Early History of Northeastern State College*, 18–22, typescript at Special Collections, John Vaughan Library, Northeastern State University, Tahlequah, Okla.

Cherokee National
~ Female Seminary Catalog ~
Excerpts

The following selections are from *An Illustrated Souvenir Catalog of the Cherokee National Female Seminary*.

~ Cherokee National Female Seminary

This building is a magnificent structure, being one of the finest in the south-west, and affords ample accommodations for one hundred and seventy-five girls, all the members of the Faculty and Steward's family. It is situated on a small hill at the northern edge of Tahlequah and affords a beautiful view of the town and the country for miles in every direction. On the first floor are the parlor, library, chapel, recitation rooms and kitchen. On the second floor are the music rooms and rooms for the teachers and students, the hospital, and the dormitory for the Primaries. The building has the advantages of modern improvements. The class-rooms are well-ventilated, bright and pleasant. It is furnished with electric lights, heated by steam and supplied with water from one of the many excellent springs for which Tahlequah is famous. The school, prior to the burning of the first building, was located four miles south of Tahlequah in the Park Hill neighborhood.

How Supported.—The Seminary, as all of the schools of the Nation, is supported by money invested in the United States registered stocks from the sale of lands to the United States Government. The interest alone on this investment is drawn and used for educational purposes. The boarders are charged a mere nominal sum as an addition to the school fund. The United States Government renders no assistance in the support of the Seminaries, Insane Hospital and Common Schools of the Cherokee Nation, except paying the interest on invested funds.

How Controlled.—The Seminary is under the control of the Supervisor of Schools and a National Board of Education consisting of three members, each elected for a term of three years. Among their duties as prescribed by the Secretary of the Interior under terms of the late treaty are to adopt and enforce rules for the examination of teachers, and for the admission of pupils to the Seminaries, and to prescribe and enforce courses of study in the Seminaries, Orphanage and Primary Schools.

Admission.—Boarders. The daughters of citizens of the Cherokee Nation are received into the school by paying the Steward the required amount for board.

Primaries.—Each of the nine districts is allowed a certain number of pupils in the Primary Department. The pupils entering this department must be at least twelve years of age.

By enactment of the National Council, all persons desirous of having their children admitted into the primary department of the Seminary shall make a sworn statement that there is not public school in the neighborhood in which they live, and that they are unable to pay the board of their children and on the presentation of such statements to the Steward, such children shall be admitted; and no class of children, except boarders, primaries and day scholars shall be admitted.

Expenses.—Boarders are charged seven dollars and fifty cents per month. This pays for board, lodging, fuel, lights, washing, tuition and text-books. Instrumental music, per month, five dollars. Vocal music, per month, five dollars.

Members of the Junior Class of Cherokee Female Seminary, 1898

Articles Furnished by Pupils.—Each pupil must bring her own bedding, sheets and towels.

Uniforms.—Each girl is required to have one blue serge jacket suit and black mortar-board cap. This, together with one dress for evening and the usual every day apparel, is all that is necessary throughout the year.

～ Cherokee National Female Seminary Alma Mater

Many years ago, some Indians
Left their homes in Alabama,
Left the red sand hills of Georgia:
Left their friends and all behind them,
And with faces stern and solemn
Set out for the western country—
For the new land purchased for them.
Many weary miles they traveled,
Many hardships they encountered
Climbing mountains, crossing rivers,
Facing wind and rain and weather
Braving hunger and misfortune—
Till at last stretched out before them
Beauteous hills and fertile valleys,
Prairie lands and herds of cattle—
Beulah land of peace and plenty.
This, the goal of all their wanderings,
Rest for weary way-worn travelers.
Here they settled with their families,
Built them homes of log and mortar,
Built their chimneys wide and ample,
Hung outside the door the latchstring;
Tilled the soil, and planted orchards,

Herded steers and drove them northward.
Prosperous was this tribe of Indians
As the happy years passed o'er them.
Spacious grew their humble dwellings,
Wide their fields and rich their orchards.
Towns they built for trade and barter—
Fairest of all—the town Tahlequah,
Nestled in a smiling valley,
Wrapped in softest summer sunshine,
Kissed by gentle fragrant breezes,
With the hill's strong arms about her—
Fairest of all the Nation's children.
In this little town Tahlequah
At the bottom of a foot-hill,
Gushes forth a spring of water,
Pure and sweet and clear and sparkling
As the one the Muses drank from;
And our fathers, as they stood there
Drinking the life-giving nectar,
Looking upward, looking northward
Let their eyes rest on this hill-top—
Felt the spell of Jove upon them,
As when in the old time legend
From his forehead sprang Minerva.

Men with axes, saws and hammers,
Men with squares, and planes, and trowels;
Men with horses, mule and wagons—
All the air was filled with rumbling
Sharp reports and heavy pounding,
Blasting rock and earth upheavals.
When at last the din was over
And the darkened sky grew clearer,
There arose from out the chaos
Bright and shining, grand and classic

Graceful arches, Gothic towers—
Fit abode for Wisdom's goddess.

Then from all parts of the nation,
From humblest homes, and from the richest
Came the bright-faced Indian maidens;
Maidens fair and maidens dusky,
Maidens tall and short and "pudgy."—
Came they to this seat of learning;
Drank they from this sparkling fountain
And with thirsty souls unslaked
Longed for more of Hebe's potion;—
Longed and all their lives kept longing
And in time sent back their daughters
That their lives might be so sweetened
And their days and deeds be fruitful.
Should you ask me whence the learning—
Whence the power and pride and greatness
Of this tribe of Indian people,
I shall point you to this college
That for years has schooled its women—
Wives and mothers of these people
Whose brief story I've related.

And the maidens now-departing
From this dear old Alma-Mater,
From this dear old second Mother
Who has cared for them so gently
Through the sweet years of their girlhood,
Leave the wish and prayer behind them
That, as future years roll onward
Blotting out our race of people,
She may stand here always ready,
Glad to welcome Indian children
And to keep alive tradition—

Monument to all the greatness
Of this proudest Indian Nation.

A Nineteen-Five Senior[1]

ENDNOTES

[1] *An Illustrated Souvenir Catalog of the Cherokee National Female Seminary, Tahlequah, Indian Territory, 1850 to 1860* (Chilocco, Okla.: Indian Print Shop). The catalog was reprinted in *Journal of Cherokee Studies* 10, no. 1 (Spring 1985), 138–44, 182–83. The original is in the archives of the Museum of the Cherokee Indian, Cherokee, N.C.

～ *Cherokee Rose Buds* Excerpts ～

This entry features articles from 1854, 1855, and 1857 editions of *Cherokee Rose Buds*, the newspaper published by the Cherokee National Female Seminary. The paper was printed partly in Cherokee and partly in English. *Cherokee Rose Buds* was devoted to "the Good, the Beautiful and the True." Catharine Gunter and Nancy E. Hicks were the coeditors.

～

[The following three pieces are from the August 2, 1854, issue. The poem was credited to "Corrinne," the second piece to "Na-Li," and the third to "Edith."]

～ *Our Wreath of Rose Buds*

We offer you a wreath of flowers
Culled in recreation's hours,
Which will not wither, droop, or die,
Even when days and months pass by.

Ask you where these flowers are found?
Not on sunny slope, or mound;
Not on prairies bright and fair
Growing without thought or care.

No, our simple wreath is twined
From the garden of the mind;

Where bright thoughts like rivers flow
And ideas like roses grow.

The tiny buds which here you see
Ask your kindly sympathy;
View them with a lenient eye,
Pass each fault, each blemish by.

Warmed by the sunshine of your eyes,
Perhaps you'll find to your surprise,
Their petals fair will soon unclose,
And every bud becomes—a Rose.

Then take our wreath, and let it stand
An emblem of our happy band;
The Seminary, our garden fair;
And we, the flowers planted there.

Like roses bright we hope to grow,
And o'er our home such beauty throw
In future years—that all may see
Loveliest of lands,—the Cherokee.

~ An Address to the Females of the Cherokee Nation

It is sometime said that our Seminaries were made only for the rich and those who were not full Cherokee, but it is a mistake. I thought I would address a few lines to the other class in the Nation. My beloved parents were full Cherokees. They belonged to the common class; and, yet, they loved their children as well [as] the rich; but they had never attended school, and therefore did not know the value of learning; and probably would never [have] made provision for me to attend school. But those beloved parents have been called from this world and left me a lonely orphan. I was very young and have but a faint remembrance of my mother's long and wearisome sickness of the consumption. At the time of my mother's death, a kind missionary teacher came and took me under her care. Under the influence and teaching of the missionaries, I was prepared to enter this institution. I should not have said so much about myself; but I feel that a great many of the full Cherokees can have the benefit of the Seminary as well as I. Our Chief and directors would like very much that they should come and enjoy these same privileges as those that are here present, and the teachers would take as much pains in instructing you. I feel it is no disgrace to be a full Cherokee. My dark complexion does not prevent me from acquiring knowledge and of being useful hereafter.

I write this, hoping that it will persuade you to attend school and thus prepare to enter this Institution. We will give you a hearty welcome. You can be instructed in Mathematics, History and studies of various characters for the improvement of our minds and though we may not see their use of the present, we will in years to come. I am much interested in the studies that [are] set before me. But a year and a half will soon pass away and then I am to go out into the Nation and endeavor to be useful; and, although I sometimes think I cannot be, yet I am resolved to try.

Once more I urge you to attend some Public School; be studious and persevering, and then after awhile you will probably be well prepared to enter our institution. If you should not succeed the first time, "try, try again."

⟶ *View from Our Seminary*

Our Seminary commands a most delightful and varied

prospect of the surrounding country. On the north, stretching away as far as the eye can reach is a wood: and though within the few years past many demands have been made upon its wealth of noble trees, yet for years to come will an inexhaustible number continue to lift their lofty tops proudly to the blue sky in defiance of the devastating stroke of the woodman's axe.

This wood is one of our favorite resorts in the Spring and Summer days, where, when school duties are finished, we often wander, a merry troop, over hill and dale in search of the woodland flowers and delicious berries. Then, laden with our treasures we set out homeward as the loud tones of the Seminary bell warn us to hasten on that we may be in time for Supper, which is relished with a much keener appetite after the exercise in the fresh open air.

But the most picturesque part of the scenery is the prairie encompassed on the south by a range of green hills rising one above another, the most noted of which is Park Hill, elevated into a peak several hundred feet above the level of the ground. From its summit a much wider view is presented: the prairie extends in from and on either side; its surface [marked] by gently rising hills and sloping valleys and covered over with flowers of every hue. Scattered in all directions are green fields, meadows and groves; and peeping from among the trees of the latter, instead of the rudely constructed wigwams of our forefathers which stood there not more than half a century ago, elegant white dwellings are seen. Everything around denotes taste, refinement and the progress of civilization among our people: well may they vie with the long enlightened inhabitants of the east.

One of the most handsome and beautifully situated of these dwellings is the residence of our Chief and his white bride, who left her native land and friends a few years since to come and dwell with him in his wild prairie home among his own tribe, the Cherokees.[1]

[The following two articles are from the August 1, 1855, issue. The first was credited to "Isabelle" and the second to "Alice."]

~ A Day's Experience

I arose one beautiful morning with a determination to spend one day of my life as I ought. The first thing was to be kind to my school-mates and all around me. I felt that I could not keep my resolution unless I asked help from above. I succeeded very well until after breakfast. Then the little trials began to creep up before me as usual. There seemed to be more that day than ever before. Perhaps it was because I was trying so hard not to give way to my temper. After breakfast I went up to my room, and as it was almost school-time, I began to look for my books, but could not find them. I got vexed, and, before I was aware, spoke unkind words to my room-mates. Very soon the school bell rang, and it was time to recite. I knew nothing about my lesson. I sat trembling for fear a question should come to me. Pretty soon I saw the Teacher's eyes turn towards me. I felt that the next question was mine. Sure enough, it was. Oh dear! What could I say? I was mum. Failure was my portion that morning. I felt sad enough, but went to my kind teacher and explained the whole matter to her, and asked her to excuse me for that time, to which she consented, and spoke a few words of encouragement to me, which cheered me not a little. Everything seemed to be set right, and all things moved on smoothly for two or three hours. I began to think that it was not so very hard to keep my resolution. I had almost forgotten it, however, for when someone came along and asked me to do something for her, which I was not willing to do, and refused, she became vexed, and I, too; but the resolution of the morning arose before my mind and I tried to control myself, but found it not very easy work to do to others as I would have them do to me. Yes, and by the close of the day, I found that this beautiful world of ours was just as full of little trials as it can hold. We should, therefore, be very watchful every day and hour, lest we be led by our own evil propensities into wrong and forbidden paths.

∽ Beauty

In creating the world, God made everything that could contribute to the happiness of his creatures. Over all he threw the mantle of beauty to please the eye.

On every side, are lofty hills and mountains; fertile valleys and spreading prairies covered with their thousand flowers. Here and there, thick forests meet the gaze; the little rippling brooks go singing by, and noble rivers roll on to the mighty ocean. These are beauties of nature.

But man, himself, in physical beauty, excels in the works of God. What more admirable than the noble form "erect in God-like majesty," or the more perfect gracefulness of woman? The blushing smiles that play upon the rosy cheek, the silken hair falling luxuriously over the shoulders, the sparkling eye;—these are all lovely and call forth many a word of praise.

But there is a beauty which exists within, worth more than all these outward ornaments and it often appears where they are wanting. It is the beauty of the intellect; the reflection of a mind which has gathered knowledge by its piercing glance from all the glorious creations that surround us. It has soared to the shining worlds which fill the universe and [bring] down wisdom; it has communed with the great intellects of earth until all that is lovely in mind and matter is stamped upon it.

But there is a higher beauty still,—before which physical,

and even intellectual beauty grow dim. It is found where right feelings and principles are cherished in the heart. Like flowers, the more they are cultivated the more beautiful they become, and if watered by dews from the Fountain of Life, they will spread the radiance of Moral Beauty over the soul. Physical beauty may pass away, and intellectual beauty decay; but moral beauty will never fade; it will only appear brighter when transplanted from Earth to the gardens of Heaven.[2]

[The Cherokee National Female Seminary had to close at the end of the academic year in 1856, effective in 1857, because of lack of funds. It reopened briefly in 1861, then soon closed until the 1870s. The following article appeared in the February 11, 1857, issue of *Cherokee Rose Buds*. The author expresses her sadness at the school's closing.]

Once more with trembling hands we have twined a wreath of Rose Buds for our friends, which we trust will not suffer in comparison with former attempts, though far from being all that we could wish it.

May it meet your sympathies; your kindly words, for it is the last bright garland we shall weave.

It is an event of sadness to us all who have so long been the recipients of our Nation's bounty. Yet we cannot but hope, that ere many months have passed, the dark cloud will be dispelled and our Seminary be permitted again to enjoy the sunshine of prosperity.

Our term has passed rapidly and quietly away. In the first few weeks during the meeting of the Council, there was much of restlessness and anxiety to know our fate, but since the question was decided, every moment has been precious.[3]

ENDNOTES

[1] "Our Wreath of Rose Buds," in *Cherokee Rose Buds*, from *The Youth's Companion*, Sept. 7, 1854, 80.

[2] *A Wreath of Cherokee Rose Buds*, Female Seminary, Cherokee Nation, vol. 2, no. 1, Wed., Aug. 1, 1855.

[3] *A Wreath of Cherokee Rose Buds*, Female Seminary, Cherokee Nation, vol. 3, no. 2, Wed., Feb. 11, 1857. For details about the closing and reopening of the school, see Mihesuah, *Cultivating the Rosebuds*, 44–50.

Joyce Dugan, Chief of the Eastern Band of Cherokee Indians 1995–99

Part 7

LEADING CHEROKEE WOMEN

In her autobiography, Wilma Mankiller speaks of her personal challenges in trying to "be of good mind." Cherokee elders use the term to describe thinking positively. At the beginning of some Cherokee traditional prayers and healing ceremonies, everyone is asked to remove all negative thoughts and to have a pure mind and heart. Mankiller describes the ways in which Cherokee women's power diminished with intermarriage and the erosion of the clan system and the practice of matrilineal descent. The Cherokee Constitution limited women's rights by excluding them from government offices and prohibiting them from voting. She writes that, under the influence of the civilization plan, "Cherokee women were expected to become subservient and domesticated like white women who were home oriented."[1] Cherokee women adapted to challenges from white society, the government, and missionaries.

In the late twentieth century, the women began to recover. They reclaimed political power, as was demonstrated dramatically when Wilma Mankiller and Joyce Dugan were elected as chiefs. Mankiller and Dugan combined traditional women's roles as wives and mothers with the roles of producers and leaders in the public sphere. Both were dedicated to working in the community. For example, Joyce Dugan was the director of education on the Qualla Boundary before being elected principal chief of the Eastern Band of Cherokee Indians in 1995. Although the tribe had never had a female chief before, Dugan ran because she believed fervently in better health care, cultural preservation, the study of the Cherokee language, and the reclamation of Cherokee lands. During her term, which ended in 1999, she helped establish the tribe's Diabetes Wellness Center, which opened on August 27, 1999; one tribal member out of three had diabetes. She also faced tremendous challenges over the gambling issue; Harrah's Cherokee Smoky Mountain Casino opened on the Qualla Boundary on November 13, 1997.[2]

On October 11, 1997, the Eastern Band, the Keetoowah Band, and the Cherokee Nation of Oklahoma came together in a moving ceremony commemorating the return of sacred land. They stood at the same site as their ancestors. Chief Joyce Dugan recommended purchasing land originally known as Kituwha, or Mother Town, a site containing a burial mound dating back to 6000 to 5000 B.C.E. The purchase price of over $3.5 million for the 309 acres that included Kituwha derived largely from the gambling enterprises. Dugan spoke on the occasion about the meaning of cultural continuity: "The significance of place is not something we have learned, for we have not lost our homes because of removal. We are indeed fortunate that our ancestors worked so hard to preserve this heritage for us." Occupied continuously for over ten thousand years, Kituwha lies east of Bryson City, North Carolina. Among the artifacts found there was a soapstone bowl over eight thousand years old. In the Mother Town, the Cherokees' ancestors received sacred ceremonies, the first fire, and clan laws.[3]

Thus, Cherokee women have come full circle from being equals within the tribe before contact with Europeans to losing power in the eighteenth and nineteenth centuries to regaining influence in the twentieth century. Through the Trail of Tears, the Civil War, and allotment and dispossession of their land, the tribe redefined what it meant to be a Cherokee woman.

The following testimonies from "Cherokee new women" include Isabel Cobb, who was a doctor in Oklahoma from 1893 to 1930, Aggie Ross Lossiah, and Wilma Mankiller.

ENDNOTES

[1] Mankiller and Wallis, *Mankiller*, 86, 226.

[2] Virginia Moore Carney, "A Testament to Tenacity: Cultural Persistence in the Letters and Speeches of Eastern Band Cherokee Women," Ph.D. diss., University of Kentucky, 2000, 238, 244, 245–46, 247–48, 268–69; section on Dugan, 236–50. See also Virginia Moore Carney, *Eastern Band Cherokee Women: Cultural Persistence in Their Letters and Speeches* (Knoxville: University of Tennessee Press, 2005), 147–56.

[3] *News Sentinel*, Knoxville, Tenn., June 5, 2001; Andrew Curry, "Cherokee Holy of Holies," *Archaeology* (Sept.-Oct. 2002), 70–75.

～ Isabel Cobb Selections ～

Isabel "Bell" Cobb was born in Cleveland, Tennessee, in 1858 and came to Indian Territory in 1870 at the age of twelve. After graduating from the Cherokee National Female Seminary in Tahlequah, Oklahoma, she taught school for a short time before entering college in Glendale, Ohio, in preparation for medical school. She graduated from Woman's Medical College in Philadelphia in 1891 and then had a two-year internship at Staten Island Children's Hospital. She came home to practice five miles southeast of Wagoner, Oklahoma, from 1893 to 1930.

Cobb's medical journal documents approximately 441 patients, 99 of whom were male. Thus, nearly 78 percent of her practice was female and 22 percent male. She recorded infant mortalities, abortions, miscarriages, and "hard, first labor." Her yearly income ranged from a high of $329.55 in 1896 to $20.00 by 1915, when her entries ended.

In her role as a physician in the late nineteenth and early twentieth centuries, Cobb was a prime example of the Cherokee professional "new woman." She epitomized acculturation on her own terms. In the context of Cherokee culture, her status as a female doctor was extremely rare. But her nurturing resembled that of female healers and shamans who had performed similar functions for hundreds of years. This remarkable woman survived the Civil War, Oklahoma statehood, and World Wars I and II, performing the duties of her career and serving as a mediator between the Indian and white cultures.

The first selection below comes from the Cobb family history. Cobb talks about her youth in the East—school, farm and social practices, the Civil War—and the family's move to Oklahoma.

The second selection is a sample from Cobb's medical record book, which she began on March 29, 1893. She wrote in a clear, concise, legible way, giving for each patient visit the history, her findings and treatment, and the charge, if any. The notes were brief and to the point but managed to convey a love of people that must have endeared her to her patients and the whole community.

⬱

In February 1870 our father Joseph B. Cobb sold his farm on Candy's [or Candies] Creek, East Tennessee, 3½ miles northwest of Cleveland in Bradley County, Tennessee, to a Mr. Julian, an M.E. [Methodist Episcopal] preacher and we turned our faces westward to the far off Indian Territory. Being part Cherokee we all had a right to land in the Cherokee Nation.

We had relatives and acquaintances who had emigrated and sent glowing accounts back. So we came.

There were six of us children—Isabel, Billy, Mattie, Joe, Alex and Sam. All of school age except the two youngest boys.

No longer would we trek a mile and a half across Candies Creek to school where Mr. Niblo taught us our first lessons in geography and guided us thro' the old blue backed spelling book and where a contest in spelling almost broke up the tie of friendship between us and one Pocahontas Cowan—one of our dearest loved cousins. And no longer would we walk the slim foot log across the Creek . . . to school—two miles to a school in a grove near Mr. Kirby's where a Mr. James Rucker with a short leg, big owl eyes and a quid of tobacco bulging out one cheek, a switch under one arm, hopped about among his students, a terror to the little ones. But he was counted a good teacher in those times. Our timid heart never swelled and beat with more pride than one evening he overtook us going home—he on his pony with his crutch across the saddle in front of him. He said, "Well, Bell, you beat them all spelling." We had had a spelling of the whole school, a string of boys and girls— some young men and grown girls standing round the room against the wall. I well remember standing at the foot and spelling them all down and going to the foot again. It was the custom to go to the foot and then climb to the head again. It was also customary for the pupils to study aloud— the humming becoming so loud sometimes the teacher had to subdue it by rapping with his cane. . . .

Martha (Patsy) Blythe, our grandmother, was sixteen when she married Alex Clingan and started housekeeping at the homestead in a cabin which was later replaced by a substantial two story weatherboard building with three chimneys and twice as many fireplaces. A long front porch looked out on the big road and the Ridge beyond at the foot of which was the family graveyard.

A cellar beneath with folding outside doors on the south side of the house—all surrounded by hard maple and cedar trees—which in the memory of the grandchildren were *large* trees—with a walk through to the front gate where there was a large plank for a mounting board. Everybody rode horseback in the early days—not even buggies had come into use—so the women and girls had to have an elevation from which to mount their horses which in those days were saddled for them with sidesaddles—disgraceful to ride astride.

What was called the Big Road passed in front of the house running north and south from Cleveland several miles north till it turned west and crossed Candies Creek Bridge and east to Georgetown. . . .

Southeast and south of the house which sat on an elevation not amounting to a hill, was a branch of clear sparkling spring water taking its origin in a spring up on the Ridge, the waters of which had been damned by a huge log over which the water fell in a cascade about two feet high and crossed the road and ran on down through the meadow with other springs along its course, one of which furnished the house with water and cool milk and butter from the log spring house and near it the family washing was done, the big black pot and wooden tubs with a bench and battling stick—not even wash boards to help get the dirt out, but plenty of soft soap.

An orchard was set which yielded in the day of us grandchildren delicious great big apples—one called the horse apple.

Children came thick and fast to this little grandmother—7 boys and 9 girls, all of whom she raised to be grown except the eldest who died in infancy. Her neighbors called her a good general and her commands, if such they might be called, were seldom questioned but usually obeyed to the letter. Tasks set for the girls to do were accomplished readily. Many a beautiful quilt and much fine needlework were wrought by these girls who also were experts at cooking. Among the older ones the spinning wheel and loom gave forth fine works of linen and beautiful counterpanes and coverlets.

The younger girls took their turn in the fields at light jobs like dropping corn or using the hoe in covering it. Our mother said she had celebrated a good many of her birthdays dropping corn on the 13th of April. The four or five grains of corn must be dropped exactly in the check where the two furrows cross—the furrow being laid off by the boys who could run the straightest row with their one horse bull-tongue plows. No such thing as corn planter and cultivators in those days, and grandfather raised fine corn on this creek-bottom land.

And when it came to wheat, no new fangled drills could take the place of the man with his sack of wheat strung over his left shoulder while his right hand scattered broadcast over the mellow freshly harrowed ground the wheat by handsfull, then followed the harrow to cover the seed, or sometimes a big brush was used to cover them, drawn by horses or oxen. And then at harvest time, in June usually, when the wheat and oats fields had grown yellow and ready to cut, men with cradles went thru them cutting and gathering into bunches which the binders picked up and tied into bundles. These in turn were bunched into shocks and carped so that rain did no damage tho' the shocks might remain in the fields for days or weeks. Finally the threshing was done by the tramping of horses feet or the beat of the flail on a floor or level clean place on the ground—then, of course, the grain must be winnowed and cleaned and stored. The first threshing machines were run by horse power—8 or 10 horses so that threshing was a big and expensive process.

If a crop of flax had to be cared for, it was cut with sickles, tied into bundles ready for the brake which crushed off the outer stiff coat of the stalk leaving the soft fibre which was hackled and made ready for the spinning wheel, the little ones the spinner sat down to and operated with her foot on a pedal. A hackle was a lot of sharp nails set in a board which could be held in the lap or set on a table. The coarse fibers were called ["]tow["] and was spun and woven for coarse towels or straw ticks.

Wool and cotton were carded into rolls and spun on the big spinning wheel turned by hand. Thread on the brooches from those wheels was made into hanks on the reel, also turned by hand, and these were then ready to be washed and dyed ready to be woven into cloth on the big loom in a vacant room upstairs or in fine weather out beside the house.

So you see those boys and girls were busy—each one fitting in where he or she could be of most use in carrying on the business of this establishment started in a tiny cabin by a young couple among the foothills of the Smoky Mountains of East Tennessee—the management of a big houseful of children.

A school was kept in a log school house across the ridge; writing school and singing school became common, and parties and dances called the young folks together. There were picnics, barbecues, shooting matches, camp meetings and singing and weddings in those early days. . . .

Much could be written of the great preparations for the weddings which occurred in the family. Old Mariah Soles was there for days baking cakes, bread, chickens, etc., in ovens round a big fire in the fireplaces. At one wedding a roast whole pig with a red apple in its mouth graced the table along with nine other kinds of meat we have been told.

The wedding cake was iced, dressed and decorated as only Old Mariah knew how to do it—and much merriment attended its cutting as it contained a ring, a thimble, and a dime. The fortunate (or unfortunate as the future might develop) young lady who cut and drew the ring was supposed to be the next one to get married. She who drew the thimble was doomed to be an old maid, while the one who drew the piece of money would marry a rich man.

The knot was tied good and fast by a minister and without any thought of its ever being untied except by death. "Until death do us part" had real meaning. No divorces ever occurred in those days among the members of our family. Indeed divorced people were considered disgraced in those days. . . .

Most of our neighbors sympathized with the Confederacy—the South. Feelings ran pretty high and bitter, even brother fought against brother and father against son. So father (Joseph B. Cobb) and Uncle William Cowan left home in the dead of winter traveling by night to avoid capture, and reached the Union line at Nashville where they found employment in the service of the government without enlisting as fighters, for they were ever opposed to shedding a brother's blood be he of the North or South.

Father was in the Commissary Department while in Nashville in 1863 while mother and her four small children were left at home to try to keep the little they had from being carried off by the Yankees, usually. But her pig pens and chicken roosts were frequently raided.

On February 21, 1863 she gave birth to her 4th baby, a boy weighing 15 pounds, named for his father, Joseph Benson Cobb who was away and did not see him until he was 6 months old. I can faintly remember the night Joe was born. A midwife, old Aunt Betsey Lane, and her husband Anderson came down the Creek in a canoe by torch light. Dr. John Long from Cleveland came later and said Joe weighed more at birth than he did at 6 months. . . .

One day there on this farewell visit at this dear old place, Billy Cowan Cobb, our oldest brother[,] 10 years old[,] went riding across the Creek (Candies Creek) with Uncle Judge and came back wet to the skin by the showers of rain—not feeling very well. The next morning he was broken out thick with measles. Of course, this meant a delay in our starting for the last chick of us had his turn but all got thru nicely except Alex who was troubled (as were our mother and father) with earache, abscess and discharge thru all our hard trip by train, boat and wagon to the Indian Territory.

As I remember the younger children were puny, whining and restless all the way, requiring ceaseless attention and care on the part of mother. At Chattanooga as we were changing trains, an unearthly blast from a nearby engine not only scared Alex but was agony to his sore ear.

Before leaving, Aunt Addie Clingan took Mattie and

me to a photographer's and had our pictures made—mine was very unnatural looking with corkscrew curls all over my head from having endured the rough curl paper bumps for a day and night! (Think of torturing a child thus to satisfy the pride of two or three aunts.) . . .

Father had gone ahead and had engaged a small house on the hill east of town (Tahlequah)—a house said to be haunted because some woman had committed suicide there. What was most to be remembered was that pigs and fleas infested the dust about the place so that we had to rid ourselves of the hoppers before getting in bed at night. [A] month or two we spent there while Father looked about for a place to buy for a permanent home. We children went to school down in town.

One memorable event was a spelling match conducted by Spens S. Stephens who was the teacher at the Eureka School some 5 or 6 miles southwest of Tahlequah—a contest for a beautiful bay pony bedecked with gay ribbons as he grazed about in the Capitol yard where the contest was held and where a long line of contestants from various neighboring schools including the town school stood waiting. . . .

Father found a place on the prairie . . . 10 miles north of Ft. Gibson . . . with a spring as the main attraction, 10 plus acres of land in cultivation, a log cabin for a kitchen and bed and living room; another log cabin chicken house, a log spring house and the hull or frame of a new cabin with roof extending over for a porch and kitchen (we made them.)

We hung up quilts and blankets and father laid a floor of rough planks to make a room in which to welcome a newcomer—a baby sister (Addie Malinda) who came the 9th of September 1870. What a place for Mother at such a time—and no doctor nearer than Ft. Gibson.

A neighbor (Mrs. Wash Mayes) who lived on the bank of the river (Grand) came after and helped—but the post doctor from Ft. Gibson had to be called before Mother was up again.

It makes me shudder now to think what that brave uncomplaining mother went through at that time—and other times when chills and fever were rampant among the children—and border warfare with the Creek Negroes when our oldest brother, Billy (William Cowan Cobb) was killed by them and Alex Cowan (a cousin) wounded in the summer of 1880.

Some men had gathered and attempted to Lynch [suspected thieves] for stealing of cattle. This, of course enraged the negroes and the battle ensued near Gibson Station and W. D. Clingan's place.[1]

—

[Mary Harvey got sick on Thursday, November 26, 1896. She came to see Dr. Cobb two days later and was given some medicine for her fever. On her return on November 30, something was added for restlessness. On December 1, she was about the same and received medicine for worms. Dr. Cobb made the following notes about her patient.]

Dec. 2—Temp. 102.5, sleeps, moans some on expiration, coughs but little, pulse bounding, respiration normal, little tenderness over liver and in right iliac region, one spot resembling typhoid, tongue dry at first, is now moist and clear, is thirsty, eats nothing, lips sore.

Dec. 3—No change—coughs a little more and looser. No worms passed—appetite better—drank some milk last night.

Dec. 4—Mouth quite sore—Temp. 102 (5 P.M.). Seemed much better this morning, sweated and seemed to have no fever at all.

Dec. 7—Thinks she is doing well—no fever since Friday night.

Dec. 8—2 A.M. —Much worse—rt. lung [involved] but thought might be hypostatic congestion—took Dr. Braziel out in P.M. —lung involvement increased—pneumonia.

Dec. 9—Rested well at night—no improvement.

Dec. 10—Died at 2 A.M.

[Doctor Cobb's bill for looking after Mary Harvey in her final illness was eight dollars. Her book contained this note beside the charge: "Dr. B. charged $13.00 hence my small bill."][2]

ENDNOTES

[1] Dr. Isabel Cobb Collection, box 1, folder 3, "Cobb family history written by Dr. Bell Cobb," Western History Collections, University of Oklahoma, Norman, Okla. See also Isabel Cobb, Interview, vol. 65, 184–218, Indian Pioneer Papers, Western History Collections, University of Oklahoma, Norman, Okla. For more biographical information, see Isabel Cobb Collection, "Partial History of Dr. Isabel Cobb: Earlyday Doctor in Indian Territory," mimeographed by Ruth Cobb Bivins, box 1, folder 5, Western History Collections, University of Oklahoma Libraries, Norman, Okla.

[2] Dr. Isabel Cobb Collection, box 1, folder 1, "Physician's Visiting List," Western History Collections, University of Oklahoma, Norman, Okla. For Cobb's original medical records, see "Isabel Cobb," vertical file, Research Division, Oklahoma Historical Society, Oklahoma City, Okla. See also "Dr. Isabel Cobb: Her Times and Ours," *Oklahoma State Medical Association Journal* 53, no. 3 (March 1960), 129–30.

⁓ Aggie Ross Lossiah Article ⁓

In 1984, Aggie Ross Lossiah's piece entitled "The Story of My Life As Far Back As I Can Remember" appeared in the *Journal of Cherokee Studies*. In her editor's note, Joan Greene offered the following biographical information about Aggie:

> Aggie Ross Lossiah, daughter of Joe and Cornelia Ross and great granddaughter of Principal Chief John Ross, was born December 22, 1880. She and her brother, Jossiah, spent their growing-up years in east Tennessee with their maternal grandparents, Jessie and Sela Techeskee. This is the story of those growing-up years as Aggie wrote it in 1960. For the first few years of her life Aggie had spoken only the Cherokee language, and her formal education had consisted of four years at the Cherokee Training School. However, Aggie mastered the English language primarily because she never stopped learning. To facilitate reading I have inserted dashes where there was no punctuation in the original manuscript. Otherwise, this is Aggie's story in her words.

⁓

When I was 3 years old I remember my brother and I and my great grand pa we were walking down the road one day—And a white man came riding down the road and over took us and he picked children up with him on his mule and we rode with him until we came to where we were going—And he let us down and we walked on then to where grand pa and grand ma were camped by the river down at the mouth of a creek they called Cit[i]co creek near the [Little] Tennessee river—And first I remember we were with them where they had them a shelter built there with four posts up and poles across the forked posts and had cane splits on top for a roof to keep us dry and cane leaves too—this is the way it looked and we all stayed under there and our bed was cane leaves but we were in the dry—I remember when we still lived at the mouth of the creek I used to wander around the corn field at the mound and gather Indian beads in the field and carry them in my hand and go back to the shelter where we lived and grand ma would give me some thread to string the beads on. And one time I went over the fence and I got scared—I thought I saw a bear and I ran home to grand ma and told her I saw a bear but I never went that far anymore afterward. Then I used to go across the creek to the white folks' house—grand ma would go with me and I would play with their children. And they would have the best food to eat like sausage and meat that I thought was the best I ever ate and good biscuits and corn bread too was so good—but I never drank milk because I never had any at home to learn to drink milk—I didn't know you drank it but I never could drink milk—and we would wade the creek and that's how we crossed to go over to McSpadons house—that was the name of the folks we went to visit— grand ma could carry some baskets to exchange for food and when they gave her food we would go home and wade over the creek again—that is the way we travelled them days when I was small—

Then one day it clouded up and looked so dark like a storm was coming and I remember then a white man came from over the river and he talked with my grand pa but I didn't know what he was saying—But my grand pa he could talk English and he said for us to go over the river to his place—there was a little cabin we could stay in and my great grand pa he took us two children over the river—this white man had a canoe which we cross the river in and then he went back and brought grand pa and grand ma over with their things and we lived in the log cabin—I don't know how long we stayed there but these folks were awful good people—the man's name was Henry Harrison and he had a daughter—her name was Maggie and after I got used to them I loved to go to their house every day—[I] used to go to milk with Maggie and gather hen eggs and pick up pea cock feathers under the house. And Maggie would give me some things to eat. That is where I learned to speak English—I thought that was something great now—I could speak English—my grand pa would laugh at me saying my English words—of course I made mistakes in pronouncing my words but that is where I started to talk English when we lived at Henry Harrison's place.

Grand ma would make baskets and go peddlin' and Brother and I and great grand pa would go with her. One time my great grand pa got sick while we were peddling— And the white folks put up a tent for him to lay under—my grand ma went back to the Harrison's and they brought a wagon after him and put him in the wagon and took us home. And I remember a white woman gave my great grand pa a rooster to take home for him to eat and I had to hold that rooster—seemed like he was as big as I was— I got so tired holdin' the rooster then—I don't remember when we got home—I must have went to sleep for I don't remember—we always went with grand ma when she went to peddle. And I never got hungry because the white folks would always give me something to eat—and I carried a little basket with me too and they would fill my basket with biscuits that was cold biscuits but they were good to eat when you never had any at home. And one time I made some little baskets—

When my grand ma was making baskets she showed me how to make them—And when she got her a load of baskets made we went to peddle. And my grand pa made some chairs and he would take his chairs too to sell—and so here we would go—we went to Maryville, Tenn.—it was a little town then—that was as far as the train came then and that is where we went to peddle baskets—and I took my few baskets that I had made and I had enough to buy me a cotton dress and a few other little things at the store— that was the first time I bought myself something myself by selling baskets that I made myself—it took us all day to walk over to Maryville from where we lived—the place where we lived they called Tallassee creek—we lived up the creek from little Tennessee river now on the other side of the river [in a place] they call Caldwood, Tenn.—

... The next I remember is when I was six years old— then our grand parents were going [to] send us to the Indian school a way up [in] North Carolina they called yellow hill—and we started one day to go to yellow hill to go to school—I remember that we started [and] my great grand pa he started with us two children up the road—and it was so hot—in August was the month we left home and as we went along the road I would stop to pick me some black berries to eat—and along the way I got stung by a wasp and that made us slow down because I got so sick after the wasp stung me on the lip—my face swole up and I couldn't see good until late in the evening before we travelled any-more—And then we started on our journey but night soon over took us in the woods and grand pa had to stop and build us a fire to stay by that night and we all went to sleep in the woods—and I remember hearing a noise sometime in the night and it was a hog—and it came [and] took our bread that grand pa had been carrying along for us to eat— and it was so dark that we couldn't follow the hog—he just got away with our bread. So in the morning we started on our way without no breakfast—and as we went on grand pa and grand ma over took us before we had gone very far— they thought we had got to Sam Blair's place, that is a white man my grand pa knew back up in the foot of the mountain on the road we were going—that was one day and night away from home on our way to school—I don't remember how long it took us to walk up to North Carolina but I remember one day we came to a house and that was where our mother lived and we stopped there—I don't remember how long we stayed there. Then next I remember when we got to the school our mother was with my grand ma—when we got to the school they took all three of us children up to school but they just kept us two—our sister went back with Mother and grand ma—I remember I want to go back too but they left me crying—and a white woman she took me by the hand and tried to make me stop crying—she would spank me and I said how [did] she expect me to stop crying when she spank me. And she stop spanking me—then she got something for me to play with and took me out on the porch where there was some little girl to play with—and this woman was the Superintendent's wife—she was good too after that time. I used to comb her hair in the afternoons when she would lie down to rest—and I never saw my grand ma any more for four years—and she came after me to take me home back to Tennessee one fall in November the day before Thanksgiving—I didn't want to go home—she just took me anyway—she took me by my hand and I went jumping along with her down the walk—and the matron came out and called me back and for me to come get my clothes to wear home—And she gave me one dress and underwear—And the matron's name was Miss Ruth Lee— I remember her well—she was a good woman—I used to work at school—I used to mop the hall and the stairs and the parlor floor—I got so lonesome before we got home I used to cry. My grand ma had a sister and we stopped at her home and stayed awhile—that was where I got so lonesome—my grand ma's sister had children but that didn't help me. I just cried anyway—and I don't remember how long we stayed—then we went on to Tennessee to our home and it was night when we got home—

. . . I remember the year 1894 [and] the month of January when we were going up the mountains of North Carolina to live and there come a white woman with Aunt Betsy Tolesky to our house—Aunt Betsy had two boys and the oldest one was about five years old and the baby was about two years old—And grand ma said for us children to start up the mountain with this white woman and they would come on after awhile because we were slow—Tom he couldn't walk fast—neither could I. Tom was bare-footed when he came to our house—I had some old shoes the white folks had given me and I gave them to him. I had two pairs that was given me. I had on one pair and let Tom have the other pair—they were too big for him but beat going up the mountain bare-footed—and it was late before granny and grand pa overtook us and we didn't go far until grand pa said he would get us some wood and we could stay there under a spruce pine tree for the night—And there was snow on the mountain there where we stayed that night but we stayed there away up in the hills of North Carolina—and grand pa left his dog with us—he said to the dog[, "]you stay with the children[,"] and he did just that. Next morning before good day this woman woke us up—said[, "]wake up we must start walking again["]—this woman's name was Laura Maney—she claim she was part Indian—and we went that morning in snow nearly to our shoe top—that was cold walking in the mountains—And every now and then we would have to run to keep our feet from freezing to keep ourselves warm too—and Tom was small and we just had to keep him running to keep him warm—And so we got [to] grand pa's cabin early the next day but it was cold walking but back when I was a small child we walked when we went anywhere—but we were happy and didn't wait to see if someone would come along and pick us up— that was away back in the mountains of Graham [County,

North Carolina] and we stayed there for awhile . . . Then Mrs. Jones wrote me a letter asking me to come up and stay with her that summer and I got ready the day I was to go—I was to go up on a steam boat—Mr. Jones was to be on the boat to take me with him—and grand ma she went with me to the landing and the boat never came that night. And Mrs. Davis she lived there at the boat landing and she said for me to just stay there with her that night and I did stay that night with her—sure enough next morning early the boat came puffing up the river—and Charley her son came and got my basket and took me down to the boat and saw that I got on the boat because Mr. Jones wasn't on the boat but got on the boat farther up the river—and I rode on a steamboat up the river and it sure was tiresome—it was four o'clock when we got to our destination and I sure was glad to get there after sitting in the boat all day from 8 o'clock until four that evening—and I stayed all summer there at Jones home and then when I went home that fall I walked home—my brother came up there and Mr. Jones hired him that summer and we both worked there—And when he got ready to go home I wanted to go home too. But brother said wait until Saturday and Mr. Jones would take me home in the buggy and I wouldn't have to walk because he was going to walk home. but I never said nothing but just hurried and wash my dishes and then I left for home too—he had been gone about an hour then but I got my pay and started home—I thought I would catch up with him somewhere and I did—about noon I passed him at a country store on the road—I didn't see him—he saw me and I went by and was a head of him then but not far a head—he over took me—I was getting tired then and I was getting slow in walking—we walked on until I was so tired—we would stop and rest and it was late in the evening—I said to my brother[, "]you go and I will come on some time to night["]—And he said[, "]no I going stay with you[,"] and so he did—and we got to our neighbors house just before dark and we were [with]in a mile of home but I was so tired [it] seemed I couldn't walk any farther that day—And the folks were all so glad to see us they say [to] stay all night [and] go home in the morning and that is what we did. Next morning Brother said for me to go on home [and] he was going to town—it was seven miles to town and people had to walk them days when you didn't own a horse to ride. And so that was our fix—we didn't own anything [and] we were just wander[er]s—but we seemed to get along good so far as we didn't own no permanent home. So we just stayed so long and then moved on somewhere else—

Our next move was when we moved to North Carolina in the fall of 1903 the last week in Sept—And we left one Sunday morning—and grand pa hired a colored man that had horses and a wagon to haul us as far as he could in half a day—and he gave him our chairs that we had and couldn't carry with us and he did haul us a long ways— then he went back and we started walking—and it took us a week to come to Whittier N.C.—that was where his brother lived then—I remember when we were coming to N.C. over the mountain we camped out on the road—and of course we had no way [of] cooking our bread and we had to have some bread for our breakfast—and so grandpa took his axe and went to a chestnut tree and peeled the bark off the tree wide enough to put the dough on to cook—and that is the way my granny baked the bread that morning on chestnut bark—stood the bark in front of the fire and when the top side baked she turned it over and brown the other side and that was good to eat—there is always a way to get help some way if you will just stop and think what to do—And then we went on after we eat our bread—we didn't have anything else to eat—we had traveled so far we had eaten all we had started with—grandpa had just got us some meal from folks we knew down in Tennessee before

we started up the smoky mountain to North Carolina—that
[was] how come we had to bake some bread to eat—then
we went on over the mountain—first we came [to] the toll
gate and stopped at the white man's house that had charge
of the toll gate and he asked us in and to have breakfast
with them and we did stop and eat with them—they were
nice and kind people—and there was a girl there too [and]
she was about my age and I had some ear bobs in my ears
and she wanted them and she begged me to sell them to
her and I did—she gave me fifty cent for them—a friend of
mine gave them to me for Xmas gift and I never forget [I
sold] my Xmas gift—then we moved on over the mountain
and when it was late in the eve we stopped at a house near
the road. It was vacant and empty and we stayed there that
night—grand pa he picked up dry wood and made a fire
to warm by—next morning we started again—this was Sat
morning and we walked all day slow but sure—that night
we came to Judson N.C. where some of the Indians lived
then—and we went to an old friend of grand pas and stayed
with them that night and spend Sunday there with them
folks—and grand pa went to church with the boys—But the
girl and her little brother and I went chestnut hunting that
day—there were plenty chestnuts them days—we spent the
day out in the hills—her brother went along to climb the
trees—And we had a grand time that day long ago—we had
chestnut bread for supper—Oh boy that was good eating
them days—[1]

ENDNOTES

[1] Aggie Ross Lossiah, "The Story of My Life as Far Back as I Can Remember," *Journal of Cherokee Studies* 9, no. 2 (Fall 1984), 89–98.

~ Wilma Mankiller Essay ~

In 1987, Wilma Mankiller (1945–2010) became the first woman elected principal chief. She remained in that position until she retired in 1995.

In an essay entitled "Womanhood," published in an anthology called *Every Day Is a Good Day: Reflections by Contemporary Indigenous Women*, Mankiller talked about the important women in her life.

~

My Great-Aunt Maggie Gourd was a very good storyteller who believed in the power of dreams. She once told us about a dream in which a large animal—a bull or a buffalo—tried to break into her house by repeatedly ramming her front door. When she woke up the next morning, her front door was badly damaged. I remember only tiny fragments of the dream stories Maggie shared, but I recall clearly that in her stories, there were no absolute lines between dreams and reality. Maggie also told us stories about Little People, *Yunwi Tsunsdi*, who live in rocky places like a bluff near freshwater wherever Cherokees reside. They are only about three feet tall. They sing and speak in Cherokee. . . . Cherokee people describe Little People as "secondhand." It is often said that if one sees the Little People and tells about it, that person will soon die.

My mother-in-law, the late Florence Soap, told me that her father used to gather medicine for her sister from a certain place. Then one day, for the first time, he took her to a new place to look for medicine. When her sister asked him why they couldn't go back to the old place, he said the Little

People told him not to come back to gather medicine there. He soon got sick and died. Florence said, "If he hadn't told my sister about seeing the Little People, he would probably have lived longer. That's what we believe." Also, if anything out of the ordinary is found in the woods, Cherokees assume that it belongs to the Little People. If a Cherokee woman goes out to gather hickory nuts and happens on a woven basket left by another gatherer, she can pick it up and say out loud, "Little People, I am taking this basket." Then it is hers to keep. That is her right.

There were other important women in my early childhood but none more important than my mother, Irene Sitton Mankiller, who has provided me with a lifetime of unconditional love. My mother worked alongside my other siblings and my father on income-producing projects as well as the dozens of daily chores required to keep a large family fed and cared for. My mother never sat me down and said[, "T]his is how you should live["] or ["T]his is what it means to be a woman.["] I learned a lot from watching her and the other women around me. I remain grateful to both my parents for never telling me, "Girls can't do that," and for letting me define for myself what it means to be a woman.

Then there were the "bless-your-little-heart" ladies. They were white Christian women who made our family one of their charities by bringing used clothing and other gifts to our small wood frame home. When I saw their big car approaching our house, I ran and hid. While walking to and from school, they would sometimes stop and offer us a ride, murmuring, "Bless your little hearts." Even at a very early age, I understood that these women thought they were better than us and that they would accept us if only we were more like them. Many years later, a white woman raising money to give college scholarships to indigenous students told me she wanted to "give pride back to the

Wilma Mankiller

COURTESY OF RESEARCH DIVISION OF THE OKLAHOMA HISTORICAL SOCIETY; FROM C. R. COWEN COLLECTION

Indians." She had such a staggering sense of entitlement; she didn't know the highly insulting and patronizing nature of that statement. She reminded me of the "bless-your-little-heart" ladies from my childhood.

After we made the wrenching move to California, a number of women reached out to me. Without them, I don't know how I could ever have become a successful adult. I especially value the time I had with my maternal grandmother, Pearl Sitton, who was a reassuring presence during a time when I felt confused, lost, and out of place in San Francisco. In school I was teased a lot and labeled as different because I had an unusual last name, spoke with an Oklahoma accent, and looked "ethnic." But the biggest differences stemmed from the very divergent life experiences of the other children and me. While they had learned to ride a bicycle, skate on roller skates, or play with the hula hoop, I had never even spoken on a telephone or used a flush commode before our arrival in San Francisco.

During my adolescence, I spent most summers with Grandma Sitton and lived with her for a year while attending the eighth grade at Lone Tree School in nearby Escalon, California. Grandma Sitton was an extremely independent and affectionate woman who had moved to California to start over again after the death of my grandfather. She liked to sing gospel songs as she worked in the house or in the garden. She was a disciplined woman who was up before sunrise each morning and in bed shortly after nightfall. It was clear where my mother got her work values.

Several single mothers at the San Francisco Indian Center made quite an impression on me as well. They held clerical or professional jobs, did volunteer work at the Indian center, and helped each other. My sister and I watched their children while they went dancing in the ballroom of the San Francisco Indian Center or some other fun place. On Saturday night, they gathered at Justine Buckskin's house to joke and tease each other as they got ready for their big night out. I loved watching the women work their hair into impossibly high hairdos, glue it together with Aqua Net hair spray, and then teeter out the front door on high heels, assuring us they would be back by midnight, a goal they never met. To a twelve-year-old, their lives seemed full and exciting. Much later I learned that they found their beautiful Saturday night outfits in the clothing bins at Saint Vincent de Paul's thrift shop on Fourteenth and Mission Streets, and that they often struggled to make ends meet, relying on one another to get from one payday to the next. Though they adjusted to life in the city, they longed to return to their tribal communities, and most eventually did. These women were resourceful, doing the best they could with what they had and taking the time to find joy in their families, friendships, and their special nights out. Even today the heavy scent of Aqua Net hair spray makes me smile and remember those resilient women.

Like my counterparts at the Indian center, a beehive hairdo was perched precariously on my head when I was married just a few days before my eighteenth birthday in November of 1963. My husband expected me to step completely away from involvement in the Indian center and from my birth family. It was a tall order. I had an avid interest in social justice issues and the extraordinary world around me. At that time in San Francisco, there were many debates and discussions of Red Power, civil rights, and women's rights. Musicians Janis Joplin and Jimi Hendrix were introducing a completely new sound to a generation now known as baby boomers, and the Haight-Ashbury district was becoming a mecca for middle-class young people. There was a free-speech movement at the University of California at Berkeley and massive anti-war demonstrations throughout the Bay Area. By the time I was twenty-three, any notion that I could live my life as a wife and mother as defined by my husband and the social constraints of that time was gone forever. I became involved in the community, started thinking about attending college, and the beehive hairdo, makeup, and heels were replaced by long straight hair and sensible shoes.

In 1976 when my daughters, Felicia and Gina, and I returned to Oklahoma, I was more independent, self-confident, and had acquired some knowledge of land and treaty rights as well as grant-writing skills. I also had an abiding faith in the ability of Cherokee people to solve their own problems, and I immediately began developing community-based programs that reflected that philosophy. At that time, there were no female executives with the Cherokee Nation—and there had never been a female deputy chief or principal chief. In historic times, women played an important role in Cherokee government and in tribal life, but that role had diminished over time. As Cherokee people began to intermarry with whites and adopt the values of the larger society, women increasingly assumed a secondary role. When I first ran for election as deputy principal chief in 1983, it seemed the strong role of women in Cherokee life had been forgotten by some of our own people. I vividly remember a man standing up in a campaign meeting and telling me, "Cherokee Nation will be the laughingstock of all the tribes if we elect a woman." Though there was considerable opposition to my candidacy, I was elected to serve a four-year term as the first female deputy principal chief in Cherokee history. I thought this was my summit in tribal government, but I was elected to serve as principal chief in 1987—the first woman to hold that position—and resoundingly reelected again in 1991.

By the time I left office in 1995, after not seeking a fourth four-year term of office, there were fewer questions about whether or not women should be in leadership positions in the Cherokee Nation. If people opposed me, it was because they disagreed with my policies, not just because I am female. Cherokee people are more concerned about competency—about whether the Head Start bus shows up on time or whether they are properly diagnosed at the health clinics—than whether a woman is leading the nation. In a way, my elections were a step forward for women and a step into the Cherokee tradition of balance between men and women.[1]

ENDNOTES

[1] Wilma Mankiller, *Every Day Is a Good Day: Reflections by Contemporary Indigenous Women* (Golden, Colo.: Fulcrum Publishing, 2004), 98.

ACKNOWLEDGMENTS

I was profoundly moved by the stories of Cherokee women whom I discovered.

I wish to thank Carolyn Sakowski, president of John F. Blair, who invited me to edit this work, and Steve Kirk, editor in chief. They were truly remarkable throughout every phase of this project. I am also grateful to Debra Long Hampton, a superb director of design and production.

I owe a special debt to Elizabeth MacDonald, whose work was crucial to this book. She spent countless hours converting the primary documents into publishable form. I am eternally grateful to Wayne Flynt and Leon Litwack, who have been brilliant mentors to me for decades. I also wish to thank Elie and Marion Wiesel for their constant encouragement and support. For their insights and enduring friendship, I thank Patricia Perez-Arce and Ed DeAvila, Jeffrey Kennedy, Xavier Landon, Mike and Sue Abram of Cherokee Heritage Museum and Gallery, William Anderson, Theda Perdue, Michael Green, Gary E. Moulton, Jewel Spears Brooker, Ralph Brooker, Catherine Griggs, Maggi Morehouse, Jared Stark, Thomas Childers, John Edwards, Linda Lucas, Santiago Nunez, Claire Bell, Chris Payne and John Galloway, Don Eastman, Suzan Harrison, Julie Empric, Lloyd Chapin, Rodney and Margo Fitzgerald, Michael Solari, Joelle Collier, all my Ford Scholars, Terri Baker, Sarah H. Hill, Alice Taylor Colbert, David LaVere, Brian Hosmer, Richard Persico, Greg Padgett, Andrew Chittick, Barney Hartston, Constantina Rhodes, Jim Goetsch, Peggy Newton, Joe Hamilton, Jesus Subero, Rayna Green, Judy and Bill Chandler, Janice Norton, Mara Soudakoff, Lia Glovsky, N. Scott Momaday, Jim Moore, James Billie, Nancy Wood, Judith Green, and David Woods.

I thank the staff of the Oklahoma Historical Society, especially Bill Welge, Sharron Ashton, and Chester Cowen. My special thanks go to the generous staff of the Houghton Library at Harvard University, where I spent many hours reading the papers of the American Board of Commissioners for Foreign Missions. I wish to thank the staffs of the Western History Collections at the University of Oklahoma in Norman, especially John R. Lovett and William Eigelsbach; I also thank those in Special Collections. I am indebted to the help of the remarkable staffs at the Newberry Library, the National Archives, the Library of Congress, the Smithsonian Institution, the Thomas Gilcrease Museum and Institute in Tulsa, especially Michelle Maxwell and Renee Harvey, and the History Branch and Archives of the Cleveland Public Library and the Bradley County Historical Society, both in Cleveland, Tennessee. I wish to thank Delores Sumner and her superb staff in Special Collections at Northeastern State University in Tahlequah, Oklahoma; Jamie Gill and the Eckerd College library staff; and the staff at the Museum of the Cherokee Indian in Cherokee, North Carolina, especially Ken Blankenship, Barbara Duncan, and Mikey Littlejohn.

I am grateful for the wisdom and stories of members of the Eastern Band of Cherokee Indians and the Cherokee Nation of Oklahoma. I express my profound thanks to my parents, Alta Ross Johnston and Eugene Johnston, my remarkable sister Nancy Smith, and the amazing Patricia Smith Higgens, Matt Higgens, and Jennifer Smith.

The great Wilma Mankiller said how important it is to "be of good mind." This book honors all Cherokee women, past and present. May we always listen to their voices.

WORKS CITED

Manuscript Collections

American Baptist Historical Society, Atlanta, Ga. (Missionary Correspondence, 1800–1900)

History Branch and Archives, Cleveland Public Library, Cleveland, Tenn. (Records of the Cherokee Indian Agency in Tennessee, James Corn Collection)

Houghton Library, Harvard University, Cambridge, Mass. (American Board of Commissioners for Foreign Missions Papers)

Museum of the Cherokee Indian, Cherokee, N.C.

National Anthropological Archives, Smithsonian Institution (Papers of James Mooney, Register to the Papers of James Mooney)

Newberry Library, Chicago (John Howard Payne Papers, Edward E. Ayer Collection)

Oklahoma Historical Society, Oklahoma City, Okla. (Grant Foreman Collection, Indian Archives)

Special Collections, John Vaughan Library, Northeastern State University, Tahlequah, Okla. (T. L. Ballenger Collection, *Cherokee Phoenix, Cherokee Rose Buds*)

Thomas Gilcrease Institute of American History and Art, Tulsa, Okla. (Hicks Collection, John Ross Papers)

Western History Collections, University of Oklahoma, Norman, Okla. (Indian Pioneer Papers, Cherokee Nation Papers, Dr. Isabel Cobb Collection, Stand Watie and Sarah Watie Papers, J. L. Hargett Collection)

Books, Articles, and Theses

Adair, James. *History of the American Indians.* London: Edward & Charles Dilly, 1775.

Agnew, Mary Cobb. Interview 5978, vol. 1, Muskogee, Okla., May 25, 1937, 289–303. Indian Pioneer Papers, Western History Collections, University of Oklahoma, Norman, Okla.

Anderson, Lilian Lee. Interview 7326, vol. 2, Eufaula, Okla., Aug. 20, 1937, 337–39. Indian Pioneer Papers, Western History Collections, University of Oklahoma, Norman, Okla.

Anderson, Rufus, ed. *Memoir of Catharine Brown: A Christian Indian of the Cherokee Nation.* Boston: Samuel T. Armstrong, Crocker and Brewster, 1825.

Anderson, William L., Jane L. Brown, and Anne F. Rogers, eds. *The Payne-Butrick Papers.* Vols. 4–6. Lincoln and London: University of Nebraska Press, 2010.

Arendell, Mary Alice. Interview 5508, vol. 3, 30–31. Indian Pioneer Papers, Western History Collections, University of Oklahoma, Norman, Okla.

Armor, Annie Williams. Interview 12635, vol. 3, Tulsa, Okla., Jan. 10, 1938, 60–62. Indian Pioneer Papers, Western History Collections, University of Oklahoma, Norman, Okla.

Baker, Mary J. Interview 13113, vol. 4, Sallisaw, Okla., Feb. 24, 1938, 241–43, 248–49. Indian Pioneer Papers, Western History Collections, University of Oklahoma, Norman, Okla.

Ballenger, T. L. "A Week at the Female Seminary." *Early History of Northeastern State College,* 18–22. Special Collections, John Vaughan Library, Northeastern State University, Tahlequah, Okla. The Genealogical Society of Utah published an edition of this work in 1976.

Barnett, Lena. Interview 7838, vol. 5, Eufaula, Okla., Oct. 15, 1937, 386–87. Indian Pioneer Papers, Western History Collections, University of Oklahoma, Norman, Okla.

Bartram, William. "Observations on the Creek and Cherokee Indians." *Transactions of the American Ethnological Society* 3, part 1 (1853): 1–81.

———. *Travels Through North & South Carolina, Georgia, East &*

West Florida, the Cherokee Country, the Extensive Territories of the Muscogulges, or Creek Confederacy, and the Country of the Cha[o]ctaws. Philadelphia: James and Johnson, 1791. See also *http://babel.hathitrust.org/cgi/pt?id=mdp.39015021105773;view= 1up;seq=59.*

Brannon, Lucille S. "Cherokee National Female Seminary." Interview 0000, vol. 10, 332. Indian Pioneer Papers, Western History Collections, University of Oklahoma, Norman, Okla.

Butrick, Daniel S. "The Journal of Rev. Daniel S. Butrick, May 19, 1838–April 1, 1839." ABCFM Papers, 18.3.3, vol. 4. Houghton Library, Harvard University, Cambridge, Mass.

Carney, Virginia Moore. *Eastern Band Cherokee Women: Cultural Persistence in Their Letters and Speeches.* Knoxville: University of Tennessee Press, 2005.

———. "A Testament to Tenacity: Cultural Persistence in the Letters and Speeches of Eastern Band Cherokee Women." Ph.D. diss., University of Kentucky, 2000.

Cherokee Nation Papers. Reel 44, RG 2, Treaty Fund Claims, 1831–83. Western History Collections, University of Oklahoma, Norman, Okla.

Clayton, Lawrence A., Vernon James Knight Jr., and Edward C. Moore, eds. *The De Soto Chronicles: The Expedition of Hernando De Soto to North America in 1539–1543.* Vol. 2. Tuscaloosa and London: University of Alabama Press, 1993.

Cobb, Isabel. "Cobb family history written by Dr. Bell Cobb." Dr. Isabel Cobb Collection, box 1, folder 3. Western History Collections, University of Oklahoma, Norman, Okla.

———. Interview, vol. 65, 184–218. Indian Pioneer Papers, Western History Collections, University of Oklahoma, Norman, Okla.

———. Medical Journal. Dr. Isabel Cobb Collection, box 1, folder 1. Western History Collections, University of Oklahoma, Norman, Okla.

———. "Partial History of Dr. Isabel Cobb: Earlyday Doctor in Indian Territory." Mimeographed by Ruth Cobb Bivins. Box 1, folder 5. Western History Collections, University of Oklahoma Libraries, Norman, Okla.

———. Vertical file. Research Division, Oklahoma Historical Society, Oklahoma City, Okla. This file contains Dr. Cobb's original medical records.

Curtis Act. June 28, 1898. http://www.accessgenealogy.com/native/laws/act_june_28_1898_curtis_act.htm. Accessed Aug. 24, 2012.

Dale, Edward Everett, and Gaston Litton. *Cherokee Cavaliers: Forty Years of Cherokee History as Told in the Correspondence of the Ridge-Watie-Boudinot Family.* Norman and London: University of Oklahoma Press, 1995.

Dawes Act. Feb. 8, 1887. http://www.nebraskastudies.org/0600/stories/0601_0200_01.html. Accessed Aug. 8, 2012.

Debo, Angie. *And Still the Waters Run: The Betrayal of the Five Civilized Tribes.* 1940. Reprint, Princeton, N.J.: Princeton University Press, 1991.

"Dr. Isabel Cobb: Her Times and Ours." *Oklahoma State Medical Association Journal* 53, no. 3 (March 1960): 129–30.

"Female Delicacy." *Cherokee Phoenix.* Vol. 01/11191828, no. 38, 4.

"Female Heart, The." *Cherokee Phoenix.* Vol. 02/11251829, no. 33, 4.

"Female Influence." *Cherokee Phoenix.* Vol. 01/08201828, no. 025, 4. http://neptune3.galib.uga.edu/ssp/News/chrkphnx/18280820d.pdf

Fogelson, Raymond D. "On the 'Petticoat Government' of the Eighteenth-Century Cherokee." In *Personality and the Cultural Construction of Society: Papers in Honor of Melford E. Spiro.* Edited by David Jordan and Marc Swartz. Tuscaloosa: University of Alabama Press, 1990.

Foreman, Grant. *The Five Civilized Tribes.* Norman: University of Oklahoma Press, 1934.

———. *Indian Removal: The Emigration of the Five Civilized Tribes of Indians*. Norman: University of Oklahoma Press, 1932.

Gordon, Mary Scott (Mrs. Raymond Gordon). Interview 1162, vol. 35, Ardmore, Okla., March 31, 1937, 30–34. Indian Pioneer Papers, Western History Collections, University of Oklahoma, Norman, Okla.

Green, Rayna. *Women in American Indian Society*. New York: Chelsea House, 1992.

Haywood, John. *The Natural and Aboriginal History of Tennessee: Up to the First Settlements Therein by the White People in the Year 1768*. Nashville, Tenn.: George Wilson, 1823.

Hicks, Hannah. *Diary of Hannah Hicks*. Hicks Collection, Museum Archives, Thomas Gilcrease Institute of American History and Art, Tulsa, Okla.

Hoig, Stanley W. *The Cherokees and Their Chiefs: In the Wake of Empire*. Fayetteville: University of Arkansas Press, 1998.

Hudson, Charles. *Southeastern Indians*. Knoxville: University of Tennessee Press, 1976.

Hughes, Ida Mae. Interview 12184, vol. 45, Muskogee, Okla., Nov. 15, 1937, 218–19. Indian Pioneer Papers, Western History Collections, University of Oklahoma, Norman, Okla.

Illustrated Souvenir Catalog of the Cherokee National Female Seminary, Tahlequah, Indian Territory, 1850 to 1860. Chilocco, Okla.: Indian Print Shop. The catalog was reprinted in *Journal of Cherokee Studies* 10, no. 1 (Spring 1985): 138–44, 182–83. The original is in the archives of the Museum of the Cherokee Indian, Cherokee, N.C.

Johnston, Carolyn Ross. "Burning Beds, Spinning Wheels, and Calico Dresses." *Journal of Cherokee Studies* 19 (1998): 3–17.

———. *Cherokee Women in Crisis: Trail of Tears, Civil War, and Allotment, 1838–1907*. Tuscaloosa and London: University of Alabama Press, 2003.

———. " 'The Panther's Scream Is Often Heard': Cherokee Women in Indian Territory During the Civil War." *Chronicles of Oklahoma* 78, no. 1 (Spring 2000): 84–107.

Jones, Evan. Journal, June 16, 1838. Missionary Correspondence, 1800–1900, microfilm reel no. 98. American Baptist Historical Society, Atlanta, Ga.

Keys, Lucy Lowrey. *The Wahnenauhi Manuscript: Historical Sketches of the Cherokees, Together with Some of Their Customs, Traditions, and Superstitions*. Edited and with an introduction by Jack Frederick Kilpatrick. Number 77, Anthropological Papers, Bureau of Ethnology, Bulletin, 196. Washington: GPO, 1966.

Klinck, Carl F., and James J. Talman, eds. *The Journal of Major John Norton, 1816*. Toronto: Champlain Society, 1970.

Kupferer, Harriet J. *Ancient Drums, Other Moccasins: Native North American Cultural Adaptation*. Englewood Cliffs, N.J.: Prentice Hall, 1988.

Lerner, Gerda. *The Majority Finds Its Past*. Chapel Hill: University of North Carolina Press, 2005.

Lossiah, Aggie Ross. "The Story of My Life as Far Back as I Can Remember." *Journal of Cherokee Studies* 9, no. 2 (Fall 1984): 89–98.

Mankiller, Wilma, and Michael Wallis. *Mankiller: A Chief and Her People*. New York: St. Martin's, 1993.

Mankiller, Wilma. *Every Day Is a Good Day: Reflections by Contemporary Indigenous Women*. Golden, Colo.: Fulcrum Publishing, 2004.

McLoughlin, William G. *After the Trail of Tears: The Cherokees' Struggle for Sovereignty, 1839–1880*. Chapel Hill: University of North Carolina Press, 1993.

———. *Champion of the Cherokees: Evan and John B. Jones*. Princeton, N.J.: Princeton University Press, 1990.

———. *Cherokee Renascence in the New Republic*. Princeton, N.J.: Princeton University Press, 1986.

———. *Cherokees and Missionaries, 1789–1839*. Norman: University of Oklahoma Press, 1995.

———. "Who Civilized the Cherokees?" *Journal of Cherokee Studies* 13 (1988): 65.

McNickle. D'Arcy. "Indian and European: Indian-White Relations from Discovery to 1887." In *The Rape of Indian Lands*. Edited by Paul Wallace Gates. New York: Arno Press, 1979.

Meigs, Elinor Boudinot. Interview 0000, vol. 62, Fort Gibson, Okla., March 2–4, 1937, 75–77. Indian Pioneer Papers, Western History Collections, University of Oklahoma, Norman, Okla.

Miller, Minnie L. Interview 13626, vol. 63, Tahlequah, Okla., Apr. 11, 1938, 216. Indian Pioneer Papers, Western History Collections, University of Oklahoma, Norman, Okla.

Mooney, James. *Myths of the Cherokee: Nineteenth Annual Report of the Bureau of American Ethnology, 1897–98*. Part 1. Washington: GPO, 1900.

———. *Myths of the Cherokees*. Cambridge: Riverside Press, 1888.

———. *The sacred formulas of the Cherokees*. Washington: Bureau of American Ethnology, 1891.

———. *The Swimmer Manuscript: Cherokee sacred formulas and medicinal prescriptions*. Revised, completed, and edited by Frans M. Olbrechts. Washington: GPO, 1932.

Moulton, Gary E. *John Ross: Cherokee Chief*. Athens: University of Georgia Press, 1978.

Moulton, Gary E., ed. *The Papers of Chief John Ross*. Vols. 1 and 2. Norman: University of Oklahoma Press: 1985.

Neugin, Rebecca. Interview, 1932. Indian Pioneer Papers, Western History Collections, University of Oklahoma, Norman, Okla.

Otis, D. S. *The Dawes Act and the Allotment of Indians*. Edited by Francis Paul Prucha. Norman: University of Oklahoma Press, 1973.

"Our Wreath of Rose Buds." In *Cherokee Rose Buds*, from *The Youth's Companion*, Sept. 7, 1854, 80. This edition includes the pieces

"Our Wreath of Rose Buds" by "Corrinne," "An Address to the Females of the Cherokee Nation" by "Na-Li," and "View from Our Seminary" by "Edith." See http://www.merrycoz.org/yc/ CHERNEW.HTM.

Owen, Narcissa. *Memoirs of Narcissa Owen, 1831–1907*. Washington: 1907.

Payne, John Howard. Papers. Payne-Butrick Papers, vol. 4, 372–73. Edward E. Ayer Collection, Newberry Library, Chicago.

Pearce, Roy Harvey. *The Savages of America: A Study of the Indian and the Idea of Civilization*. Baltimore: Johns Hopkins University Press, 1953.

Pennington, Josephine. Interview 7783, vol. 70, Hulbert, Okla., Oct., 12, 1937, 398–99. Indian Pioneer Papers, Western History Collections, University of Oklahoma, Norman, Okla.

Perdue, Theda. "Cherokee Women and the Trail of Tears." *Journal of Women's History* 1 (Spring 1989): 14–30.

———. *Cherokee Women: Gender and Culture Change, 1780–1835*. Lincoln: University of Nebraska Press, 1998.

———. "Southern Indians and the Cult of True Womanhood." In *The Web of Southern Social Relations: Women, Family and Education*. Edited by Walter I. Fraser, R. Frank Saunders Jr., and Jon I. Wakelyn. Athens: University of Georgia Press, 1985.

———. "Women, Men, and American Indian Policy: The Cherokee Response to 'Civilization.' " In *Negotiators of Change*. Edited by Nancy Shoemaker. New York: Routledge, 1995.

Perdue, Theda, and Michael D. Green. *The Cherokee Removal: A Brief History with Documents*. 2nd ed. Boston and New York: Bedford/ St. Martin's, 2005.

Perdue, Theda, ed. *Sifters: Native American Women's Lives*. New York: Oxford University Press, 2001.

Philippe, Louis. *Diary of My Travels in America: Louis-Philippe, King of France, 1830–1848*. New York: Delacorte, 1977.

Phillips, Joyce B., and Paul Gary Phillips, eds. *The Brainerd Journal:*

A Mission to the Cherokees, 1817–1823. Lincoln and London: University of Nebraska Press, 1998.

Prucha, Francis Paul. *The Great Father: The United States Government and the American Indians*. Vols. 1 and 2. Lincoln: University of Nebraska Press, 1984.

Rackleff, Kate Neugin. Interview 7382, vol. 74, Fairland, Okla., Aug. 31, 1937. Indian Pioneer Papers, Western History Collections, University of Oklahoma, Norman, Okla.

Records of the Bureau of Indian Affairs. Records of the Cherokee Indian Agency in Tennessee, 1801–35. RG 75, microcopy 208. History Branch and Archives, Cleveland Public Library, Cleveland, Tenn.

Robinson, Ella. "Cherokee Seminaries." Vol. 108, no. 13812, Apr. 12, 1938, 9–18. Indian Pioneer Papers, Western History Collections, University of Oklahoma, Norman, Okla.

Robinson, Ella Coody. Interview 13833, vol. 77, Muskogee, Okla., May 6, 1938, 94–127. Indian Pioneer Papers, Western History Collections, University of Oklahoma, Norman, Okla.

Rogin, Michael Paul. *Fathers and Children: Andrew Jackson and the Subjugation of the American Indian*. New York: Alfred A. Knopf, 1975.

Sixkiller, Emma J. Interview 6468, vol. 84, Fairland, Okla., June 29, 1937, 49–51. Indian Pioneer Papers, Western History Collections, University of Oklahoma, Norman, Okla.

Stremlau, Rose. *Sustaining the Cherokee Family: Kinship and the Allotment of an Indigenous Nation*. Chapel Hill: University of North Carolina Press, 2011.

Timberlake Henry. *The Memoir of Lieut. Henry Timberlake*. London: printed for the author, 1765.

Ulrich, Laurel Thatcher. *The Age of Homespun: Object and Stories in the Creation of an American Myth*. New York: Alfred A. Knopf, 2001.

Warde, Mary Jane. "Now the Wolf Has Come: The Civilian War in the Indian Territory." *Chronicles of Oklahoma* 71, no. 1 (1993): 69–87.

Washburn, Wilcomb E. *The Assault on Indian Tribalism: The General Allotment Law (Dawes Act) of 1887.* Edited by Harold M. Hyman. Philadelphia: J. B. Lippincott, 1975.

Watts, Elizabeth. Interview 0000, vol. 95, Muskogee, Okla., Apr. 27, 1937, 527–31, 536–38. Indian Pioneer Papers, Western History Collections, University of Oklahoma, Norman, Okla.

Whitmire, Eliza. Interview 12963, vol. 97, Estella, Okla., Feb. 14, 1936, 398–401. Indian Pioneer Papers, Western History Collections, University of Oklahoma, Norman, Okla.

Williams, David. *The Georgia Gold Rush: Twenty-Niners, Cherokees, and Gold Fever.* Columbia: University of South Carolina Press, 1993.

Williams, Samuel Cole, ed. *Adair's History of the American Indians.* New York: Promontory, 1930.

"Woman." *Cherokee Phoenix.* Vol. 01/08131828, no. 24, 4. http://neptune3.galib.uga.edu/ssp/News/chrkphnx/18280813d.pdf.

Woodall, Bettie Perdue. Interview 7551, vol. 100, Welch, Okla., Sept. 20, 1937, 66–68. Indian Pioneer Papers, Western History Collections, University of Oklahoma, Norman, Okla.

Wreath of Cherokee Rose Buds, A. Female Seminary, Cherokee Nation. Vol. 2, no. 1, Wed., Aug. 1, 1855. This edition includes the pieces "A Day's Experience" by "Isabelle" and "Beauty" by "Alice."

Wreath of Cherokee Rose Buds, A. Female Seminary, Cherokee Nation. Vol. 3, no. 2, Wed., Feb. 11, 1857.

Wynn, Lizzie. Interview 12286, vol. 101, Dustin, Okla., Nov. 29, 1937, 57–59. Indian Pioneer Papers, Western History Collections, University of Oklahoma, Norman, Okla.

Yarbrough, Fay A. *Race and the Cherokee Nation: Sovereignty in the Nineteenth Century.* Philadelphia: University of Pennsylvania Press, 2008.

INDEX